In Her Hands

Africa is seen as the next large growth economy, but with this potential comes concerns about exploitation from outside interests. Based on the real-world experiences of Demi Samande, award-winning entrepreneur, this book provides a toolkit for aspirational and savvy African entrepreneurs, as well as insights for responsible investors to seize the opportunity and to help transform the African economy for the benefit of Africa.

As a practical guide, the book will inspire a new generation of entrepreneurs to tackle the challenges of doing business and the steps to creating sustainable, successful companies, both large and small. It features interviews with entrepreneurs who are already having success, as well as business executives, artists and creatives who are inspiring the transformation of African business from within and from overseas. Demi's own story, which she draws upon to illustrate how to build a successful business from scratch, starts in a London flat and traces the development of her company in Nigeria to becoming the premier manufacturer of luxury furniture in West Africa. It also tells her story from the perspective of a female entrepreneur.

The book provides a hands-on roadmap for building and sustaining a business of any size and can be used on its own or in conjunction with training, either for entrepreneurs who are already in the process of building a business or for budding entrepreneurs in the classroom.

Demi Samande, a visionary entrepreneur and podcaster, blends technology with traditional craftsmanship in Africa's manufacturing sector. Her passion is emphasising ecofriendly, scalable solutions and empowering artisans across Africa.

'The narrative is not just an inspiring blueprint for budding entrepreneurs; it is a vivid testament to the resilience and ingenuity of Nigerian business leaders. Having meticulously followed her journey from the United Kingdom back to the heart of Lagos, I am profoundly impressed by her dedication to nurturing talent and fostering entrepreneurship among our youth. Demi's exceptional commitment to teaching valuable skills like upholstery, woodworking, furniture design but most importantly entrepreneurship is more than commendable—it is transformative. This book does more than recount the successful establishment of Majeurs Holdings; it invites us into the very essence of what it means to build a business that is both locally rooted and globally recognised. I am confident that Demi's story will ignite a passionate fire in the hearts of many young Nigerians, propelling them towards creating their own paths in our vibrant city and beyond. Her journey resonates deeply with the spirit of innovation and community that is crucial for our continued growth and prosperity.'

—**Professor Akin Abayomi**, *Honourable Commissioner of Health, Lagos State, Nigeria*

'What an inspiration and a profound demonstration of what faith and determination can achieve. Demi's journey through challenges and triumphs provides a compelling glimpse into the resilience required to excel both as an entrepreneur and a creative spirit in the demanding world of furniture design and manufacturing. I commend Demi's unwavering commitment to transforming lives through her business. By providing skills, employment, and new opportunities, she offers not just livelihoods but hope and a future to many young Nigerians. Her book is a powerful tool in our collective mission to uplift the next generation. It is with great conviction that I recommend this book to anyone seeking to understand the true impact of visionary leadership in business. Let us embrace the lessons it offers and be inspired to make a significant difference in our communities.'

—**Ituah Ighodalo**, *Lead Pastor of Trinity House Church, Lagos, Nigeria*

'I commend Demi for her exceptional dedication and vision in publishing this insightful book. Demi's journey embodies the very essence of leadership: a clear vision, unwavering responsibility, and an earnest commitment to serve. Her endeavor to establish a furniture manufacturing business in Nigeria not only showcases her entrepreneurial spirit but also her perseverance and commitment to excellence. This narrative serves as a profound demonstration of the hard work and dedication required to overcome substantial challenges. Demi's story is a testament to what is possible when determination, faith, energy, and investment are aligned towards a common goal. Her influence extends beyond her business, inspiring her employees, community, and indeed all Nigerians. As we aspire to position Nigeria and Africa as future global manufacturing hubs, her book emerges as a crucial guide for anyone willing to undertake the rigorous journey of entrepreneurship and make a lasting impact.'

—**Femi Gbajabiama**, *Chief of Staff to the President of Nigeria*

'What a captivating read! Demi offers invaluable business and life lessons that transcend borders, making them applicable to anyone, anywhere. In Africa, entrepreneurship isn't just a career choice, it's a fundamental aspect of life itself. Lagos may appear chaotic at first glance, but within that chaos, there's a remarkable orderliness waiting to be understood. Samande masterfully navigates this environment, drawing from her own successful startup journey in Lagos, Nigeria, and weaving in insightful interviews with a diverse array of African entrepreneurs spanning tech, design, fashion, and manufacturing. The book brims with engrossing real-life narratives that will leave you eagerly anticipating how you can implement transformative strategies in your own business or personal growth journey. Offering a fresh perspective on business lessons through an African lens, this book is poised to become indispensable for companies of all sizes. It's an original work that resonated deeply with me—I couldn't put it down.'

—**Brendan Boyle**, *Stanford University Adjunct Professor,*
Founder of the IDEO Play Lab, Associate Director Fuse London

'A candid and compelling showcase of entrepreneurial spirit and innovative prowess within Nigeria's vibrant business landscape, the United Kingdom and the United States. As Honourable Commissioner for Commerce, Cooperatives, Trade, and Investment in Lagos State, I recognize the profound impact that resilient dedicated entrepreneurs like Demi have on our local and national economy. Her journey from the diaspora to establishing a successful furniture manufacturing enterprise in Lagos offers invaluable lessons in perseverance, innovation, and sustainable business practices. This book not only charts a path for budding entrepreneurs but also highlights the critical role of trade and investment in fostering economic growth and development across Africa (all the more crucial with Africa poised as the New Frontier of the world, not only in terms of natural resources, but also in terms of infrastructure, telecommunications, urbanisation, and financial and consumer markets). I wholeheartedly and proudly endorse this inspiring work, which promises to inspire, motivate and guide future generations towards entrepreneurial "demystified" excellence. Bravo Demi!'

—**Folashade Ambrose-Medebem**, *Honourable Commissioner for Commerce, Cooperatives, Trade and Investment (MCCTI)*

'A groundbreaking exploration of manufacturing in Africa. Demi's insightful experience coupled with her strategies and innovative solutions align with Tolaram's vision for empowering local industries long term. A must-read for anyone passionate about sustainable development and entrepreneurial success in Africa.'

—**Haresh Aswani**, *Managing Director Africa, Tolaram*

In Her Hands

Shaping the Future of Manufacturing in Africa: A Woman's Story

DEMI SAMANDE

Routledge
Taylor & Francis Group

LONDON AND NEW YORK

Designed cover image: Tolu Aliki

First published 2025
by Routledge
4 Park Square, Milton Park, Abingdon, Oxon OX14 4RN

and by Routledge
605 Third Avenue, New York, NY 10158

Routledge is an imprint of the Taylor & Francis Group, an informa business

British Library Cataloguing-in-Publication Data
A catalogue record for this book is available from the British Library

Library of Congress Cataloging-in-Publication Data
Names: Samande, Demi, author.
Title: In her hands: shaping the future of manufacturing in Africa – a woman's story / Demi Samande.
Description: Abingdon, Oxon; New York, NY : Routledge, 2024. | Includes bibliographical references and index.
Subjects: LCSH: Manufacturing industries—Africa. | Entrepreneurs—Africa. | Africa—Economic conditions.
Classification: LCC HD9737.A352 S36 2024 | DDC 338.4096—dc23/eng/20240730
LC record available at https://lccn.loc.gov/2024027369

ISBN: 978-1-032-58762-2 (hbk)
ISBN: 978-1-032-59283-1 (pbk)
ISBN: 978-1-003-45399-4 (ebk)

DOI: 10.4324/9781003453994

Typeset in Dante and Avenir
by Apex CoVantage, LLC

To God Almighty, the designer of my path and the inspiration of my journey, I offer my profound gratitude. He has implanted within me an undying vision, nourished it with the gift of ambition and bestowed upon me the courage to make a meaningful difference in the world. From the age of 12, my pilgrimage started with His guiding hand. His divine providence, faithful even when I faltered, provided me with an anchor and a beacon in life's most tumultuous seas. This book is dedicated first to Him and then to my cherished family.

Contents

About the Author

Demi Samande, 2022. Image courtesy of Majeurs Holdings.

Demi Samande stands out as a visionary leader in the furniture manufacturing industry, bringing over 15 years of experience in spearheading a high-end furniture manufacturing venture across the UK and Nigeria. As the CEO of Majeurs Holdings, Demi has shown exceptional prowess in both the practical and conceptual realms of design, specialising in blending traditional craftsmanship with contemporary aesthetics. Her work ethic revolves around sustainable practices and innovation, ensuring every piece is not only luxurious but also environmentally conscious.

With a solid background in architecture from the London Metropolitan University, Demi's expertise extends to designing innovative spaces. Her communication skills, coupled with a charismatic leadership style, have been instrumental in mentoring young talents in the art of fine craftsmanship.

As a certified Leather and Upholstery Expert, Demi has lent her skills to various high-profile projects, both in the UK and Nigeria, showcasing her ability to meet the sophisticated demands of a diverse clientele. Her passion for quality and sustainability is matched by her commitment to continuous learning and improvement, a philosophy that has driven her personal and professional success.

Accomplishments

- Founder and CEO of Majeurs Holdings: Established as a benchmark in sustainable luxury furniture manufacturing.
- High-Profile Clientele: Successfully designed and built furniture for dignitaries in the UK and Nigeria.
- Artisan Training and Tech Innovation: Spearheaded programmes to formalise local artisans, elevating the standard of craftsmanship by utilizing and leveraging technology in aiding their job security.
- Majeurs Academy Launch: Initiated a training academy for individuals aged 18–35, addressing skill deficits in African manufacturing.

Acknowledgements

Writing this book has been an incredible journey, and it would not have been possible without the support, guidance and encouragement of many wonderful individuals. I am deeply grateful to all those who have contributed to making this work a reality.

My heartfelt thank you go to my parents Folasade and Olusegun and my sisters, Toyin, Pelumi, Bimbo, Bisi—your unwavering support and encouragement kept me going through the toughest times. Your belief in me and this project was a constant source of motivation.

My family, who not only prayed for me but also meticulously read over the chapters to ensure the essence of my messages was captured. Your love and faith have been my anchor.

To my partner, your patience and willingness to listen to my ideas, contemplations and doubts were invaluable. Your conversations helped me find clarity and direction.

I am profoundly grateful to my mentors, whose words of wisdom came at just the right moments, providing me with the guidance I needed.

Special thanks to my friends at Stanford for their expertise and their readiness to help me focus on what would best serve my audience.

To my dedicated staff, thank you for holding the fort while I took the time needed to write this book. Your hard work and dedication are deeply appreciated.

A special thank you to my editors, Robert and James—your meticulous attention to detail and insightful feedback have been wonderful.

To David, my photographer, and Timothy, my graphic designer, your talents have beautifully brought my vision to life. Denys, thank you for your exceptional illustrations.

Tolu, your creativity as a visual artist has been a tremendous asset. Toyin, your research contributions have been indispensable.

I am also grateful to all the consultants who provided valuable insights, feedback and expertise.

To all the guests on the SUSU podcast who shared their stories and contributed to the research for this book, I am deeply thankful.

A heartfelt thank you to all the people I interviewed, including Folasope Aiyesimoju from UAC, Iyinoluwa Aboyeji, founder of Flutterwave, and Adenike Ogunlesi. Your insights have enriched this work immensely.

For those who gave me access to research and their work, including Tom and David Kelley from IDEO, authors of *Creative Confidence*, and Irene Yuan Sun, author of *The Next Factory of the World*, thank you for your support and encouragement throughout this process.

Thank you to all those who endorsed this book. Your support helps to validate the quality and credibility of this work, including Haresh Aswani, Oswald Osaretin Guobadia, Akin Abayomi, Ituah Ighodalo, Femi Gbajabiamila, Tom Kelley, Bayo Udunlami, Towun Candid-Johnson, Hon. Folashade Ambrose-Medebem, John Ugochukwu Uwajumogu, Yemi Keri, Brendan Boyle and Tunde Adeola.

A special mention to Toyin Owoseje, who was instrumental in assisting with research and permissions. Your support has been invaluable.

I am deeply inspired by thought leaders such as Irene Yuan Sun and the many inspirational entrepreneurs and intrapreneurs whose passion for young enterprise fuels my own.

Thank you to Gaia Africa, my women's network group, whose journeys and stories offer inspiration at every turn and who provided valuable connections. To all the women who shared their stories, network, knowledge and time with me, I am eternally grateful.

To all my clients over the past 14 years at Majeurs, your support has made this book possible. Without you, I would not have a story to tell or the experience to share. Your trust in me has been a profound source of encouragement.

To everyone who took the time to read the drafts and provided genuine feedback, I am very grateful. To all those who will buy this book, thank you so much for your support. I can only hope that my journey sows a seed that paves the way for you to begin your own journey and body of work. May our collective light and contributions inspire the tomorrow we all dream of.

With gratitude, *Demi Samande*

Foreword

When I first met Demi Samande during one of her visits to Silicon Valley, I was fascinated to hear her stories about entrepreneurial struggles and successes from London to Lagos. As she talked about her unique experiences, it seemed like she could write a book about it someday. For many of us, those 'someday' dreams of the future get lost along the way, but Demi has the kind of energy and perseverance to make hers come true. So it is my great pleasure to introduce her debut book, *In Her Hands: Shaping the Future of Manufacturing in Africa: A Woman's Story*, which is equal parts autobiography, entrepreneurship handbook, and call to action.

This engaging book invites you on a journey of discovery that not only spans three continents, but also lights the way toward entrepreneurial success in Africa and beyond. Demi shares her personal story as she navigates her way from the architecture studios of London to the vibrant startup environment of Nigeria, with side trips to California's Silicon Valley. Throughout her narrative, she points to lessons learned, sharing them to benefit the next generation of leaders in Africa and around the world. So Demi's story is not just hers alone. It is a beacon of possibility for aspiring entrepreneurs everywhere.

Some parts of Demi's business will sound familiar to startup founders around the world, but then she surprises you with moments that are truly unique. For example, there is the extraordinary day when Prince Charles (now HRH King Charles, of course) visited her company in London and sat on one of the classic Chesterfields she had restored.

Like many of us, Demi went through a lot of trial and error before finding work that was not just a job but truly a calling. She ran a car wash, sold products to beauty salons, and eventually worked as an architect, which seemed like the perfect job until she realized she didn't have a passion for the field. She gained relevant skills from each role however, and her experience across multiple industries helped fuel her entrepreneurial ambitions. Demi's growth mindset helped her pivot from being stuck at an unfulfilling job to becoming a startup founder and CEO.

Throughout her story, Demi recognizes that she hasn't done it all alone. For example, she gives her mother a lot of credit for being an influential role model, since her mother's informal shop in London, overflowing with African textiles and goods, helped plant the seeds of her own entrepreneurship. One of her kind and generous uncles was the catalyst for starting her Nigerian business, as well as a trusted advisor along the way. And when Demi acknowledges her former partner for 'doing the heavy lifting,' she meant that quite literally, because those big Chesterfield sofas certainly aren't light.

Demi's voyage from London to Lagos was both a geographic shift and a cultural homecoming, as she entered a market brimming with potential. Describing her enterprise there, she touches on universal leadership challenges—like finding good, skilled people—as well as distinctive regional challenges like frequent power outages, which many entrepreneurs have never had to worry about.

Near to Demi's heart is the Majeurs Academy she founded, a teaching program that stands as a testament to her belief in nurturing talent and fostering sustainable economic growth. The academy is not just an educational institution. It is the embodiment of Demi's philosophy that skill development and empowerment are the engines of economic transformation for Africa.

As you read this book, I hope you will have the chance to be inspired, to learn, and maybe even to find a spark that ignites your own entrepreneurial spirit.

Tom Kelley, co-author of *New York Times* bestseller, *Creative Confidence: Unleashing the Creative Potential Within Us All*

Tom Kelley. Image courtesy of Tom Kelley.

Tom Kelley is Founder and Chairman of D4V (Design for Ventures), a Tokyo-based venture capital firm renowned for connecting startup companies with unmatched design and business expertise. As a best-selling author of Creative Confidence *and* The Art of Innovation, *Tom's decades of experience in Silicon Valley contribute to D4V's global outlook. In his role as a professional storyteller, Tom has presented to business audiences in over 30 countries, sharing insights on fostering innovation and unlocking creative potential. At IDEO, Tom helped lead the firm from a small team of designers to hundreds of professionals, having managed areas including business development, marketing, and talent. In addition to work at IDEO, Tom also served as the first-ever Executive Fellow at the Haas School of Business at UC Berkeley.*

Finding Your Ground 1

The origins of the tufted leather Chesterfield sofa are unknown, but thought to be first commissioned by Phillip Stanhope the 4th Earl of Chesterfield, in the early 1700's. The goal of the stately sofa was to create seating that allowed gentlemen to sit comfortably without wrinkling their garments. Stanhope was patron of the arts and known for his trendsetting tastes and his Chesterfield sofa was a trend that caught on.[1]

How could a humble Chesterfield sofa teach me or anybody anything? Particularly, how to be an authentic and successful businesswoman in London and now in Lagos, Nigeria. Sofas, couches—or in the UK specifically, leather Chesterfields—are typically graceful, elegant, and timeless pieces of furniture normally situated in a common living area with a quiet authoritativeness.

Without getting overly poetic, we tend to imbue this ubiquitous object as a special place for families and friends to gather and sit to chat, argue, love, cry, fight, grieve, or even just plop down to read a book or watch our favourite television programmes. However, I seriously doubt that many contemporary couch sitters *of both sexes* now worry about wrinkling their garments. It is not without irony to state that Phillip Stanhope's grand furniture idea that tufted leather 'Chesterfields', built originally for the English nobility, could change the life of a young Nigerian woman who grew up in a middle-class family in East London.

The Chesterfield has taught me many things. First and foremost, that there is no need to shout to the mountaintop or raise my voice in celebration about a new creative invention because Chesterfields have quiet usefulness built in—suggesting universal conviviality and comfortability in any

DOI: 10.4324/9781003453994-1

room or space. Learning these timeless lessons and values gave me a front-row seat to everything that makes a design truly authentic.

My long(ish) story with Chesterfields begins rather ordinarily when I purchased an abandoned leather Chesterfield sofa and restored it to its former glory in my London flat. This restoration work allowed me to find my true calling, and authenticity, as a young Black businesswoman. It also propelled me to heights that I never would have imagined in a remarkably short period of time. My business acumen and interest grew alongside this work, more out of necessity than anything.

★★★

From a very bootstrappy beginning in business that developed in fits and starts, including driving a rental van all over England and Wales with my former boyfriend to pick up and then restore leather Chesterfields—to showcasing and selling my furniture restoration projects all over the UK—to literally inviting HRH Prince Charles, now King Charles, to sit on one of my restoration projects! I delve into this story in a later chapter. I can say from the outset that Prince Charles was extremely curious about the recycling of vintage furniture (yes, we sat on my Chesterfield and chatted!). I also met with former British prime minister, David Cameron, and was

Figure 1.1 HRH King Charles with Demi in Majeurs' London studio, 9 September 2014. Image courtesy of Majeurs Holdings.

*Figure 1.2 Prime Minister David Cameron with Demi Samande,
22 September 2013.* Image courtesy of Majeurs Holdings.

asked to restore a vintage leather chair at 10 Downing Street that belonged to Winston Churchill. I politely declined, and I'll explain that decision in another chapter.

My story is not unique, and many entrepreneurs find success from very simple beginnings, but rarely, if ever, do they find early success in a major global city like London, before deciding to pack up and move to Lagos, Nigeria with the plan to build a furniture, design, and manufacturing company, and now an operational training academy, from scratch.

As of January 2023, I've opened the doors and welcomed the first students to a brand-new entrepreneurial training academy in Lagos. I hope it will create an entirely new generation of Nigerians who want to break the mould and change the view held by some of Africa as a broken group of countries, still dealing with the traumas of postcolonial horrors and corruption.

Knocks and Failures

I'm acutely aware that I am not the perfect role model for my students or staff at the training academy in Lagos, and my learning curve in Nigeria over the past seven years has been steep and profound. What this chapter is truly about is finding your ground, or your voice, and being authentic to that ground, wherever it is.

As a businesswoman, and entrepreneur, I've certainly had my share of knocks and failures, and all of these have given me new strength to carry on and then make a bold, and some may say risky, move to Africa. As I stated in my foreword, my faith has been a constant guide, and for the students who have come forward to sign up, I'm in constant awe of their desire to build something completely different and tread new paths to find their own authentic success.

Teaching someone to become an entrepreneur in Africa can be somewhat daunting, however, in a country where everyone seems to have a small home-based business or side hustle, not unlike my mother's back in London. The buying and selling of all kinds of goods on street markets, corner stalls and homes is common practice, like my Mum's chaotic informal market. Lagos is a city-state that from an outsider's point of view is a chaotic jumble of street vendors and never-ending traffic jams. However chaotic, entrepreneurship is everywhere.

Thus, the idea of training entrepreneurship to Nigerians seems rather lame when almost everyone is haggling, dealing, and flipping goods to pay for food to put on the table for their families.

However, to build a business, hire trained artisans, administrators, and technical staff and then scale that business takes a much larger set of skills that must be learned.

The fairly straightforward analogy to be drawn here is that being an entrepreneur in business is much like becoming a film director. There is so much that can be learned and studied in a classroom, but until that director or young entrepreneur is confronted with making real-time decisions for the camera and actors, or a team of employees, and success or failure rides on their clarity of vision and decision-making, it is the practical and 'creative thinking' training and learned classroom skills they can fall back on.

To begin my classroom talks, I like to ask students to think about two concepts, authenticity and 'knowing your ground'. For some students it is a big question and often met with awkward silence. In my experience, the Nigerian school system tends to knock down any kind of creative thinking. It is more about not asking too many questions, keeping your head down, and knowing your place in life. A creative idea might be a repetition of something that already works. Stultifying to say the least, but given the opportunity and a safe space with like-minded students, the resulting conversations are always surprising.

In my own personal research while setting up a business in Africa, possibly the only book that deals with the new realities facing African businesses and entrepreneurs is Irene Yuan Sun's groundbreaking volume called *The Next Factory of the World: How Chinese Investment is Reshaping Africa*.[2] Her book is a comprehensive study of manufacturing in Africa, with a critical and fascinating eye on Chinese manufacturing companies who have a long history of success and failure in several countries including Nigeria.

Since data is slow to be developed for studies of manufacturing in Africa, her book became a kind of how-to, and how-not-to, guide for me as I was starting my furniture manufacturing factory in Lagos. Not much has been written on this new wave of African investment and I want to personally thank her for the inspiration the book has brought me—her words of wisdom lend an understanding of what is happening on the continent and are essential reading for anyone interested in investing or starting up a manufacturing company in Africa.

In her statement about Chinese factories in Africa, Yuan Sun boldly quotes Dani Rodrik's speech from 'An African Growth Miracle', at the Ninth Annual Richard Sabot Lecture (Washington D.C. Center for Global Development, April 2014):

> This is the future that will create broad-based prosperity for Africans and usher in the next phase of global growth for a large swath of the Chinese economy. This is what will make Africa rich and achieve dramatic and lasting change in living standards. To be clear, Africa today is not defined by poverty: it is characterized by promise and optimism with eight of the ten fastest growing economies in the world over the next decade projected to be on the continent.[3]

Bold words indeed, but in my thinking, what about products and services created and developed by and for Africans and that might be then scaled for a global marketplace? Some of the issues Yuan Sun writes about are what I'm dealing with on a day-to-day basis, and I'm sure if she were to travel to my factory in Lagos today, she would see that small and bold changes are happening all over the country, *but investment sorely lags behind almost all other regions*. In my experience when speaking with potential investors, the tropes that Africa is too broken, too poor, too corrupt do not add up to the reality on the ground.

Yuan Sun's study does not try to soft pedal the contemporary African business environment, and realities on the ground:

> But just as it is wrong to cast Africa in the tired stereotype of pitiful, hopeless destitution, it is problematic to ignore the fact that more than half a billion of the poorest people in the world still live in Africa. Over the past half century, Africa has become the testing ground for multiple waves of Western ideas about poverty alleviation. To be sure, Western

development programs that help with things like educating children are important for other reasons, but they will not create 100 million jobs and lift half a billion people out of poverty.[4]

Yuan Sun concludes this introduction by making a clarion call directly to her readers and indirectly directly to me as a Nigerian businesswoman who is building a factory:

> If we are serious about raising the living standards across this vast region of the world, it is time to try something new. That something new has already started moving to Africa: factories. Factories are the bridge that connects China, the current Factory of the World, to Africa, the next Factory of the World.[5]

Her words are indeed inspiring and the numbers are staggering, however, as the geopolitical business and trade world begins to turn away from China due to its spiralling labour costs, demographics in a death spiral due to harsh family planning programmes, the disastrous mismanagement of Covid-19 pandemic and a political focus on top-down control and militarisation rather than trade and development, Africa is the logical 'Next Factory of the World'. But is it ready?

This is a question I've given a lot of thought to, and for both the new students and instructors at the academy, it is the existential question that must be asked. How may you ask? The answer is clear to me: by doing it, and to prove my point, we have already secured a new building to house the academy, so that we can quadruple our intake of students over the next five years.

There is no question that Africa faces innumerable issues, and I'll address them in future chapters, but overall, the top ones that I've identified are the massive problems with infrastructure and consistent power supply for factories, corruption, supply-chain problems, and a lack of trained factory personnel. Why Africa? The Chinese investors have seen the light for many years and profited from lower costs. There is a burgeoning new high-tech sector, as well as a growing middle class that aspires to have luxury goods like handmade Nigerian furniture.

I'm not stepping out of line when I state that I firmly believe the future *is* Africa. Its global impact on the world economy through design and the way Africans do business is exploding. Just look at the tsunami of Afrobeat musicians making a huge impact on the global stage. Social media and instant communication drives interest even higher, and in turn, this interest drives a deep desire for products created, developed, made and sold in Africa.

I'll explore this theme in later chapters, but like jazz music in New Orleans, hip-hop that came from the streets and clubs of the Bronx, Afrobeat makes the world think about Africa in an entirely new way.

How do I know this? At 28 years old, I left London and booked a one-way ticket to Lagos. I was determined to find what was missing in my entrepreneurial journey. I went looking for Africa and I may just have found far more than I bargained for. Like the Chesterfield sofa, Africa has taught me incredible things, and doing business here has opened a dynamic world of possibilities and introduced me to remarkable people and business opportunities.

After graduating from London Metropolitan University with a degree in architecture, I had never intended to leap directly into entrepreneurship. I initially joined an architectural firm, and let me be honest—it was anything but fulfilling. The daily commute from East London to Luton was its own brand of chaos, exacerbating the dissatisfaction I felt in my work environment. Picture this: a cramped office, the size of a shoebox, shared with five colleagues who, to put it kindly, had a lax attitude toward organisation and cleanliness.

In stark contrast, I had always envisioned a very different professional reality for myself. Imagine walking into a glass-walled office on the 14th floor of a premier architectural firm, located in the pulsating heart of London. Each morning, I'd don my quirky Le Corbusier glasses and select an outfit from my carefully curated wardrobe that screamed 'Architectural Digest'. Hopping on the tube, I would head to my chic office space where most of my day would be spent in spirited debates with my team. We'd delve into the intricacies of lavishly elaborate designs for clients who had no financial constraints. In my mind, I was the Zaha Hadid of East London, the female counterpart to David Adjaye. This was the dream I had nurtured since my first year at university.

The reality? A far cry from my aspirations. I found myself confined to a grimy office, tasked with drafting rudimentary floor plans for council flats in the least affluent areas of Luton. Needless to say, the dream was rapidly disintegrating. I began to make excuses to avoid the office until, eventually, I found myself jobless. Though financially strapped, the sensation that washed over me was one of sheer relief.

It had become very clear to me that I had the genetic code from my mother about paying my own way. I was lucky enough to continue my studies in Architectural Design at London Metropolitan University, and then selling body shapers as a side hustle paid my way through university.

I was a restless student and was never really happy with how my life was panning out. There were family tragedies, like the sudden passing of my older sister, but that truly devastating event brought me even closer to her husband, Chinedu, who turned out to be a wonderful mentor and advisor. He was the person who advised me to think about moving to Nigeria. I'll delve into that narrative in a later chapter. If there is anyone to blame for that decision, I can happily point my finger at him.

After I left college to set about finding my ground, there was a lot of activity, buying and selling, trials and errors, fits and starts and yes, the early success when I began restoring vintage Chesterfields. When I speak to my staff and to the students at the factory in Lagos, I'm always reminded of my very humble beginnings in London; my mother's chaotic informal home-based emporium, and her deep desire to teach me about paying for all the things that you need, even if you don't have the direct means to do so.

Through my Mum's actions and her love for her children, she also ingrained in me that it doesn't matter what your background is, or where you come from, or whether or not you come from a family of means, or no means whatsoever, sometimes all it takes is a spark to light an idea, to get the creative and industrious wheels turning. She quickly figured out that the Nigerian community in London wanted to feel closer to home, and by supplying a range of goods imported to England she created a demand and cash flowed into her family. She was certainly not what I would call a businesswoman, and I'd say that whatever strategy she had has a plan, she certainly was not going to scale it beyond a home-based business.

When I began my furniture restoration business with leather Chesterfields, I always thought to myself, how can this actually work? What are my creative resources and how do I learn to do this very precise work? Yes, there was a steep learning curve to understand and source all the particular dyes and materials, to taking a leather Chesterfield apart and then painstakingly restoring it to its former glory. I learned the trade by doing, asking questions and finding resources that I'd never even considered or realised existed. I was an architectural and design student, and none of that training really prepared me to become a major player in furniture restoration.

I'll also admit that sometimes divine intervention, and a little bit of luck, also helps answer the nagging questions about finding your ground and it pays to be restless, and a little edgy—never truly happy with the reality of being tied to a 9 to 5 job.

This entrepreneurial restlessness can be problematic, and the toll on family and relationships can be difficult, but the rewards can be very good, and that includes the greatest pleasure of being your own boss.

In Nigeria and elsewhere, the education system tends to dissuade students from thinking creatively and taking risks to find a service or a product they feel they could either build better, or a better idea from scratch.

I don't want to sound overly optimistic, because a lot of startup businesses fail due to many factors, and in Nigeria and in Africa the odds are even steeper because of preexisting bias to providing secure investment.

What did a distressed Chesterfield couch really teach me? With the right idea or the right product, a lot of doors can open that you never thought even existed. The Chesterfield also taught me about craftmanship and attention to detail, which imbue all my furniture creations.

If you combine those ideas with my family background in London, where my mum was not afraid of opening our doors to the public to sell all kinds of products from our home, then the leap to selling body shapers in hair and nail salons, fundraising for cancer and other good causes, was not so huge, because the ground I was raised in was literally an African marketplace.

Role Models

When I speak with new students about the entrepreneurial spirit, I often like to open the conversation about role models. I like to ask them, 'What are you exposed to? What is right in front of you?' 'If you are not exposed to anything, or have anyone to inspire you, how do you look for that exposure?' 'What is within your reach?' Then I ask them, 'What are you looking for, a business idea, or creating a specific product?'

I was first exposed to this entrepreneurial spirit by my mother, Elizabeth, but to me it was not called entrepreneurship, it was simply survival. She had a full-time job as a nurse and raised five kids, all while going to university for ongoing training. She also had a small 'home-based' emporium, meaning that she traded in all kinds of goods.

Initially Mum would buy goods for X amount and then flip them. She would purchase various goods that she knew would appeal to the Nigerian expat community, sell them, and add a little profit for herself. She was very dynamic, and her business was moulded by her work schedule which was hectic. While she was at work she would make phone calls with customers and arrange pickups and deliveries. My sisters and I would package every-thing together and make sure the deliveries were made.

Over time, she expanded to food, fabrics, and hard-to-get products from Nigeria, importing traditional food items that were not available in the UK. She would sell these food items wholesale. A supplier would drop them at the house, and then she would organise people to distribute them to the Nigerian community. It was so successful that she branched out and began selling electronics and small appliances, which I can tell you filled up the corridors and rooms throughout our flat in East London, turning it basically into a home-based Nigerian market.

Without a doubt my mother was a huge inspiration for me. I literally saw her buy and sell a bit of everything, and I saw her make things work and make extra money for the family budget. In retrospect it probably shouldn't have worked but it did, particularly because she had so little time. I have a lot of admiration for her and how she juggled kids, schoolwork, a full-time job, her university coursework, and the business. She really wanted to make sure she could feed her family, and make sure we had everything we possibly needed. The profits allowed us to go on school trips and holidays. My Mum was possibly the closest person I had to a female business role model. However, I also saw how disorganised it was, I saw how chaotic it was. We were conscripted to run the distribution operations. It wasn't an ideal situation, and as I've mentioned, it was very chaotic.

In looking back at this period in my life, I'll have to say that her home-based emporium inspired me to create something much more structured. I realised that chaos did not work for me, and I believe at that point I recognised that if I ever had my own business I would need to create structure and something that was more organised and scalable.

Our flat was always filled with various goods coming in the door, then my sisters and I would package them, and make sure everything was properly paid for. That is a lot of additional stress for young kids, and I would not recommend that lifestyle, unless for survival purposes. I think my family members would all agree and say that running an emporium is a very nontraditional family setting and we were unpaid participants, perhaps grudgingly, in my mother's informal market. Also, it was unavoidable, because it was literally right outside my bedroom door. My Mum was an entrepreneur, and the buying and selling of all kinds of goods to London's Nigerian diaspora was in essence her desire to provide income for the family but also to supply a fairly large community with products that reminded them of home, and they could not get elsewhere.

This work experience was inevitable, as it was happening right outside my bedroom door. My mum was an entrepreneur, and her business of buying and selling all kinds of goods to London's Nigerian diaspora was not just a way to support our family, but also a way to provide a large community with products that reminded them of home—items they couldn't find anywhere else.

★★★

This brings me to an essential concept I introduce to students and future staff: the idea of authenticity and knowing your ground. To me, your "ground" is the foundation of who you are—your passions, skills, strengths, and even the desires you've left behind. When you truly understand this, it becomes the starting point for building something that can have a lasting impact. This approach shapes how we teach at the academy, and it's just as crucial for the designers and craftspeople on the factory floor.

It's a big question because many young people have never been asked to reflect on what makes them unique. They might think, "I don't have what it takes," simply because they haven't identified their ground. But without that self-awareness—without recognizing what drives you—you might feel ill-suited to start your own business or enter a business environment.

For me and other businesspeople, this is a personal challenge we face daily. Yet, knowing your ground—your strengths, limitations, and what makes you authentic—is the most valuable starting point for training future entrepreneurs. That's why at Majeurs Academy, we focus on helping students identify their ground. No matter the challenges they face, this grounding provides the clarity and resilience to see any project through to completion.

★★★

I also relate these stories that give some personal background. Prior to moving to Lagos, I attempted several small-scale business ventures. This period of my life was before I discovered my passion for creating beautiful furniture.

I got involved in a car wash business, several years after my older sister had suddenly and tragically passed away. It sparked the idea that I could raise money for charities. It was not that difficult, and I thought I could make that a business by being a professional fundraiser.

We would wash cars for donation to a good cause, and for me and my friends, the car wash was a great exercise in community building, but as a career, I quickly learned that it was not my ground, just a great idea. Following that period I started university and was studying Architecture. I knew I needed extra money for university, and as mentioned earlier, worked with a Spanish woman, who lived in Sevenoaks in London, who sold body shapers from a little hole in the wall. One day I actually accidently stumbled into her shop and asked her about these spandex girdles—called body shapers. The idea was to give women who didn't want to go to the gym that perfect hourglass figure.

We immediately struck up a good working relationship and she'd literally give me all her new stock. These body shapers were made in her hometown in Spain, and she brought them into England to sell.

I thought to myself that I could sell these things for a small markup on the price and she worked quite a distance from where I lived so I wasn't directly competing with her. I thought this could be a very good business. She had an amazing body; I suppose because of the shapers. I told her she was really cute! I somehow convinced her to give me the new stock to sell without putting any money down.

Then I'd get on my scooter and travel back to my neighbourhood and I'd go into all the hairdressers, nail salons, really anywhere you could find women who were making themselves beautiful. I'd walk in, and stand in the middle of the salon, and say, 'Hello ladies, my name is Demi and I'm selling these body shapers!'

I was hawking body shapers and it became a very good side hustle. Selling to customers gave me confidence as a businesswoman. I stood in front of complete strangers in various salons and told them about my body shaping product to get them intrigued and basically get them to part with their money.

It became a 'thing'; the owners of the salons asked me to come every other Saturday and sell to their clients. The owners would also buy the body shapers and of course show them to their clients proving to them that they actually worked.

In a very basic way, I was able identify a market, women in hair salons who were thinking about beauty. I had the right product and was bold enough to tell customers that the body shapers would make them more beautiful. I was kind of a classic street hawker, but I can say that the Spanish lady loved working with me because I moved a lot of products and body shapers paid my way through university.

★★★

My story has a lot of deeper meaning now, particularly when I sell my furniture today or my team are struggling with something that must be dealt with, or I have to meet investors and have to do the whole founder's pitch, I can literally hear myself on that salon floor. I use that same confident tone of voice saying how can I convince this person to either buy from me or invest in my company. What sets my product apart? I can still hear that young girl in London's hair salons hawking body shapers!

★★★

By relating my personal story, I provided you with the deeper background—the kind of hands on, creative, and practical training I had—when I decided to build a scalable manufacturing business and training academy in Nigeria. In retrospect, I believe I had to take baby steps before making the massive step to leave England. After all, those family comforts cannot be easily replaced or found in a new country. Did all this activity prepare me for moving to Africa? In some small ways, yes. However, I never had any dreams or plans to move to Africa. My family were a part of the large diaspora who left Nigeria for good. I'd visited some family but really had very little to do with them. My father and mother were deeply embedded in England as immigrants, and then with hard work built a growing family in London. Nigeria was so far out of my reality that it could have been Mars.

I am working with the team at the academy to rapidly develop these ideas into a pedagogy that can be learned and repeated by a new generation of students. My ambition is to have 25,000 students go through this training over the next ten years, so I've set my sights high. I want my students to be inspired to take the next steps and make their Africa the 'Next Factory of the World'.

In the following chapter on creative thinking, I've provided a step-by-step guide on a very specific process, and I've included an interview with Brendan Boyle who is a professor at the d.school at Stanford University, and a celebrated toy inventor. Brendan is also an instructor at the Lagos academy, and I'm forever grateful for his guidance and inspiration to the first group of students. In that chapter, I've also included an interview with one of the students, who is learning new ways to become an entrepreneur in Africa as well as using the creative thinking pedagogy developed at the d.school.

So how did a struggling girl from London find her authentic ground by buying a distressed vintage Chesterfield couch and turn it into a success and have the now King of England sit on it?

Answer: creative thinking, perseverance, bootstrapping, and literally thousands of unpaid hours of sweat equity.

Notes

1 Whitney Wood. 2014. 'The Chesterfield Sofa: A Classic Piece for Any Interior.' *Decoist*. 22 January. https://www.decoist.com/2014-01-22/Chesterfield-sofa-interiors-inspiration/?Exc_D_LessThanPoint002_p1=1

2 Irene Yuan Sun. 2017. *The Next Factory of the World*. Harvard Business Press. Page 6.

3 Ibid. Page 6.

4 Ibid. Page 6.

5 Ibid. Page 6.

Creativity

2

Sofa So Good/Embrace Your Mistakes

> Creativity is much broader and more universal than what people typically consider the 'artistic' fields. We think of creativity as using your imagination to create something new in the world. Creativity comes into play wherever you have the opportunity to generate new ideas, solutions and approaches. And we believe everyone should have access to that resource.
>
> —Tom Kelley and David Kelley[1]

My journey with buying, restoring and selling Chesterfields really began when I made a huge mistake. I, along with my boyfriend at the time, had purchased what I thought was a classic English Chesterfield for our small flat in London. However, the moment it was being loaded off the delivery van, I knew it was a fake. It just did not live up to what I saw as one of the greatest English furniture designs ever created. I was truly frustrated that we'd paid for something that was not the real thing. I wanted the big, generous classic Chesterfield sofa with arms that embraced you, with big buttons and buttery-soft brown leather.

My boyfriend said, 'It's fine, we should just keep it.' He was not invested in authenticity but rather just wanted a sofa to sit or lay on. He was practical like most men—design was secondary to function. We needed a sofa, we bought a sofa, mission accomplished.

Sofa So Good

I became even more frustrated that in effect we'd been ripped off. We had bought it off of the website Craigslist, and it really bothered me that

DOI: 10.4324/9781003453994-2

someone would have the audacity to sell a fake Chesterfield (the leather was not even real). I was a recently graduated architecture and design student and I'd certainly developed an eye for size, shape and texture and the fact that I had been tricked was doubly insulting.

A few weeks later, I was shopping for groceries at our local Sainsbury's supermarket with my sister. She noticed a small poster pinned on the community billboard and drew my attention to it.

> Chesterfield set for sale, a three-seater, two-seater, two armchairs and a foot stool.

My sister said to me while eyeing the notice, 'Isn't that the sofa that you have been complaining and obsessing over?' She knew I was obsessed with finding an authentic Chesterfield.

There was a phone number attached to the poster. I immediately called the number. The woman on the end of the line invited us to come over straight away and have a look.

She was an elderly white English lady, who was obviously downsizing. The entire collection of authentic Chesterfields and armchairs was in excellent condition. I asked her the price for the three-seater, thinking that I could sell the fake and replace it. She immediately said, no, that she wanted to sell the entire set for £300 and I would need to hire a van to come and take them away.

At the time I was working in a clothing store, and I only had £350 in the bank. The price for the entire set was ridiculously low which made it even more enticing. My sister thought so as well.

The upside was I thought this some kind of sign from heaven or at least Sainsbury's. The downside was that I'd need to drain my bank account, hire a van, and deliver these gorgeous leather set pieces to our extremely tiny flat, all without talking to my boyfriend.

I called a local van driver in the neighbourhood, and I had to borrow £10 from my sister to pay the driver. In the back of my mind, I could only think, I have finally found what I was looking for and what I thought I had paid for, an original, authentic leather English Chesterfield.

Needless to say, my boyfriend was absolutely livid. He was perfectly happy with the ugly replica, and now our flat was crammed with all of these oversize leather furniture pieces—we even stored some in the hallway and ignored our neighbours' constant complaints.

My boyfriend asked bluntly, 'Demi, what are your plans for this furniture?' He was so irritated by my random actions. Not only had I invaded his space without consent, I had now rendered myself completely broke and this meant I would now be relying on him to take care of me completely. He loved me and didn't mind supporting me, but I could tell he felt the pressure of my rash decision to buy the entire set as a sign of bad financial judgement.

The tension was mounting. Still, he smiled and on most occasions went along with my crazy ideas. He worked at the local council and wasn't earning a great deal with his salary, but we got by.

I had big dreams that he didn't always understand. Often, he would give me the most puzzled facial expressions, underlying a squint of fear on his eyebrows. I could tell he was always so fearful of my curiosity and free spirit. Our relationship often felt like a dance of push and pull. Me always pushing forward, him always wanting to pull me back to reality and financial safety.

I told him frankly, 'Don't worry, I am going to sell them.'

I cleaned all the furniture pieces that I wanted to sell, and used some photo techniques that I had learned in university to create far more enticing photos and posted them on Craigslist.

In short order we had strangers in our flat looking over the leather armchairs and sofas.

A woman asked about the two-seater. I took a deep breath, then stated clearly that it was an original and the price would be £600. I sold the armchairs for another £300 and in a very short time period, I'd made a very tidy profit flipping authentic English Chesterfields.

By rejecting the fake and searching for the authentic leather Chesterfield a business literally grew in my living room (sound familiar?). Was I being fearless, foolish, or just stubborn? I believe my sister thought I was all three.

My boyfriend was more than pleased because by selling the vintage furniture at such a profit, so much so, that I made half of his monthly salary in one afternoon.

***

In Tom Kelley and David Kelley's must-read book *Creative Confidence, Unleashing the Creative Potential Within Us All* (that I encourage all staff and students at the academy to read), they include a section called The Clay Horse.[2] It is a story told by David Kelley about a boy named Brian who was shamed in his class when a fellow student told him the clay horse he had made was terrible and useless. Brian never did a creative project like that again.

The Kelley brothers write, 'Our fear of being judged is something we learn at a young age. But we don't start out with it. Most children are naturally daring. They explore new games, meet new people, try new things and let their imaginations run wild.'

If I had to dissect my decision to buy the entire set of leather furniture and basically bankrupt myself so that I could have an authentic leather Chesterfield, the first words that might come to mind are impulsive and headstrong, but it was also linked a very strong creative impulse to reject the fake replica and allow my imagination to run wild at all the possibilities of owning an authentic Chesterfield sofa. My sister and boyfriend could have called out 'clay horse' and ridiculed me. I understood very well that this purchase was literally going to take every penny of mine, but in retrospect my life changed the day I decided to buy that furniture set.

Creativity is many things to everyone. My business really grew out of buying, restoring, and then reselling leather Chesterfields, but it was also born out of necessity: we literally had no room in our flat—we had to sell the pieces.

My creativity and discerning eye developed even further as I began buying more Chesterfields—and a quite few of them were not in perfect sellable condition. I needed to find out how to restore leather furniture and that led me to hire —for the purposes of his privacy, I will call him 'Jamie'— a fourth or fifth generation leather furniture restorer, who held on tight to the family secrets of furniture repair—at least until he met me...

I should state for the record that Jamie was an excellent furniture restorer, and when he showed up in our flat, that had become a de facto leather Chesterfield storage and repair shop, I asked him if could share any of his furniture restoration secrets. He firmly believed in the old British WW2 warning to its citizens that 'Loose lips sink ships.'

My Secret Apprenticeship in Leather Restoration

Jamie was a man wrapped in an enigma, coated in the paradox of his own character. The air around him hummed with an electric charge of nervous energy, yet his hands moved with the precision of a surgeon—never hurried, always intentional. Picture this: a man with a quiet demeanour that seemed almost contemplative, but a firm resolve that belied his silent exterior.

After scouring the market for leather restorers for months, Jamie emerged as a craftsman willing to come to my location. The timing was impeccable; he'd arrive at my flat during those sun-soaked afternoons when my boyfriend was away at work. A clandestine observer from the sidelines, I watched Jamie pour himself into the art of leather restoration with a meticulousness that was almost ritualistic.

Each step was an act of devotion— from the initial preparation to the intricate colouring, followed by the meditative sanding, and finally, the meticulous application of hues before the drying process. It was akin to watching a maestro, each movement flowing seamlessly into the next, forming a symphony of craftsmanship. Jamie never sprinted through his work; instead, he meandered, savouring every stroke and curve like a sommelier with a vintage wine.

But alas, the man was a sealed vault. When it came to his unique skill set, Jamie would politely, yet firmly, deflect my inquiries. 'No, Demi, these are trade secrets. No restorer will freely divulge this kind of knowledge, and those who might, well, they'd charge a pretty penny for it.'

Thus, began my covert operation. On his subsequent visits, I'd stealthily film Jamie, my phone concealed within the folds of a casual magazine or behind a curtain of plants. Each time he'd make his way to the bathroom, I'd seize the opportunity to snap pictures of his tools—tools devoid of any identifying labels or tags. What were they? Where could I find them? I was clueless, but I banked on the hope that I'd recognize them when I saw them elsewhere.

After months of this discreet apprenticeship and countless hours immersed in YouTube tutorials, my patience bore fruit. A training academy in Yorkshire caught my eye, and I enrolled for a week-long course. Armed with the surreptitious knowledge I'd gathered from my afternoons with Jamie, I walked into that academy not as a novice, but as someone who had glimpsed the arcane world of leather restoration through the eyes of a reluctant mentor.

The week in Yorkshire was transformative, solidifying the fragments of skill and knowledge I'd collected. But it was those stolen afternoons with Jamie, observing his quiet but firm demeanour, his meticulous yet nervous craftsmanship, that had set me on this path. Though Jamie might never know it, he'd unwittingly become the catalyst for my journey into the secretive craft of leather restoration—a craft I would eventually make my own.

Ahmed and the Next Generation of African Entrepreneurs

In the classroom and on the floor of the furniture manufacturing business, we are developing what we hope will be a very scalable model. Using the descriptions set up by the d.school, we are very much in the prototype phase, although we ramped up very quickly to the implementation. Well-trained, creative staff have been essential for the long-term growth of my company, and I would argue to any investor, competitor, or governmental policymaker that active, professional, engaged responsible employees are the key to success of any business, but particularly in Africa. The question is, are there enough trained, dynamic workers who ascend to become managers and owners of factories?

In Irene Yuan Sun's book,[3] she relates the story of Ahmed. His story is worth telling here because it strongly relates to many family and work situations in Nigeria I've encountered and it also puts a final nail in the coffin to the tired arguments that Africans are not worth hiring, except for the lowest menial positions.

> Ahmed started at the bottom. He is from Sokoto. One of the poorest states in Nigeria. After secondary school, like many Nigerian men, he was underemployed and surviving by working odd jobs...In 2009 Ahmed got a call from a Chinese man he had once met on the street. This man had a buddy, Mr. Wang, who was fresh from China and hoped to start a business in Nigeria. Ahmed agreed to work for Mr. Wang, first as a driver, then quickly morphing into a sort of all-purpose local fixer.
>
> The key moment in Ahmed's career came when Mr. Wang needed to buy a car for his nascent company the way local Nigerians do by bypassing Nigeria's high import tariffs via Benin. (That meant Ahmed travelling to Benin for at least two weeks.) Many of Mr. Wang's Chinese colleagues thought he was out of his mind and basically kissing that money goodbye.
>
> ...Mr. Wang locked eyes with Ahmed and handed over the wad of cash for the brand-new vehicle...To their surprise, Ahmed came back with the car two weeks later—and even handed over some change. He was full of apologies, however, because he had spotted—in his own words, a pair of beautiful shoes that could not be resisted...Needless to say, Mr. Wang was not upset in the least about the shoes, and from that day on, Ahmed was his right-hand man.

Creative, trustworthy, professional, perhaps with a good eye for footwear, Ahmed proved to his Chinese boss that indeed he was a man to be trusted with money, and responsibility. It should be noted that Ahmed has become the plant manager of Mr. Wang's cardboard box factory having earned the hands-on and practical degree in trust and knowledge, and dependability.

The question begs to be asked, who and where are the next generation of Ahmeds in Nigeria and Africa? In part, it will be the goal of the academy to discover, nurture, and train an entire new generation of entrepreneurs, managers, designers, and creatives. The first students have begun training, and this small but very engaged group are what I hope will be our Ahmeds.

Brendan Boyle and the d.school

Creative endeavours come in a myriad of ways and means, and with the development of the academy in Lagos, the underlying skill I am trying to nurture is creativity in all my staff and students.

I feel honoured to have built a connection to the d.school at Stanford—in particular with Brendan Boyle[4] who is an Adjunct Professor as well as the founder of IDEO's PlayLab.

Full disclosure, Brendan is also on our advisory board, and is now giving classes online to our first group of students at the academy in Lagos. Brendan is an amazing toy designer, and a terrific and super-creative individual. For my students it was a revelation that a fully grown man could design toys. Amongst many toys and games and play items, Brendan has designed a whole range of accessories for Barbie, but that is another story.

I invited him to engage with my team, to think about design and manufacturing of not only furniture design as play, and in an interview included in this chapter along with students, you will see how lively his conversation is. Brendan also visited Lagos and toured our facilities and witnessed perhaps

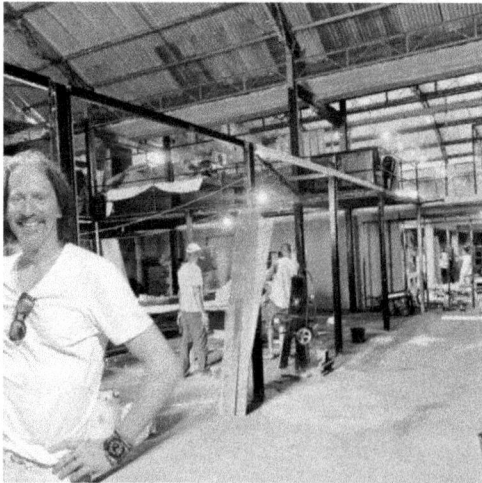

Figure 2.1 Brendan Boyle visiting the Majeurs Factory in Lagos, 2023.
Image courtesy of Majeurs Holdings.

one of the most chaotic cities on earth, at least from an American's point of view.

I'm a big believer in active empathy and allowing the students at the academy to not only thrive but also become problem solvers, team builders, and skilled craftspeople. My furniture manufacturing business needs creative people with a big range of skills. The academy aims to help them develop and create their own entrepreneurial chops, with *creativity serving as the foundation of all its pedagogy.*

Tom and David Kelley's book[5] reminds the reader, in a section called Creativity Now, that,

> Creativity is a much broader and more universal than what people typically consider the 'artistic' fields. We think of creativity as using your imagination to create something new in the world. Creativity comes into play wherever you have the opportunity to generate new ideas, solutions and approaches. And we believe everyone should have access to that resource.

Their broad and inspiring statement makes sense in a North American and European context, but how could it translate to present-day Lagos, Nigeria? I wondered how I could unleash that kind of creative thinking and confidence in a culture and country where creativity was basically drummed out of school children at a very early age. Don't get me wrong, Nigeria, and Africa, definitely has a creative class, but they are the one per cent of the one per cent. Nigeria has a long history of producing great artists, writers, actors, and poets who have left in the diaspora.

As I wrote in Chapter One, the explosion of Afrobeat musicians is making a huge impact on the Nigerian economy, but my questions were more localised. Why can't creativity and playfulness be taught for all levels of craftspeople, and even for workers at a small furniture manufacturer in Lagos? After all, Nigerians are some of the most naturally creative people in the world when it comes to survival. I emphasise the word survival. Creativity should not be viewed merely as a lifeboat, deployed only in the tempest of trials; rather, it ought to be the wind in our sails, propelling us forward even in calm seas. When we confine our creative impulses to moments of survival, we risk cultivating a mindset that is reactionary, rather than visionary, often settling for immediate solutions that lack depth and foresight. A culture that celebrates and encourages creativity fosters an environment where innovation can flourish without bounds, ensuring not just survival, but thriving growth. It is in the steady practice of creativity that we find the seeds of true resilience, enabling us to not just weather the storms, but to chart new courses towards unexplored horizons. Can this sense of creativity be extended within the school system and for the growth of our businesses and innovation that translates to the rest of the globe?

I spoke with Brendan Boyle[6] who travelled from Palo Alto, California to Lagos to visit our factory and gave a series of classes to our first group of students. We spoke again in spring of 2023, and these are his impressions:

> It really reminds me of the very early days of d.school in Stanford[7]— it started off with one class in a trailer that was outside the campus and a handful of students. Fifteen years later, now it is housed in a 50-million-dollar building and has other schools in Germany.
>
> Majeurs is building their own version, which is a prototype, but I felt it would be the right thing and travel to Lagos and I really felt that I should see in person the furniture factory and meet potential students in person. I'm also really interested in this because Demi and Majeurs have really taken the first steps, and I have a lot of admiration that they have taken up the d.school mantra, *put aside all the talk and planning stuff, which can go on forever, forever, and start to start doing.*
>
> The d.school was started from one tiny class, and from that you learn from that class what you need and at least learn how to take the next step. I was able to see that this idea of taking positive steps, finding the first group of students and getting them trained and then into the workforce.
>
> I'm impressed by the first group, and by giving lot of lectures around what are the concepts of design thinking and entrepreneurship, I can see that eventually Majeurs will likely need a director of curriculum— someone who is going to plan what is happening, day-to-day courses and hands-on activities. It was also great to connect with the Academy Lead Franklyn White, who is starting to develop a pedagogy that can be taught and repeated, from all the little experiences that you and Franklyn are already doing.
>
> Something that really impressed me when I was in Lagos and by Nigerians is their entrepreneurial spirit. A huge cultural difference is that in California, you choose to become an entrepreneur. We say, 'I am going to be an entrepreneur and create a start-up around an idea or a product.' Then find the money and try building a startup.
>
> In Nigeria, becoming an entrepreneur, either large or small tis not a lifestyle choice, it's a way of life. What I mean is that to make a living for your family, buying and selling, negotiating prices, haggling, street sales, are really a huge part of daily living. Every price is negotiable,

and this gives Nigerians this bred-in-the-bone attitude that to get ahead you need street smarts, and probably a side hustle. I say this in positive way, because in many ways you cannot teach that attitude. It is really grass-roots creative entrepreneurship and reminds me of a book called *Creative Hustle*[8] written by fellow d.schoolers about how to put yourself forward by becoming an entrepreneur.

In Nigeria there is a lot of that 'Creative Hustle' and energy and—not necessarily a choice—it's a way of life.

After visiting the factory, I actually believe if they can bottle that incredible energy in the Academy then they will be setting up so many students for all kinds for successful outcomes.

In my career and my teaching, at the d.school, the initial basic premise is very clear: *everyone is creative*, however, when students begin, most don't have creative confidence. I saw that in Lagos, and with the classes I've taught I can say that the wider the experiences you give to students, like hands-on classes with students learning drawing, or woodworking, the more confident they become. Confidence is grown overtime and not taught, so I can see that as more students arrive at Majeurs Academy, perhaps having never held a crosscut saw in their hands, to graduation as fully trained craftspeople, with confidence to solve problems, and strong potential for employment, their lives will literally be changed. That is a very powerful message.

I'll also be very clear that there are plenty of challenges and obstacles to overcome in Nigeria, particularly around infrastructure. Something that we take for granted is our power grid. In Nigeria, blackouts, brownouts are part of daily living, and it is tough to witness for an outside viewer.

Imagine if the power went out in California on a daily basis—I'll guarantee that everyone would be panicking, running around with fear in their eyes because the power is off and there's no Wi-Fi. And demanding to their employers that 'we should all go home!?'

While I was in Lagos, I saw that basic infrastructure is pretty weak, and to operate a business that depends on having consistent power supply is a huge challenge.

Despite these challenges, what truly impressed me was that instead of whining about the loss of Wi-Fi, and panicking when factory the power went several times every day — the worked stopped momentarily, while the batteries turned on and the generator kicked up and no one bats an eye. Then the work proceeded normally, as if nothing had happened.

However, I absolutely believe if Nigeria and Africa are to make the leap in manufacturing they must invest in building strong infrastructure and power grid—this is critical, including all the way down to school systems.

There is a vast, young, and creative workforce just waiting to be trained, and then brought up to speed in terms of filling jobs. Nigeria and Lagos is teeming with entrepreneurs and I was really taken by how many creative people are designers and creative folks with different world views and it is definitely two worlds—I can see clearly to goals and plans for Majeurs Academy, to actually train and inspire a huge workforce.'

***

Brendan's commitment to working with the class at the academy was really an eye opener, for him and for our first group of students. I'm eternally grateful for his commitment to working with our team. Once we get the academy truly off the ground, we will have a template for success for the academy and which way it is run. We are creating a road map of how to get the students into the workforce and earning a salary. The formula we have mapped out is that we simply need 16 other graduates who know our system and can build 16 other academies in order to scale it beyond what we are physically able to do and achieve at the moment.

If we can get 16 other people who completely understand our system and can take the academy template and open up in other locations and follow our training and teaching modules, and literally just let them grow, we will hit our target in no time. Sixteen is the magic number to scale the academy to work alongside us.

Brendan and I have discussed these plans that on first look are ambitious, but totally realisable, goals—inspiring the development of satellite Academies all around the country makes perfect sense. He explained to me, 'If you look at the d.school in Stanford, now there are other d.schools at Northwestern University[9] and in Germany. It's like putting out a blueprint and freely offering a programme.' He says the process is open:

Take our d.school pedagogy as a starting point and come back and tell us what you are learning. I love that openness and I believe this will make a huge change in people's lives in Nigeria and Africa.

Brendan explained to me and my students that at the d.school the philosophy is very clear:

You are never the lone sage on the classroom stage. There has to be a multi-disciplinary group of professors or instructors teaching the class of students who also come from different disciplines. What makes the d.school work so well, is that we always encouraged admission from an interesting mix of genders, interests, academic or non-academic backgrounds, because as he explained, everyone one is creative. From what I can tell at the Majeurs Academy, there is a mix of different ages and backgrounds.

I asked Brendan to sum up his impression of the first group of graduates:

Majeurs Academy is unique in that they are using furniture manu-facturing or entrepreneurship as background, and I truly think you're going to have some special people come out of the Academy.

I could not have said it better and I couldn't agree more.

Notes

1 Tom Kelley and David Kelley. 2013. *Creative Confidence: Unleashing the Creative Potential Within Us All*. New York: Crown Publishing Group.
2 Ibid. Page 53.
3 Irene Yuan Sun. 2017. *The Next Factory of the World*. Harvard Business Press. Page 69.
4 https://dschool.stanford.edu/team-directory/brendan-boyle
5 Tom Kelley and David Kelley. 2013. *Creative Confidence: Unleashing the Creative Potential Within Us All*. New York: Crown Publishing Group. Page 3.
6 https://ecorner.stanford.edu/contributor/brendan-boyle/
7 https://dschool.stanford.edu/about
8 Olatunde Sobomechin and Sam Seidel. 2022. *Creative Hustle: Blaze Your Own Path and Make Work That Matters*. Ten Speed Press.
9 https://dschool.stanford.edu/how-to-start-a-dschool/

Nigerian Industry and Creativity

3

My Mother's Home Emporium vs. the Lee Group

In the late 1980's the Nigerian textile industry encompassed two hundred firms and was the second largest employer after the government. Beyond factory jobs, there were jobs for the growers who supplied the raw cotton, the ginners who did the initial processing, the parts suppliers who provided the machinery and the distributors who sold the finished cloth. At its height, the industry employed a million workers and was also indirectly responsible for several million other jobs along this value chain.[1]

When you pull the lens back on this brief but shocking statement, that an entire industry that made absolutely some of the most beautiful cotton cloth in the world had collapsed, it demands the question: how this could happen so quickly? Famous brands, The Kaduna, Arewa and United Nigerian Textiles were globally recognised for excellence. Today in Nigeria there are but a few remnants of the massive industry that affected the well-being of almost every Nigerian family, through work and income and the pride that Nigerian cloth and designs were highly sought after. The companies created national pride, knowing that their goods were marketed and sold successfully around the world. They had created a global demand and market and that was sustained by lower labour costs plus the high quality of textiles, and lower export duties.

To leap forward to my home in 1990s London, Nigerian textiles were also sold at my Mum's home emporium in London. directly imported cloth and lace from Nigeria along with other goods. She knew the demand was there and understood very well that Nigerians from the diaspora had plenty of house pride when it came to their designs and textiles. In her small but

DOI: 10.4324/9781003453994-3

highly successful methodology *she created a market* that met the demands of her customers but also helped sustain our family. In turn that cloth made it into many coverings and traditional garb worn by Nigerians for weddings, and big family occasions.

Why did she succeed? My mum was highly attuned to attitude of service, which really means listening to your customers, and responding with alacrity and promptness, and more than likely also listening to your suppliers. Try to stay one step ahead, so that once you state to your customers you can get a certain item, you *must* deliver.

This is particularly true when dealing with nonessential items such as cloth, textiles and now in my case, furniture design and manufacturing.

My Mum's small home-based business was always humming with activity, and it provided me and my sisters with a kitchen-sink-reality lesson in both micro and macroeconomics. She was actually creating demand for all kinds of products, a market which included goods that I thought would never sell.

As a girl growing up in London, I never really appreciated all the hours of extra work the business created for my Mum, and the enormous efforts she made to keep our family fed and it was certainly not all rosy. There were moments of despair and uncertainty, times when her business faced rough patches and profits plummeted, customers became scarce, money was tight, and it seemed her emporium was on the brink of collapsing. Yet through it all, my mother stood firm, her indomitable spirit never waning. She held on to her belief that she was doing it for us, her children. The pain of those moments was overshadowed by the vision of a better future for us.

My story of understanding what a market is is not only based on some vague and long-winded economics class or what I learned in university. In a sense I'm very privileged to have had this homemade insight. It gave me a deep appreciation of what entrepreneurs must give up in order to succeed. Through observation and participation in my Mum's emporium (I call it that for lack of a better word), I understood what sold, what didn't, how to create pricing, create profit, and how to create an attitude of service by listening and then responding to the needs, desires, and yes, the complaints, of the customers. After all, we were in living London where complaining about the weather and just about everything else is a national pastime.

I also learned about the brutal realties of outside market forces that were out of my Mum's control like price gouging, excessive importation taxes, currency manipulation and corruption. The latter topic I'll deal with in a later chapter.

As I've outlined in previous chapters, there are plenty of dos and don'ts when planning your business, whether it's service-based or product-based. If you are considering a long-term, sustainable, successful and scalable operation—either in Africa or anywhere else in the world—I've created a top ten list. Many of these I've learned the hard way by bootstrapping and *by doing it*. My furniture business did not grow in a vacuum, and I've essentially built and scaled it using many of these values and rules listed below.

Ten Essential Rules for Anyone Starting a Business

1. Identify your passion and expertise—no matter how small or inconsequential you may think it is. You will be surprised how you can scale it to be something substantial.
2. Study your market and what is working for those already there.
3. Develop a solid business plan but understand that this is a living document, and you must be malleable and visit it often as you pivot.
4. Get an accountant onboard from the first day. Outsource if you cannot hire full-time.
5. HR is your most important hire. Have them outline the company structure and processes from the very first day.
6. Put your customers before your big ideas. If you fail to tailor your goods and services to the requirements and or needs of your customers, then you deserve to fail (my most painful lesson so far).
7. Stay flexible and open to change. Covid-19 made people rich because of their ability to be flexible and move with the market at the right time.
8. Familiarise yourself with the legal and regulatory requirements to avoid legal issues.
9. Develop a strong brand identity and marketing strategy that you can implement at every stage of your growth.
10. Network, network and network some more. As a founder it is your job to meet people and get access to information.

Moving to a New Market

I moved to Nigeria for many reasons, some personal, religious, and cultural, I want to be perfectly frank and tell you that I was also highly motivated because I truly despised the English climate—wet, damp, cold, plus I was struggling against constant setbacks, red tape, slammed doors, and always living hand to mouth. I was also trying to manage the cost of labour and hiring, and high taxes. I don't want to give the impression that I faced racism living in the UK, because as a Black woman that was just not my reality. In many ways my obvious youth, gender and minority status actually gave me a leg up over the competition. I stood out in places people like me did not frequent—I was a young Black girl doing a job that you typically see old white men doing.

***

In the heart of Lagos, the air is warm and pulsating with life—a stark contrast to the chilly, damp winds that sweep through England. Having called Nigeria home for several years now, I've come to appreciate the distinct ambience and energy of a city so incredibly different from London, where I spent the first 30 years of my life. There's a richness in the soil and a rhythm in the air that harmonises with the cultural and religious chords in me.

Yet, England was also a land of opportunities for me, and in this complex tapestry, there were silver linings. As a Black British woman in business, my uniqueness became a sort of spotlight that often shined favourably upon me. I occupied spaces where people didn't expect to find me, and that element of surprise became a power I could wield. By no means should our differences be a reason to feel small; rather, they are something to leverage, a source of strength, and an occasion for excellence. This is a lesson I often emphasise when speaking to young people, particularly those who belong to minority groups.

In Nigeria, the lens through which I'm viewed is fundamentally different. Here, I am not an exception but a part of the norm, a component of the majority. For the first time in my professional life, my identity as a Black woman doesn't have to be a talking point or a pivotal focus—it's just one thread in the rich tapestry that is Nigerian society. And yet, the skills and talents that set me apart in England remain my strengths here, just channelled in new directions.

In Lagos, I am doing ground-breaking work in manufacturing, driven by technology. I'm working toward boosting artisans' quality and output, achieving ISO standards without factories—a mission that feels all the more poignant on my native soil. My venture aims to scale beyond Nigeria, beyond Africa even, but the foundation remains here, nurtured by a community that represents the majority of my identity.

Both countries have been a classroom of sorts for me. England taught me how to stand out, how to navigate spaces where my very existence was an anomaly. Nigeria, on the other hand, allows me to stand up, to rise within spaces where I can be a leader without the constant weight of racial prejudice holding down the scales. Each experience has its value, each environment its lessons, but it's here, under the warm Nigerian sun, that I find the freedom to grow in directions I never considered before.

And so, I work passionately in my field, the same passion with which I gather my friends and family around me, the same passion with which I travel and explore the world. I've traded the grey, cloudy skies for brighter horizons, yet carry with me the strength and resilience that navigating the murky waters of England imparted upon me. Here, in Nigeria, the sky isn't merely the limit—it's the starting point.

Lunch with Uncle Chinedu: Part 1

I was having a hurried and depressing lunch with my brother-in-law, Chinedu. I was at a low point in my life, and basically dumped all my troubles on the table. He listened very carefully to all my problems.

He was excellent at this. At the time he was working for Boris Johnson, when Johnson was Lord Mayor of London. I assumed that he was well tuned to sorting through Johnson's dramas from facts. (I'm being polite here as there are better but non-publishable words to describe Boris Johnson's political shenanigans.)

My brother-in-law put his cutlery down and smiled at me, then in the calmest, most considered voice, he suggested, 'Perhaps you should go and take a look at Lagos, Nigeria as a potential place to start a design and furniture factory.'

I thought to myself, Nigeria!? Did he actually say the words, Lagos, Nigeria?

Note: I'll go deeper into this story in a later chapter to give a wider context of relocating to Lagos.

Figure 3.1 Demi with Chinedu Igobokwe, 2 October 2015. Image courtesy of Demi Samande.

To be perfectly clear, I was not sold immediately on the idea of Nigeria and had to really convince myself that my brother-in-law's idea could work. To me, the negatives were certainly outweighing the positives.

The near total death of the textile industry in Nigeria, except for a few luxury textile manufacturers, is enough to put off any entrepreneur, and a lack of basic infrastructure like having access to consistent electricity underlined my fears that it was the last place on earth I should set up shop.

In the immediate aftermath of my lunch in London with my brother-in-law, I thought that one, I loved my brother-in-law dearly, and two, why on earth was he suggesting that I relocate to Lagos?

Something stuck with me was that Nigerians have a very long history with manufacturing, design and then marketing their goods to the world.

My Dad used to tell us stories growing up about Nigeria's production of rich textiles and that Nigeria once dominated in Africa for export. I knew that Nigeria had the largest population in Africa, far bigger than the UK... surely, I could find a market there?

The Nigerian textile industry employed over one million workers, which is massive by any standard. Manufacturing, design and creativity was in their collective DNA. Irene Yuan Sun explains it this way, and it is a reminder of the birth and death cycles in manufacturing.

> Factories live and die; They take root in a place and then fade away. From British textile factories in the 19th century, to Detroit auto plants and Japanese TV makers in the 20th century, factories come and go.[2]

I had many questions about why Nigerian cloth manufacturing dried up. Could the Nigerian companies not compete with others in Asia, or was the cost of labour too high? What was it that killed this vibrant and powerful industry?

Yuan Sun is blunt: 'What Happened to Nigeria's textile industry? The decline of this once dominant sector defies simple explanation and is a result of the interplay between three macroeconomic forces: the resource curse, short-sighted government policies, and global competition.'[3]

The 'resource curse' is the tragic love affair with oil and gas, Yuan Sun expounds: 'The paradoxical sounding "resource curse," refers to the phenomenon whereby a windfall of natural resource discoveries, ironically results in the country becoming poorer not richer.'

One example of a modern-day resource-cursed country is Venezuela, as well as Nigeria.

Yuan Sun explains that money poured in and caused the (Nigerian currency) naira to appreciate against the global currencies, making it nearly impossible for textile manufacturers to compete on price. The succession of governments also ignored the need to build basic infrastructure like secure power sources so that factories could operate seamlessly. The final death knell was when textile factories in Asia learned to make cloth much more efficiently, and then Nigerians began importing cheaper textiles.

So, given all that negative information, why on earth would my dear brother-in-law suggest that I take such a big gamble on a country whose current economy was described by Wilson Erumebor in 2023 (for the Brookings Institute, at the Nigerian Economic Summit Group at SOAS University of London) as:

> The last seven years (2015–2021) have been tough for Nigerians. During this period GDP growth averaged 1.1 percent, as the country experienced two economic recessions. Unemployment and under-employment rates increased to all-time highs of 56.1 percent, pushing Nigerians into multidimensional poverty according to the latest data from the National Bureau of Statistics.

Given those grim numbers, why would I or anyone else decide to take such a risk and start my business from scratch in Nigeria?

I was very hesitant to travel to Lagos alone, although the chance to get away from the dreary English winter and to the heat of Africa more than made up for my reluctance.

I packed my bags, arranged the workshop, locked it up and told my staff not to come in for the next two weeks. I was well and truly taking the much-needed break I craved. I felt a mix of emotions—was I really returning to this strange jungle on my own free will? The last trip I took to Nigeria, my mother had forced both me and my sister Toyin to go, because she felt we needed to learn our culture. My second trip to Nigeria was for the funeral of my brother, making me well and truly hate Nigeria. Yet here I was going again and this time of my own free will. It felt less like I was going to Nigeria, and more like running from England.

My brother-in-law's suggestion was a huge challenge, however, the more I spoke to colleagues and family, the more supportive they became. I was curious and restless and definitely ready to make a change.

Full disclosure: my brother-in law not only encouraged me, but he also funded my exploratory trip, which certainly made the decision much easier.

However, when I travelled to Lagos to perhaps find a place to start from scratch, how would I begin to navigate the world of manufacturing? Where do I start from? Who do I speak to? Out of habit I began mind-mapping my steps backwards (who makes furniture here, who sells furniture, where are their factories, where do they buy materials, who are the suppliers? I needed to know all of this). I started with the stores selling—they were disorganised, difficult to find and to be honest most sold outdated, poor-quality pieces with what seemed like irregular price points. I saw mass-produced pieces tagged 'luxury'; I could not understand the chaos. The markets were even worse. I dedicated an entire month to just following recommendations and leads on where to find the answers to my questions. I travelled around Lagos with a guide—we ventured as far as Ogun State in search of wood suppliers, factories who would be OK to show me their setups, I wanted to know it all. I ventured to the fabric suppliers of Mushin Market then explored the trail to Abia State looking for the traders. There wasn't anywhere I was not prepared to go. It was all an adventure to me. I jumped on motorbikes with no helmet, very much the culture in Nigeria. I walked into strange and unscrupulous looking places off the beaten track, fearlessly searching for contacts and knowledge.

To build a factory and find a market for my furniture, I was literally swept up in many emotions and gobsmacked by the chaos, the insanity of the traffic, gridlock and the masses of humanity, most of them Black and in one of the largest and poorest cities in the world.

In the back of my mind, I kept reminding myself that while the numbers that economists and researchers quote don't lie, they also couldn't quantify the energy and optimism I felt when I was on the ground touring Lagos. It was very to me clear that if I was to set up shop, there were so many missing pieces, including basic services like consistent power supplies and an upskilled workforce, a reliable supply chain and very little data to track down who would be my market for fine leather furniture.

I consider myself somewhat privileged to be on the ground floor and realise that Nigeria and indeed all of Africa is on the brink of a massive manufacturing breakthrough and renaissance.

Only in Nigeria have I ever seen a multimillion-dollar house with several luxury cars parked in its driveway, but walked outside the perimeter of the building or the front gate and seen a flood of people living below the poverty line, decorating the environment doing one thing at a time. The facilities filled and rubbish overflowing its gutters and blocking sewers just outside. Nigeria has me in awe. The rich and the poor cohabitating. I am very aware of the opportunities to go from zero to hero overnight. I hear such stories frequently. You are just one deal away from starting a new life. Every day I see people clamouring at the hope that today is their day, their turn to get to the next level, to acquire the wealth, the social class, the luxury cars, the notoriety and respect of their peers. The juxtaposition of rich vs. poor coexisting in tight quarters here is unlike any I have ever witnessed.

★★★

Later in his article, Wilson Erumebor describes the current Nigerian manufacturing sector:

> At the middle of the productivity ladder sits manufacturing. The sector has a much higher productivity level than agriculture and can accommodate, in large numbers, the kind of labor that is abundant in the country. Nigeria's rising population [which is projected to reach 428 million by 2050], the existence of mineral resources, and the adoption of a single market in Africa—the African Continental Free Trade Area (AfCFTA)—present a case for why manufacturing would thrive in Nigeria. The priority, therefore, for the incoming government must be to address the burgeoning infrastructure deficit and inadequate power supply, which limit the competitiveness of the manufacturing sector. In addition, the government will need to develop an industrial policy that seeks to support the scale, efficiency, and competitiveness of local firms within the manufacturing sector; bearing in mind that developing the sector is key to building economic resilience against vulnerability and future shocks. *Such policies must be integrated with Nigeria's AfCFTA strategy and support transition of small-scale firms that are often the drivers of job creation in the country.*

From London to Lagos

I derived so much comfort knowing this was an opportunity that would provide me with a journey, fuelled not only with the opportunity itself, but one filled with necessity.

Eruembor captures a sentiment that resonated deeply with me when I made the move from London to Lagos. This wasn't just a change in geography, it was a paradigm shift. You see, London was more than just a home for 30 years: it was the birthplace of all my businesses. But moving to Lagos was about fulfilling a different kind of purpose, a sense that there was a lifetime of meaningful work to be done in Nigeria.

While in London my focus was on restoration, in Lagos it was building—building businesses, building a future for a continent brimming with potential. In Nigeria every challenge—from infrastructure deficits to policy gaps—is an opportunity in disguise, waiting for solutions that are both innovative and scalable. And let me tell you, that's an entrepreneur's dream.

It's more than a lucrative market, It's a call to action. It's the reason I could venture into tech for manufacturing here. To solve real-world problems with an immediate and long-lasting impact. When I started my training academy earlier this year, it was another step in that direction. It's about equipping youth, who are the very backbone of this nation. With the skills they need not just to survive, but to excel.

My journey from London to Lagos has been about chasing opportunities that are not only financially rewarding, but also emotionally and intellectually fulfilling. It's a lifetime of work, indeed, but one that promises to leave a legacy, and perhaps inspire a new generation of entrepreneurs to build the Africa we dream of.

This it is exactly what I witnessed on the ground in Lagos and was not information buried in an academic report for economists, and for the political class. Energy, optimism and a vast, young workforce waiting to be upskilled, retrained or whatever buzzword works for you. Everywhere I turned there was an incredible young African dynamic and energy just waiting to be tapped into.

I also understood what my Mum had been doing with her emporium while we were growing up in London, albeit on a very small scale, by creating a business with a strong foundation in attitude for service. She was also creating a sustainable future for her family. I saw this in myself, that by creating a long term, scalable furniture manufacturing business in Nigeria, I too would create sustainable futures for my family of workers.

I also knew that by creating exquisitely designed furniture pieces, made exclusively in Nigeria, with upskilled Nigerian labour and as many raw materials as possible sourced in Nigeria, then my nascent small-scale furniture manufacturing firm would become a driver of the new Nigerian economy, essentially leapfrogging into the 21st century. Possible, or a pipe dream?

Find a Support System: Family First

I've truly honoured my Mum, Elizabeth, and her unstoppable spirit and work ethic. I highly recommend speaking to family members who may be in business or know small businesspeople to get a clear-eyed view of what you may be heading into. I also should not neglect my dear father, Charles, who is an academic and worked for many years as a civil engineer. He was always engrossed in his studies and research, and he studied with a generation of engineers that hand-drew their blueprints. He would have these large rolled-up sheets at home, and as a young girl I was totally fascinated by them. He certainly supported my education at university, to become an architect and then work in an architectural firm. Though my father was vaguely supportive of my mother's home emporium, he was never fully involved. It was a stark difference, to see them side by side—the scholar and engineer and the nurse and entrepreneur. I have often found myself wondering how different things would have been if my father had taken a more active role in her business. Would it have flourished more? Would it still be thriving today? It was not his nature to get into the chaos of her emporium. He was the quiet bystander watching from the sidelines, saying very little but swiftly weaving between the bags and bags of product like a skilled yet unphased runner through a maze. His lack of reaction or unmoved stoic gazes were his way of showing support. He never complained. He stood behind her bustling energy, always there but never too involved.

It was clear to us in the family that my mother yearned for my father's involvement in her business, and I would catch glimpses of longing whenever she spoke about the business to him. She dreamed of building a business legacy that would stand the test of time and set us on a path for financial safety. However, with his lack of involvement that dream seemed to slowly fade away.

However, those huge sacrifices my mother made were not in vain and ignited a spark in me, a burning desire to continue her legacy. I saw the potential of what her business could have been, and it fuelled my drive to venture into the world of entrepreneurship. My mission became clear—to not only build a business but also create a legacy for future generations.

As I've outlined in this chapter, my decision to move to Nigeria was not part of a larger plan that I had as a young person nor was it impulsive. It was where my parents had emigrated from, and it was never a point of discussion that I should move there.

***

When my brother in-law suggested the move, my initial reaction was mixed. It wasn't part of my original roadmap, however, the proposition was intriguing enough for me to consider. Still, before making such a monumental shift, due diligence was non-negotiable. I spent three rigorous months conducting feasibility studies, examining market trends and assessing the socioeconomic landscape of Nigeria. I wanted to ensure that my skill set and entrepreneurial aspirations would not only be viable but transformative in this new context.

My final decision to relocate was not based on sentiment or a romanticised notion of returning to my roots (although romance is needed, you must build on it with research and data to confirm your instincts are indeed right and not just baseless passion). It was rooted in data, research and a concrete understanding of what lay ahead. This analytical approach might seem cold to some, but in the complex world of business and entrepreneurship, numbers often speak louder than words. And the numbers, alongside the tangible prospects of manufacturing and technology, told me that Nigeria was ripe for innovation, growth and meaningful impact.

My move to Lagos, far from being an emotional whim or a preordained plan, was a calculated business decision backed by thorough research over several months (if not years). It was a new chapter. Dictated not by destiny or nostalgia, but a well-studied opportunity that promised to be mutually beneficial. And it turns out it has been an incredibly rewarding journey—professionally, personally and for the broader goals I have for manufacturing in Africa.

In fact, I was probably like many readers, mostly aware or partially aware of the many historical and political disasters, including religious and tribal terrorism. I was painfully aware of what the oil and gas industry had done to the social fabric of the country, and that indeed Nigeria and Africa is littered with business failures of Western companies trying to tap into the vast marketplace. However, if I was to start over in Nigeria, failure was not an option.

***

The market is a fickle thing and because Africa is so culturally diverse, with many languages, religions and taboos, there is never a one-size-fits-all way to market to the public.

There are numerous pitfalls to avoid that I have run into and by highlighting them, I want to allow readers to clearly see how confounding but rewarding it is to identify the market.

I'll chronicle one very successful manufacturing company that has come into the West African market that is a lesson and an eye opener for any business considering coming to Africa. It is also a lesson about learning the culture or understanding economies of scale and laying the groundwork to finding your market.

Insights into the Giants: The Story of the Lee Group

In addition to manufacturing bottled water, bread, plastic bags, and steel, the Lee Group manufactures 1.2 million flip-flop sandals a day. This single firm makes more than enough flip flops for every man, woman and child in the United States—or two pairs for every man, woman and child in Nigeria— each year.[4]

The Lee Group's reach into everyday life in Nigeria is staggering, and there is no doubt that this company is in for the long haul. And as Irene Yuan Sun points out:

> There is no better proof that Africa can industrialise, than the humming of this [flip-flop factory] owned by people who have survived the worst and came out believing even more in the promise of African manufacturing.[5]

For the record, in no way am I comparing my small-scale furniture and design firm to the Lee Group's mighty grip on the Nigerian economy, but there is something that they profoundly understand about the market in Nigeria and Africa, and it is critical for anyone starting up a business to pay attention to.

Yuan Sun underscores the Lee Group's deep understanding of the African marketplace:

> The Lee Group has 99.9 percent of market share in Nigeria and surrounding countries, it doesn't use this monopoly power to raise prices. The company understands that its business model relies on consumers who are unwilling or unable to afford more so it continues to sell its flip flops at a price no smuggler can possibly match.

What can we learn from the Lee Group's massive success? It is so successful that when Walmart, the American and global retailing behemoth, was seriously considering opening retail stores in Nigeria and elsewhere, it asked the Lee Group if they would consider becoming its global flip-flop sandal supplier.

I was surprised to read in Irene's book, 'that the Lee Group said no'.[6] Walmart was attempting a top-down retail marketing practice that worked in many places around the globe, but not in Africa. By top-down I mean build gigantic stores that eventually will grab most of the market share, that put small 'mom and pop' shops and distributors out of business and force many to have to travel to larger centres to their superstore. To meet demand, Walmart would need to import most of the goods, and put many smaller Nigerian manufacturers out of business.

What Walmart failed to understand or care about was that the Lee Group had comprehensive, local and small-scale distribution of their flip-flops to every corner of West Africa, and it was already working exceedingly well. It did not need the 'World's Biggest Retailer' to show them how to improve their marketing, manufacturing and distribution.

Yuan Sun ironically caps off her chapter, 'In some sense, [The Lee Group] had out Walmarted Walmart.'[7]

Understanding the Giants

This rather audacious story really piqued my curiosity about the Nigerian manufacturing titan, the Lee Group. With some luck and good timing, I began with an interview with a senior member of their team in December 2023. Our conversation illuminated the company's strategic decision to refuse collaboration with Walmart for exporting flip-flop sandals. As a very brief background, the Lee Group can be considered a powerhouse in manufacturing and communications, but is also thriving in sectors like bottled water, cement and steel manufacturing, and they chose not to compromise their successful model for Walmart's demanding terms. After all, it's not every day in Nigeria that Walmart comes knocking and looking for a local business partner. I asked the Lee Group if Irene Yuan Sun's book was an accurate portrayal of the story.

Please note: for the purposes of this interview, I've called my Lee Group guest, LG.

Demi:	The Lee Group basically said no, why? Irene's account didn't really delve into the crux of how that conversation went down. Was Irene's book accurate?
LG:	Yes, she [Irene's book] was pretty accurate. But it's actually a lot simpler than what she wrote about. Walmart have this refund policy. The policy is they won't pay you for your goods. I believe the terms were that they we wanted to buy X number of [flip-flops] somewhere in the thousands or hundreds of thousands. What they told us was, 'we'll pay you in 60 or 90 days after delivery. In addition, if our clients refund the product, it will be considered as void and for that we'll need credit.'
Demi:	Very interesting, so you declined.
LG:	I believe the Lee Group said that's it's not worth their while. We already export mostly to Europe and to South America and to the rest of Africa. Why would we want to jump through hoops? The Lee Group's APIN Footwear is making about 2.5 million pairs of flip-flops a day.

His answer was actually quite refreshing, and I was able to delve deeper into their success, considering all the hurdles in the Nigerian economy.

The Ecosystem Approach

My guest shared insights into the Lee Group's ecosystem approach, where needs like water and internet services led to the creation of respective companies. This self-reliance also extended to cement and trucking companies, reinforcing their independence and community-building.

Demi: The Lee Group employs around 30,000 locals. With that scale, they're a business that actually grows out of their own need. They are the first customer. It's an ecosystem, right?

LG: Yes, it's an ecosystem. They need water. So instead of buying water from wherever, they started a water company. They need to access the internet? Instead of buying from internet companies, they did a joint venture. The Lee Group is constantly building factories and warehouses. They need cement to build? They built their own cement company. Then they started to say, 'Okay, how do you sustain yourself without the Group?' At first, you're within the Lee Group ecosystem. You supply the group; however, the group should not be your sole client. Once you got the foundation, you should now be competitive and independent and start selling outside the Group. You have a construction company; you have a trucking company. The only reason why they have the trucking company is because in the past, they were shipping six hundred containers a month of raw materials. So, think about the business they were giving to all these trucking companies. They're thought, why? So, their solution was their own trucking company, which means they started owning trucks, and then their own garage for repairs. I mean, it's just keeping it within the ecosystem, but always starting off slow. They're not telling new businesses in the Group that were only going to support you for a year and then we're gone.

The Humble Beginnings

Starting in 1962, the Lee Group's founder exemplified humility and dedication, starting from the factory floor and reinvesting earnings back into

Africa. I asked the member of the Lee Group about the founder's remarkable story. His lifestyle set a tone of frugality and commitment within the company.

LG: It is remarkable. When they first started, they were working in the factory. Then started their own company, but they still worked in the factory. His wife lost four fingers and she still worked. They were very frugal, very humble. Then the company progressed to Mr. Lee because he started one factory. Honestly to this day, we still can't figure out how he did it. But I think one of the components for the Lee Group's success is that he truly felt that Africa was his home. If you look at a lot of the Asian-owned businesses in Africa…it isn't their home. They considered it as a workplace and then they go home. The founder was fully dedicated. It wasn't even about the money. It was his passion. He would re-invest 90 cents of every hour back into Africa.

Building a Community

The Lee Group's community focus included negotiating land for factories and developing surrounding areas with accommodation, schools and hospitals. This strategy fostered community development and symbiotic relationships with local governments.

Demi: Can you explain to the readers how it works with local and national governments?

LG: We are like the Walmart of the Africa. What do I mean by that? When Walmart picks a location, every governor, every state legislator, every local mayor knows that when they set up shop, it brings in other business, and communities are created around Walmart, like gas stations, restaurants. So, what happens is they [local governments] give Walmart a very sweet deal.

Demi: Okay, but how does a land deal work for Nigeria, where land is often tied up in tribal and local politics?

LG: Every Lee Group factory employs at least 2,000, 3,000, sometimes 5,000 workers. What the founder would do is he would tell the government, 'I need the land. I'll pay for it, but I need a good deal.' Then he'd say, 'On the land around my factories I'll build accommodation, schools, a hospital.' Because in a lot of the rural areas, you need a lot of workers, and there's not enough [services, like schools or hospitals]. In the past, they used to have to bring the workers in. Then he decided, you know what? I'm just going to build a community. The Lee Group had its own construction company to develop projects, and the cost to build these communities was done at cost. If the government would give him the land, he could develop it. Then he would give it to the people. The Lee Group wouldn't own that land. He would actually donate the hospital, donate the accommodation, donate the school. However, the Lee Group would own the land under the factories. The land around his factory would belong to the government. The land that was for his factory, he would get a sweet deal from the government.

Visionary Leadership

The founder's vision integrated global best practices with a localised approach, ensuring adaptability and independence from singular technologies or expertise. I asked my guest how the Lee Group built capacity and set the vision so rapidly without overreliance on imported expat expertise?

LG: He always had the vision and he told it to everyone...everyone understood his vision and they were heading in the right direction. Now, whether or not it was a two-lane highway or a 20-lane highway, remains to be seen. But I think in his particular field, so you talk about manufacturing, right? You're talking about manufacturing. He would learn from the best. He would go to Italy, buy the best, buy one set of the best equipment. He'd travel to Germany, buy the best equipment. Then he'd go to China and try to copy the Italian and German equipment, then he bought the company that was the best at replicating. Just like Japanese did after World War II. They replicated manufacturing equipment from all over the globe, Germans, Italian, Americans. They found all the best experts for providing skill set, training and knowledge. Then like the Japanese he said, 'Okay, thank you very much. It's now ours.'

My understanding is that the Lee Group's founder took the same approach and then he localised it. He made the outside experts *dispensable*. He didn't rely on any particular person. He was more like a PIC: a person-in-charge, and so the company structure is more horizontal.

Reflections and Insights

The interview on the Lee Group provided a realistic portrayal of their journey. Their story is one of resilience, adaptation and a balance between profitability and responsibility. My research also highlighted the Lee Group's readiness to invest in agriculture, reflecting their dynamic approach to local market needs. This story is a testament to the resilience and innovation needed for success in the African business landscape.

Data, Data and More Data

Why is data so critical to understand for any new entrepreneur considering starting a business? In some ways it is simple—where do I find a market for my product or service? Knowing your ground, and how to get your products into the hands of your customers, is essential, but also understanding that local economies are actually thriving, and in a young, vibrant population, where growth will be exponential, it will be essential to build databases. For instance, for my furniture company, I needed to know where in Nigeria my potential customers were, and how I could find and keep this data on hand, so that when we are designing and creating new furniture ideas for the Nigerian market, we had the data to back up our products and knew precisely where and what these potential customers wanted.

But collecting data isn't a one-off task. It's an ongoing process that evolves with your business. The initial data that I gathered for my feasibility study wasn't static; it was the foundation on which we continuously built. Market trends shift, consumer preferences change and economic variables fluctuate. A static database is as good as no database.

However, I must stress that collecting data should be conducted ethically and responsibly. It is not about hoarding information for unscrupulous advantages. This is about understanding your business environment deeply to offer products or services that genuinely meet a need. Therefore, privacy concerns, data security and ethical considerations should be integral components to data strategy.

Data-driven decisions are not modern business jargon; they're the cornerstone of successful, sustainable enterprises. In an economy as vibrant as diverse as Nigeria, where local economies are growing and the population is increasing, leveraging data is not just smart—it's essential. And if we're to avoid the pitfalls that have befallen businesses in the past due to the lack of data, then let's make a pact to record everything responsibly. I believe we must treat every byte of data as a building block for a more informed and successful future.

Takeaways

Currently, I'm creating a new line of affordable furniture that is in the early planning stages, but supply-chain issues continue to dog our rollout. Because furniture is considered nonessential and the effects of a double recession are forcing families in Nigeria to focus on what is deemed essential, we will be monitoring this launch over the next few years.

What are the lessons learned in making a decision to move to another country? I'd say research, and above everything else, investments and financial backing that allow the company to survive and hopefully grow into the future.

Whether it is flip-flops or fine leather sofas, market demands are always in the driver's seat, so it's important to constantly seek new markets. To compete on the global market, a small-scale furniture manufacturing company based in Nigeria should be constantly looking around the globe. This is not a small task when you are knee deep in the day-to-day, but it is critical. I have failed at this on many occasions and learnt the hard way. Today I have learnt that reaching for those customers is integral to the business, even if it means sacrificing some aspects of the day-to-day. Marketing and finding customers should not be underserved for the sake of admin tasks.

For entrepreneurs, find your support system, whether it be a family member, a teacher or a businessperson. For me it's my London friends— Flavia, Shilla and Nancy from secondary school. Ramone and Ade from my university days of studying architecture. My closest and dearest Lagos friends (and Gaia Africa members), both Yemis, Fola, Oche, Bukky, FK, who are always so gracious to let me vent on the hardest days.

Turn to friends for help to make the critical early decisions. Success may not come to you right away and I can honestly say that hurdles will be the norm, until you have recouped all the initial funding and you are actually creating profit.

Put your advisory board together early if you can. Do not pay them initially but ensure that you choose people who believe in you and ensure you are updating them regularly with the progress of the business. We are all busy so a quarterly update email or newsletter with all your numbers of challenges, wins and requests is a fantastic way to get everyone in the loop. This strategy works well for both investors and your advisory board.

My Mum's home-based emporium in London taught me many essential lessons—attitude of service, knowing your market and being responsive. It also taught me what bootstrapping is, and how to survive the inevitable downturns and make difficult decisions. It is these lessons and more that I'm passing on to a new generation of young workers and entrepreneurs in Nigeria.

As a preview to Chapter Four, I'll also describe current issues in Africa that will adversely affect every new entrepreneur. Certainly, the biggest hurdle that I have faced is watching how our incredible raw resources are literally stripped away before being sold at embarrassingly low prices. These resources are then resold back to manufacturers at a premium, just because we lack the creativity and manufacturing base to make them here. Are we lazy or just uninterested in the opportunity to transform our fortunes in this wealth game?

Sadly, in Africa, we do not yet have this level of production. For instance, African cattle producers sell 'blue skins' to the West, which are processed and then sold back to us as finished leather with an average 2900% markup. This is a ridiculous situation, and it will require not only design thinking but real industrial strategies to solve. Unfortunately, exporting resources and imported manufactured goods happens across all our sectors.

For the sake of clarity, if India is selling one sheet of wet blue cow leather for $57, Nigeria is selling the same wet blue sheet for $5.42 to Italy, then buying it back for $356: that is a 6468.27% mark up.

India: The markup percentage is approximately 522.92%.
Nigeria: The markup percentage is approximately 2900%–6468.27%.

These percentages reflect a significantly higher markup for the leather sheet sourced from Nigeria due to its much lower cost price compared to the Indian counterpart.

The reason Nigeria is selling its raw blue skin leather at a lower price compared to other countries like India can be attributed to several factors:

Quality and processing: The quality of leather and the processing methods used can significantly affect the price. Nigerian leather might be less processed or of a different quality compared to Indian leather.

Market demand and supply dynamics: The demand for Nigerian leather in the global market and the supply capacity of the country can influence pricing. If there's less demand or a surplus in supply, prices may be lower.

Economic factors: The economic context in Nigeria, including labour costs, production costs and export policies, could lead to lower pricing to remain competitive in the international market.

Global trade agreements and tariffs: Trade agreements and export tariffs that Nigeria is subject to could affect the pricing to ensure competitiveness in international markets.

Industry development and investment: The level of investment and development in the leather industry in Nigeria might be different from other countries. A less developed industry could lead to lower prices due to simpler processing techniques or less value addition.

Exchange rates: Currency exchange rates also play a crucial role. A weaker local currency against the dollar can lead to lower prices when converted to USD.

***

In Chapter Four, I also argue for stronger and more complete education that puts a big emphasis on design thinking. I will not minimise the complexities of these processes but emphasise that we must get creative and simple in our approach to big ideas. Once we learn how to do it like China, we keep it simple, then scale it, replicate it over and over again—with all key natural resources—like wood and leather—designed, created and sold by Africans to manufacturers like Majeurs Furniture and other new startups.

The issue of raw materials being exported only to be sold back at a staggering markup is a glaring problem that hits home for many African entrepreneurs, including myself. It signifies a lost opportunity and reflects an imbalance that we can no longer afford to sustain.

However, in the face of these challenges, I've developed a set of key principles that I believe can serve as pillars for entrepreneurial success in Africa. These principles aren't just theoretical; they've been honed over years of real-world experience and have proven their worth.

Five Key Factors

- **Localised production:** The first factor emphasises the importance of local production to counteract the 'export and import at a premium' issue. The idea is to add value to raw materials within the continent. For example, my furniture company sources timber locally and ensures the entire production process occurs within Nigeria, thereby adding value right here at home.

- **Resource mapping:** Knowing what resources you have and where to find them is crucial. Create a detailed resource map that not only lists what is available but also identifies the quality, costs and logistics involved. This puts you in a position of power when negotiating with suppliers or even when considering exports.
- **Innovation through data:** The use of data analytics to inform design, production and distribution cannot be stressed enough. This involves tracking customer behaviours, preferences and needs to inform our product development strategy. It is by using this data that my company has been able to create furniture pieces that are not only beautiful but also functional and ecofriendly.
- **Collaborative partnerships:** If there is one thing I know for sure, it is that you can't do it alone. Establishing partnerships with local artisans, educational institutions for research and development, and even with government bodies for sustainable practices can make a difference. Such collaborations help by sharing knowledge and resources, which can be particularly useful for startups. However, I must emphasise that you should tread carefully with this, as often these are based on relationships because the normal channels can prove to be abortive. Find the person who will take you directly to the source by way of an introduction to the men and women in charge. This will save you a lot of 'sitting around time'. The truth is, our government officials love to keep people in the waiting areas for hours, if not weeks. Legend has it that many have been known to wait months and never be seen. Joking! Just don't get tricked into waiting in reception areas to be seen chasing a carrot on a string.
- **Customer-centric sustainability:** The last factor focuses on merging customer needs with sustainable practices. It's not just about creating an ecofriendly product; it's about creating a product that customers want and can afford. At Majeurs, we've married sustainability with customer needs—as well as selling new products we offer a renovation and restoration service, taking old furniture and bringing it back to life. A staple of our business from inception. We believe in reuse not just for our customers' pockets but for our environment, thereby making our products more appealing to a broad demographic.

In Chapter Four, I delve deeper into how an educational overhaul, with an emphasis on design thinking and creativity, could serve as a cornerstone for solving some of Africa's most pressing challenges. But remember, these aren't just buzzwords; these are actionable strategies that I've seen work. Simple in concept but profound in impact, they've been instrumental in steering my company through the complex economic landscape, and they hold promise for other new startups as well.

Notes

1 Irene Yuan Sun. 2017. *The Next Factory of the World*. Harvard Business Press. Page 34.
2 Ibid. Page 33.
3 Ibid. Page 35.
4 Ibid.
5 Ibid. Page 46.
6 Ibid.
7 Ibid.

Real Recognises Real   **4**

I have major issues with Nigerian Afrobeat music star, Burna Boy. He made me wait along with thousands of his fans for nearly seven hours for a concert on New Year's Day in 2023. It was supposed to begin at 8 p.m. He did not start his concert until 3 a.m. the next morning! Once he finally showed up to his fully paid fans, he had the gall to only play a one-hour set of his most famous tunes and then walked off the stage. I, along with his more loyal fans, were massively outraged—I have other choice words but I'm being polite. We all left the event in a very sour mood.

After a lot of public pressure, he issued this apology:

> I still love you na why I dey here, so if you like no love me, na God go punish you.

The rough translation of his gloriously pathetic apology is that 'He still loves us, and if you don't love him back, don't worry, God won't punish you.' Talk about rubbing salt in an open wound? This is a sure-fire way to kill your brand and any mutual respect. If he had pulled that prank in London, New York and LA or anywhere outside of Lagos, he would have played his songs to an empty hall and faced endless lawsuits. He broke the bond of rule number one of 'real recognises real': show up, be on time, and always give it your best effort. Period. And when you do mess up, keep trying to fix it until your customer sees that you are committed to their satisfaction. Let me warn you, this will at times cost you money, but it goes a long way to ensuring you keep that customer.

This was the antithesis of the hip-hop idiom real recognises real. Did I and others earn any more respect for Burna Boy after his debacle and

DOI: 10.4324/9781003453994-4

half-baked apology? Categorically, NO! He lost my respect and thousands of others who paid for the tickets, found childcare, transportation, meals and all the other thousands of ways we all pay for and organise our lives to attend live music events.

You may be asking yourself, why does a book about the emerging manufacturing sector in Africa really have any relation to the Nigerian music scene?

In my opinion, this massive cultural industry has scaled up rapidly, and must be part of any discussion about the various economic sectors in Africa and Nigeria. I believe that we have a lot to learn, embrace and gain from understanding a culture, and more specifically the Nigerian music scene that has literally exploded over the past ten years. To give readers some background, in a recent report published by the US Trade Department, it noted the rapid and global reach of music from Nigeria:

> The music sector of Nigeria's entertainment industry also recorded significant growth over the years. Stakeholders include artists, musicians, producers, promoters, managers, distributors, and marketers. As of 2021, the music industry employed about a million people and generated over $8 billion for the economy. In the past six years, the growing numbers of new production studios and artists enabled a more vibrant and self-sustaining industry, producing globally recognised music. In this environment, Nigerian musicians have developed a vast spectrum of music genres. The industry has won prestigious awards with artists like Wizkid and Burna Boy claiming Grammy awards, attracting more and more investments from several sources. Spotify, the global leader in music streaming, is also moving into the Nigerian market as part of a broader global expansion.[1]

This rapid growth is well earned and mostly well respected—sorry Burna Boy, you have a long way to go to regain my respect— and as the article suggests, giants like Spotify are looking to Nigeria to expand.

If we drill down to the reality on the ground, these developments are incredibly well timed for the burgeoning creative and tech workers who are creating and demanding better incomes from this industry and in turn creating a new group of middle- and upper-class music industry professionals who are able to purchase luxury items for their homes like leather furniture and other goods that are well designed and hopefully not imported from Italy or China, but manufactured in Nigeria.

When artists recognise each other's authenticity—real recognises real. Whether they are musicians or furniture designers, they tend to build and support economies that then create sustainable futures. Owning a new sofa might be a status symbol, but it is also an investment in your community.

If the sofa is made in the same city or country where you live and not imported from China or Scandinavia, then the benefits are compounded. You are supporting local designers, artisans and craftspeople who become part of the cultural and manufacturing ecosystem. For African manufacturing, I argue that this music and cultural industry is attracting the top producers and technicians, but also attracting investment in Nigerian and African products.

When we buckle down to do the work, we position ourselves to also attract the global best. So, what does that mean? The Nigerian music scene is not the overnight success many like to think it is. Many of these artists were behind the scenes grinding for years, honing their skills, gaining traction, with no income. Track after track, slowly, before opportunity met preparation. The same must be done for our manufacturing. We stay the course. At times it will not make sense, it will seem like a colossal waste of time, people will laugh, they will mock us for even trying to compete. We will lose money on bad choices. Many will lose their entire investments. But one day you will find us amidst the conversations, in the exhibitions, on the committees, inside the global 'who to watch out for'. Recognise our names amongst the listed companies in our industries and wonder how we got the attention of the world.

Hurdles to Consider

As I've made abundantly clear, I did not move to Africa with rose-coloured glasses, and there are major hurdles for any new entrepreneur to be made aware of.

Certainly, the biggest hurdle that I have been faced with, and believe we must overcome, is watching how our incredible raw resources are literally stripped away before being sold for embarrassingly low prices. These resources—leather, metal and wood—are then resold back to manufacturers at a premium, just because we lack the creativity and manufacturing base to make them here.

As a designer and furniture manufacturer, I can say that I am a leather enthusiast. My deep love for leather shows in my work and my personal style. However, to find high-quality leather hides, I actually need to import them from outside of Africa! Sadly, in Africa, we do not yet have this level of sophisticated production (see the issues mentioned with internal leather production in the previous chapter).

***

Figure 4.1 *Staff working in the factory on a piece, 16 August 2021.* Image courtesy of Majeurs Holdings.

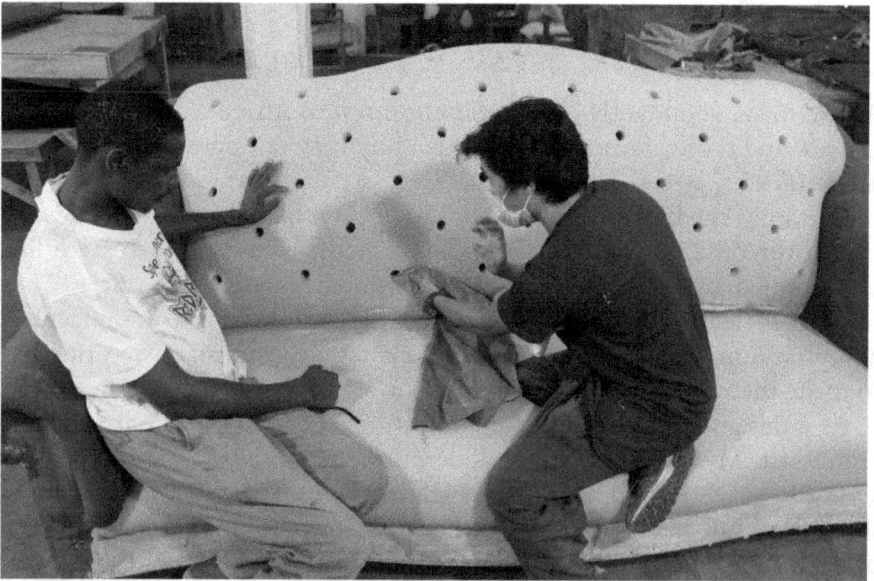

Figure 4.2 *Majeurs staff building a sofa, 6 October 2022.* Image courtesy of Majeurs Holdings.

My second biggest hurdle is finding trained craftspeople to work in our factory. Nigeria's massive advantages of a lower-cost labour force must be matched with high value and comprehensive training. I'll address this more in a later chapter, but it is a pressing need that we have begun to address by creating our own training academy.

In many of my podcasts, I've spoken publicly about the fact that I'm also a huge promoter of many layers of the Nigerian creative class, and constantly on the lookout for designers, artisans and craftspeople to join our team, much like the music industry, where real recognises real.

There is no doubt that we have a very long way to go to match the huge Nigerian music industry, and our respect is being earned on a daily basis. Our larger goal is to make Lagos and Nigeria into a global hub of furniture manufacturing.

The third hurdle is more practical, but it is a priority. We must push all layers of government and industry for a more stable and REAL power grid. Brownouts and blackouts all reduce efficiency. If I gave you a tour of my manufacturing floor on any given day, you would be shocked at how many power disruptions there are and the amount it costs to have generators running so that the manufacturing can continue. Getting real about the power grid is not only my demand, but also every Nigerian's.

Real recognises real. You can't fake authenticity.

—Unknown

★★★

In a previous chapter, I wrote about how I made the instant discovery of a fake leather Chesterfield sofa that was delivered to my door. This led me on a search to find an authentic sofa, and then I built a business that sourced and restored many leather Chesterfield sofas all over England.

The furniture manufacturing world is full of fakes and rip-offs, with various companies promising a cheaper version of the original. There are exceptions of course, but in general, the public is mostly unaware about the sophistication of these fakes.

Authenticity is also linked to old values like craftsmanship, beauty, and for leather furniture, warmth. When you sit on an authentic, well-made and beautifully designed piece of leather furniture, your senses are immediately rewarded.

As an example, if you look at the classic Eames lounge chair and recliner made of rosewood and leather, the replicas give the feel of real without the huge price tag. I'll be honest, you could probably buy a used car for the same price of this grand piece of furniture and art. On the website link below, you will note that there are at least 22 replicas available on the market.[2]

However good the replicas are, I would ask you just to sit on the famous recliner, put your feet up and immerse yourself in authenticity. What is it that immediately comes to mind? Certainly, the buttery soft leather, the smell and of course the absolute perfect ergonomics. Almost everybody relaxes and melts into this furniture and becomes surrounded by warmth, and an uncanny understanding that the Eames lounger is a work of art and total comfort.

This is the same intuitive feeling that I had when I sat on the authentic Chesterfield sofa. It is like a place you never want to leave. You want to invite a friend to sit and have a good long chat, or just kick off your shoes and relax.

The question then becomes, how can you replicate those deep feelings of real recognising real, while making it affordable? Craftsmanship, care and attention to detail all help to recreate authenticity. These are all human attributes that have costs attached to them, particularly training and materials. But what are the trade-offs and compromises that must be made to make manufacturing furniture affordable?

TRADE-OFF 1: Craftsmanship

The cost of skilled labour is a significant factor. To make this affordable, one approach could be implementing training programmes, like the one we initiated in our academy, to nurture local talent. This not only reduces the cost of importing skilled labour but also empowers the community. The trade-off here could be the time invested in training versus immediate production.

TRADE-OFF 2: Materials

The choice of materials greatly influences both cost and authenticity. Locally sourced materials can be more cost-effective and environmentally sustainable, aligning with our belief in ecofriendly manufacturing. The compromise might be in material consistency or the range of available resources, which could limit design options or require adaptation in manufacturing techniques. I must admit though, when you are competing with a global market this can be very hard to convince customers.

TRADE-OFF 3: Technological Integration

Our venture into tech for manufacturing with an AI-powered SaaS for vertical integration is a game changer. It streamlines processes, reduces waste and optimises resource allocation, making manufacturing more cost-effective. The trade-off here is the initial investment in technology and the learning curve for artisans in adapting to new ways of working.

★★★

These questions and problems always become an issue when I am working with my team on designing new pieces, and in a further chapter I'll explain all the steps in a flow chart from idea and design to the finished piece being boxed and shipped from our factory in Lagos. It will also be a great visual guide for any entrepreneur in how a product is developed to its final polish.

I firmly believe in design thinking, prototyping and problem-solving and always being alert to your local market, with a very strong eye on the global market, but behind every choice and decision is the key element that real recognises real, and the goal is to strive to create this feeling of well-being, warmth, even joy from a small manufacturing base in Lagos. The next challenge for all manufacturers is to how to scale up (we have battled with this for seven years), but not lose that feeling of a small-scale furniture design business and move towards larger production while maintaining the highest level of quality control. This has got to be the hardest thing to do, not just for my business but for many businesses here. I struggle to find many who have maintained local manufacturing at a consistent level of quality without importing prefabricated furniture to be assembled in Nigeria. I would love for this to change, mainly because those prefabs can also be made here in Nigeria providing those jobs to locals whilst still maintaining a high quality.

Real Recognises Real: Scale Up

There are many decisions to be made, both large and small, when scaling up. I'll tackle the funding issue as a separate chapter.

Once your product has been established in the marketplace and the demand is there, with orders coming in, the question is when do you begin to scale up. I'll be brutally honest here, this is often the make-or-break point for many startups, because it requires capital infusion, proper staffing, space, a guaranteed supply chain (or at least a well-structured pipeline for your needs), and the management and the design and manufacturing team all on the same page, pulling in the same direction.

Difficult indeed, and this is where your entrepreneurs need to fall back on design thinking.

What I mean specifically in this case is both an ideology and a process that seeks to solve complex problems in a user-centric way. Design thinking focuses on achieving practical results and solutions that:

1. Can Be Developed into Functional Products or Processes

There is a vast amount of literature written on failed products and companies who misunderstood the market, or did not dig deep enough into creating functional products. We can't all be manufacturers of flip-flops. This is where every entrepreneur must look at themselves in the mirror and say, is this product or service of value to the general public, no matter what income level or where they live.

2. Are Technically Feasible

The team must also solve all problems with the physical plant. Is there enough space to expand? Is it convenient for large-scale shipping and receiving? Then the giant questions that I'm faced with every day: do we have access to a consistent power grid, do we have enough trained, skilled craftspeople to learn the manufacturing workflow, so that building becomes streamlined and efficient? The other major decision to consider in the scale-up phase is the supply chain. Can you get the raw resources on time, in the proper format and with consistent delivery? Remember the massive problems with surgical masks and PPE during Covid-19? The world learned more about supply chain issues that we ever wanted to know. We quickly came to realise that without a working good supply chain, the system quickly dries up and companies fail.

For manufacturers the supply chain is the river of raw materials that must be flowing consistently, otherwise scaling up becomes very difficult, and can literally stop manufacturing. In fact, I would suggest that before any scale-up process, check and then double-check to make sure your materials are available, and can be guaranteed delivery, so that the scale-up process can deliver what you have promised to the distributors and the buying public. Trust me on this one!

3. Are Economically Viable and Desirable for the User

This is always a great discussion point, not only for young entrepreneurs and manufacturers, and I encourage all readers to consider what their price point is for their products. The book you are reading has a price point, and it is set by the publisher working with distributors, and I'm sure a sales department who are monitoring competitors. They are also looking at what the wholesale and retail price point of the book will be. What is the hardback price, paperback price? They are looking at the global book market, but they are also interested in making a profit.

The Lee Group's flip-flops were priced so that no smuggler would make any profit by importing flip-flops, thus having a near monopoly of sandals in West Africa.

What is critical for a manufacturer and investor is whether or not the product or service is making profit for the company, and the ROI, or return on investment, in the scale up is matching what the investors expected. Certainly, a product that is overpriced vs. one that is underpriced is always a good discussion point, but I would also suggest another question—is it desirable for the user? Desire is always an intriguing question for all entrepreneurs.

It can be broken down to two distinct feelings or sensations when it comes to products or services and this is where real recognises real—respect, critical thinking, plus cultural, regional understanding of what the market is looking for, what the public *desires*.

In my opinion, this authentic choice and understanding is the key to *real traction* in the marketplace and for commercial success. And these feelings are also the trickiest and most complex to understand but in essence, not taking them into account can make or break many startups. That is why prototyping and beta testing are an essential part of product development.

One final aspect that is essential at this stage of development is respect and attitude of service. Decisions are very critical at this stage, because management and the workforce all need to be on the same page.

There are also soft decisions also to be made. What I by mean by that is do your team believe that all the indicators that the product is useful, wanted and will beat the competitor on price and quality. It is a high bar to set, but to fund the scale-up could cost millions.

Real Recognises Real: Training for the Future

The solutions are clear. The ongoing education of workers, designers and entrepreneurs is at the heart of everything we do. I'm also proud to announce that as of July 2023, we have already graduated the first two students from our academy. This is a major milestone that is further developed in Chapter Thirteen in a conversation with the Majeurs Academy Technical Drawing Facilitator, Lateef Balogun, and Carpentry Facilitator, Damiola Ogunbiyi.

The overarching goal is to create a stronger and more complete education and human resource development plan that puts a big emphasis on design thinking. I will not underplay the complexities of these processes, but emphasise that we must get both creative and simple in our approach to big ideas. Once we learn how to do it, we keep it simple, then scale it, replicate it over and over again—with all key natural resources like wood and leather that are designed, created and sold by Africans to manufacturers like Majeurs and other new startups.

Need to Have vs. Want to Have

Think about the above heading and jot down ten *need-to-have* products and ten *want-to-have* products.

Need-to-have products can be classified into basic products for health, home, safety, transportation and education. If you think about products that are in these categories, it becomes quite straightforward and generally they exist or there is a space for new and improved products to disrupt the existing market.

Categories for want-to-have products include personal space, comfort, style, convenience, beauty and of course status and trends. This is where my company and many of thousands of other furniture manufacturers fit in.

Furniture per se does not precisely fit into the want to have—yes, we need to have furniture in our homes, however basic. Want-to-have items are aspirational, and linked to how others view you and your choices. Successful furniture designers and manufacturers are looking both into the future, for what the next and younger generation are looking for, and back to see what classics pieces still resonate with the public and still sell. A gorgeous handmade leather Chesterfield will always have a specific market, but so will IKEA sofas that are stamped out mostly by robots. They share the same value.

Takeaways

In my experience, scaling up can be an extremely difficult process and for any small company, my suggestion is always to seek out outside help, because there are so many factors and details to cover. You may need advice from commercial lawyers, trusted friends, family members or business leaders, who have piloted their own business through scaling-up turbulence. I'm not being facetious when I say that it can be an extremely difficult time, but getting quality advice is always the best solution.

You might think I'm repeating myself, but I'm very clear that with design thinking, problem-solving and teamwork, the hurdles and headaches can be overcome.

I'm a big believer in communication and building consensus from the manufacturing floor to management team.

Added to the complexity is the distinct cultural and economic realities of setting up a new company in Africa, and that is why this book and topic is essential. For African entrepreneurs, it is also critical to keep one eye on the future and keep focused on building your authentic brand, and build global respect like the incredible Nigerian music business.

There is always a myriad of issues to deal with on a daily basis, but one teaching moment always stands out for me as I was starting up in Lagos. When you've spent years of your life cultivating a vision and working tirelessly to see it to fruition, the last thing you expect is for your own personal life to almost dismantle it all.

The last thing you need is to burn out or to find yourself alone amidst the storm of business difficulties. In the middle of Covid, my factory flooded and I was totally overwhelmed. I needed my network and friends more than ever. You must surround yourself with friends before you need them. My friends and network came through for me first during Covid then again when my health was on the line. Your business success is very much hinged on the moments when you simply carry yourself through the tough times and realities of the toll the challenges take on you emotionally.

Notes

1 https://www.trade.gov/country-commercial-guides/nigeria-media-and-entertainment
2 https://www.irreverentgent.com/best-eames-chair-replicas/

Simplicity   5

Ten Laws of Simplicity, by John Maeda

1. REDUCE; The simplest way to achieve simplicity is through thoughtful reduction.
2. ORGANISE; Organization makes a system of many appear fewer.
3. TIME; Savings in time feel like simplicity.
4. LEARN; Knowledge makes everything simpler.
5. DIFFERENCES; Simplicity and complexity need each other.
6. CONTEXT; What lies in the periphery of simplicity is definitely not peripheral.
7. EMOTION; More emotions are better than less.
8. TRUST; In simplicity we trust.
9. FAILURE; Some things can never be made simple.
10. THE ONE; Simplicity is about subtracting the obvious and adding the meaningful.[1]

★★★

This chapter is by nature the most theoretical in my book. I've purposely written short, simple and humorous sections, with some exercises to consider. There are many points of argument and departure, although there is plenty written about the topic of simplification, or how to simplify furniture design for modern lives.

I'm a big believer in simple design, although some of my ideas may come from more Eurocentric privileged economies and consumerism. I've been an incredibly fast learner since moving to Nigeria and I acknowledge that

DOI: 10.4324/9781003453994-5

many theories don't always work in an African context, and certainly don't need to be amplified here.

However, in Africa, we are on the verge of creating an entirely new generation of thinkers in creative design, that would have been inconceivable ten years ago. Why am I so positive? Because the astounding demographics of young Africans, who are seeing the light that things designed, made and sold in Africa have real value. Simplicity plus bold and creative thinking are part of the answer.

Understanding the African lifestyle: Good design in Africa should reflect how people live—from communal living spaces to outdoor gatherings. It should consider the social dynamics, like extended family living and the importance of communal areas. Furniture should be designed for these interactions, fostering community and conversation.

Functionality and versatility: The functionality of furniture in an African context often requires versatility. It's about designing pieces that can serve multiple purposes, catering to the dynamic and sometimes fluid use of space in African homes. Furniture that adapts to different uses, from family gatherings to individual relaxation, is key.

Cultural rationality: Every design must resonate with the cultural rationality of its users. This means understanding the cultural significance of certain forms, materials and uses. In some cultures, certain seating arrangements might be preferred, or specific materials might have cultural connotations. Integrating these aspects into design ensures that the furniture is not just physically in a space, but also belongs there culturally.

Movement and flow: The way people move around furniture and utilise space is crucial. African homes have different spatial dynamics compared to Western homes. Furniture design should accommodate these patterns, ensuring ease of movement, space optimisation and a natural flow that aligns with daily activities.

Sustainability and local resources: Considering the environmental impact and the availability of local materials is crucial. Designs should leverage locally sourced materials not only for sustainability but also to support local industries and economies. This also adds a layer of authenticity and connection to the region.

Adaptability to environmental conditions: African climates vary greatly, and furniture should be designed to withstand local environmental conditions. This includes using materials and finishes suitable for different climates, from humid coastal regions to dry inland areas.

Ergonomics in an African context: Ergonomics isn't a one-size-fits-all concept. The design should consider the ergonomics suitable for the diverse body types and physical needs prevalent in Africa. Comfort and usability should be tailored to the local populace.

Reflecting the African narrative: Beyond using African fabrics or motifs, design should tell the African story. This involves incorporating elements that reflect the rich history, diverse cultures and contemporary realities of Africa. It's about creating pieces that are conversation starters, that tell a story about where they come from and the people they are designed for.

Goldilocks and Mari Kondo

The term simplicity in design these days is overused. If we look around in popular culture and media, it is a clarion call to be what exactly? Leaner, less fussy, sleeker, better organised? We all have seen the Japanese clutter reduction queen, Mari Kondo,[2] imploring us to simplify our lives by reducing the stuff that surrounds our daily lives. Simplicity sells, because the alternative is what? Chaos, disorder, mess.

There is even a line of stainless-steel rubbish bins called Simple Human.[3] As if by simplifying the mountains of garbage by purchasing a fairly ordinary, although elegant, rubbish bin called Simple Human, we'd somehow feel less negligent about how much plastic, metal, wood and fabric we toss out. Simple? Human? Really?

How many times have we reminded ourselves to, 'Keep it simple'; look at all the other variations in furniture design—like the Scandi-Nordic IKEA's seemingly effortless design—that have captured the world in creating mass simplicity for all.

Supported by television, media and internet publicity, we are constantly urged to consume both must-haves that ignite our imaginations and desires, as well as the 'I want to haves'.

Simplicity is all the rage these days. It is a design philosophy that is championed by many successful companies and fans of those companies alike.

However, in furniture design there is paradox. I have found that simple can be harder than complex design in many ways, because it requires more attention to detail. Particularly so in a market such as Africa that struggles with quality products. Many attempt these so-called simple designs with enthusiasm and skill but put very little effort into execution. Simplicity requires a detailed mind free of chaos and noise.

I'm not against simplicity per se, but as our planet gets filled up with more and more stuff, and that includes furniture, and as the next generation of product designers emerges, they will need to work harder to find better ways to design furniture that is regionally appropriate and appeals to local cultural aesthetics as well as being adaptable to the global market. This paradox is what I believe in—simplicity driven by complex ideas, cultural and aesthetic needs, available materials and resources, and understanding that overarching goal to get their thinking clean to make it simple.

The payoff is that it's worth it in the end, because once entrepreneurs and designers figure it out, they can achieve great heights in every facet of manufacturing.

As an example, it was a great feeling of personal satisfaction when customers complimented our furniture products because they thought they were imported.

If new African designers can build and sustain international standards locally and market effectively, there are almost no reasons why they cannot sell more internationally and thereby earn foreign exchange.

If I use the brilliant MIT designer and TED Talks superstar John Maeda's *The Laws of Simplicity* as a reference list, that I've outlined at the top of this chapter, and adapted more or less to contemporary African context, then my simplicity in design would be something like this:

My first step is to reduce Maeda's laws of simplicity from ten to four.

REDUCE

How simple can you make it versus how complex does it have to be?[4]

A chair is the perfect design for the human body. I'm sure as soon as carving with tools became a skill set that became developed, chairs for sitting, resting, eating and standing on became useful. After sitting on rocks and tree stumps for millennia, look at the incredible variety of chairs that every culture on the planet has built. I could fill this book and several others with the incredible designs of chairs, but they all fill a function. The human in resting position and not sitting on the floor.

I could bastardise Rene Descartes' famous quote to read, 'I sit therefore I am.'

This exercise in simplicity in design would begin with almost any easily acquired material—paper, glue, toothpicks, sticks, metal scraps, cardboard—and then build a 'simple' chair that could support your own weight.

Once you begin the task, it will become very clear that the chair is actually not that simple. How many legs does it have? How is the back attached to the seat and how do you fasten the legs on the underside, and most importantly, will it support your weight? In fact, the engineering of even a simple wooden chair is quite complex when we look at the stress points, with the aim of making a chair that others, large or small, can sit upon.

Thinking about how to reduce for my simple design a chair exercise, reducing or removing the chair back would create a stool, and not a chair. If we remove some legs, then it becomes quite comical. However, I would challenge a new generation to make use of materials that are discarded, and recycleble and look for creative ways to either restoreto their former glory or upcycle with a new identity

Now the big tests would be to see if it would support your weight, and if it has a basic design that supports a range of bodies.

One solution comes from Goldilocks and the Three Bears. I'll remind you of the part of the story:

> Having eaten the bowl of porridge, Goldilocks walks through to the living room, where there are three chairs. She tries sitting in each of them. The first is too big, as is the second, but the third is just the right size. However, it's a small chair and Goldilocks manages to break it by sitting in it. So, we can add destruction of property to the list of growing charges.[5]

Now to be perfectly honest, I'm not really championing the infamous blonde Mother Goose juvenile delinquent but there something to be said about the Goldilocks Zone when it comes to design, comfort and function. If your chair is too small, too light or you skimp on support systems, the chair could break. There is something deeply comforting to the statement, 'Just the right size.'

Sitting is something that we do over and over again in our daily lives, and finding the Goldilocks Zone should be the goal for every designer.

In my opening chapter, I wrote about acquiring my first authentic leather Chesterfield sofa. In my experience, and I've sat on plenty of sofas, the Chesterfield it is quite possibly the perfect sofa. Yes, there are a million updates, and contemporary designs, but when sitting on this singularly perfect piece of English furniture design, surrounded by tufting and the warmth of the leather, you will know what I say about the Goldilocks Zone. It is just right. Your body recognises it as soon as you sit on it.

ORGANISE

For most of us, clutter is the bane of our existence. Yes, we've watched in awe as Marie Kondo[6] decluttered our homes and computers, secretly wishing she'd be more like the rest of us—stuffing unused items into a drawer, slamming it shut, and thinking, 'There, clutter gone!'

For designers, designing spaces to park or hide clutter will be the next big thing. It is naturally human to be messy, inefficient and clutter-bound. However, as John Maeda points out in his book, solutions exist for our stuff. And I don't mean stuffing it all on a rocket and shooting it into orbit.

Maeda states comically (I urge students and readers to look at his TED Talks):

> The home is usually the first battleground that comes to mind when facing the daily challenge of managing complexity. Stuff just seems to multiply. There are three consistent strategies for achieving simplicity in the living realm: 1) buy a bigger house, 2) put everything you don't really need into storage, or 3) organise your existing assets in a systematic fashion.[7]

For a potential furniture designer, when you read the words *home, battleground* and *managing stuff,* they present a huge opportunity. We can take option one off the list, because very few people are in this position. Number two will work, but then there will be a constant need to find larger and larger storage, and really who has the time to drive to a remote facility to look for a some long-forgotten piece of furniture or piece of electronics?

We can look at option three as the opportunity for designers to simplify. Then the challenge will be how to create these systematic organisational units, or wardrobes, and look for spaces in homes that are underutilised.

As an example of storage space, if you look at the clever design of the Italian bed design company Flou,[8] their Nathalie bed utilises the bed frame to create a storage box under the bed and a simple hydraulic piston mechanism that allows the mattress and bed frame to raise easily, and close much like a car bonnet. This found space under the mattress actually has a lot of storage, if you consider the size of a queen or double mattress. This is a clever solution to reduce clutter. What other organisational furniture can be designed so that we can declutter and organise as families grow, people move in and through homes and apartments?

Or the genius of Ori, the robotic furniture company founded by Hasier Larrea, who is building the furniture of the ever-shrinking living spaces of large cities. The company is not just creating furniture; it's redefining the way we use and perceive living spaces in urban environments. The company's products are a testament to the fusion of technology and design, aimed at enhancing the functionality and sustainability of modern urban living.

Ori's solutions represent a significant shift in how living spaces are designed and used. They reflect a growing trend toward making smaller spaces more liveable and sustainable through innovative technology. The company's efforts are a response to recognising the increasing need for more efficient use of space in cities worldwide.

As I stated at the outset of this chapter, simplicity is actually difficult to achieve, and as our lives fill with objects and clothing and we adapt to living in small spaces, furniture designers will be tested more and more to come up with comfortable, affordable, space-saving designs that also use refurbished, recycled materials to help a sustainable planet.

There are plenty of challenges, and I am very bullish about young designers in Nigeria, once they unlock creative thinking. They can experience and prototype in a hands-on training programme that I'm positive will unleash the imagination of a new generation of designers and manufacturers.

Maeda's book also suggests two critical laws to consider when aiming for simplicity in design and life. One key takeaway for students is understanding the importance of acknowledging complexity by stating that some things simply can never be made simple. This insight can motivate students to strive for simplicity while recognizing the inherent complexities in certain tasks.

FAILURE

One should never stop creative thinking when looking for solutions but make failed attempts. In fact, failing is a critical part of the creative act. We learn from failing, and getting it just right takes many versions and attempts in almost everything we do, including writing my first book!

That is why I encourage prototyping, to allow designers and students to try and work with a wide range of materials to give them a feel of texture and what is possible, and what is impossible.

When aiming for simplicity in furniture design, don't look for what has been done, or what has been deemed classic and tried and true. We actually don't need another version of Ikea furniture or imported Chinese rip-offs. Originality and simplicity are vastly different for different cultures and localities, and what is popular in Europe may get mocked in Africa. What is essential, however, is for designers to have the space and the time to fail and learn and build from their failures, both large and small.

Maeda calls this process an ROF, or return on failure, when you try to simplify, which is to learn from your mistakes. When faced with failure, any good artist, or any other member of the creative class, leverages the unfortunate event to radically shift perspective. One person's failed experiment in simplicity can be another's success, as a beautiful form of complexity. Simplicity and complexity shift with subtle changes in point of view.[9]

THE ONE

The final law of simplicity is rather elegant:

Simplicity is about subtracting the obvious and adding the meaningful.[10]

How can that be done? When students are faced with the task of designing a simple chair from found materials? What is obvious, and what is meaningful? The answer is up to the individual designer and in the eye of the beholder. To a designer in the UK, it might be that the legs are too bulky, or the chair might fall backwards. To an African designer, it might look too low to the ground. It must give the *meaningful* emotions of comfort, safety, warmth, security—all emotions that excellent designs bring to consumers, or as Goldilocks stated: it feels just right.

Meaningful is a subtle word that cuts across many territories. John Maeda ends his book with a very poignant story about a former student called Marc. It begs telling the full story because it is deeply connected to what is meaningful:

Marc volunteered in shelters for poor people at the end of their lives...Even though he came from a well-heeled family and could easily turned his back on the impoverished. Marc always felt compelled to help others in need. He told that how while working in shelters, he noticed that each patient *held a single shelf by their bed that held the total sum of their worldly belongings*. Seeing this situation made him silently ask, 'What are the few precious things you can afford to keep at the end of your life when you have so little?' A ring, a photograph, or another small memento what he consistently found. Marc surmised that memories are all that matter in the end.[11]

To unpack this touching story for furniture designers, and consider the overarching ideas of simplicity, that if designers approach every single design with a goal to strip away excess, but add layers of meaning, the story of the simple shelves is indeed profound. A place to keep all of your worldly goods, a simple shelf display that honours loved ones, and objects that induce deeper feeling of the warmth of memories, and emotional connection to their pasts before they pass on. It is very inspiring and—I believe—the essence of simplicity in a world where the accumulation of objects, including furniture, makes the economy spin.

Yet, Africa is no stranger to intergenerational poverty, so simplicity is not created but made out of necessity and survival is not a wilful act of design. Their memories and how they display their family histories and lives have a deep meaning, even though the objects may seem to the outside eye worthless. However, they are *meaningful* because they are displayed in a place of honour and therefore imbued with the powerful place for memory and connection to the past.

Like Marc's story, I also see one of the multipronged goals of the academy as reaching out to the extremely poor and homeless. And inviting them to attend our academy to give them practical hands-on training tools, inspiration to work with their hands and minds.

The deep question then is, how do the next generation of Nigerian and African furniture designers design simple but also meaningful pieces? It is a very intriguing challenge, because more often than not, meaningful is in the eye of the beholder, and it is definitely not a one-size-fits-all solution, like designing a kind of medicine cabinet to store valuable objects.

However, as I've outlined in an earlier chapter, if future designers know their ground, focus on real recognises real and do the research, and look to their own lives and ask themselves questions of what is meaningful, I am very positive that a new generation of African creative thinkers will emerge. They will begin to totally transform how we look at furniture that is more than an object to be desired, but create pieces that have function, comfort, beauty and are imbued with meaning that is built in.

Checkmate with the Future

In a very exciting outreach programme, we have teamed up with Tunde Onakoya who is a Nigerian chess master and coach who founded Chess in Slums Africa in 2017. He is driven by the conviction that chess can serve as a powerful educational tool to improve young lives and foster a new generation of intellectuals, even among underprivileged communities.

Figure 5.1 Tunde Onakoya with Demi, 29 March 2023. Image courtesy of Majeurs Holdings.

I encourage all readers to look and listen to a SUSU Podcast[12] where I interview Tunde and his incredible work with kids in Nigeria's homeless communities.

Tunde is an exemplary Nigerian, who we plan to team up with to find young, poor, but perfectly able children to start training at our academy. It just takes a spark to light a fire, and I'm incredibly humbled and honoured that Tunde will work with us to help find and train these students, and I'm positive that soon they will develop an entire range of chess tables to fit any family and budget.

I'll close Chapter Five with this thought: the power of African youth is at a crossroads, it can go two directions. The first is the predictable old-school thinking about Africans and how they work and will only increase mass out-flow of young people to Northern Africa and then to Europe's growing hostile shores. The second direction is one of innovation, empowerment and investment in local talent and industries. By fostering entrepreneurship, providing education and training, and creating sustainable job opportunities, we can harness the potential of African youth to drive economic growth and transform the continent from within. This path will not only stem the tide of emigration but also build a prosperous future for Africa led by its own vibrant and capable young population.

★★★

I'll remind you that it was not too long ago that the outside view of the Chinese attitude and aptitude for work was pejoratively described similarly to how Africans are generally thought of today—lazy, unskilled and unproductive. It is amazing what can be achieved in 25 years when there is great conviction and dedication to change.

Africa is poised to become the next global hub of manufacturing. A massive, young, dynamic but untrained workforce is ready to begin work immediately. To harness this energy, it will need thought leaders, but also on-the-ground training that perhaps only the Chinese can provide, because they have that skill set and long history working in Africa. It may sound controversial, but a made only in Africa workforce and a training solution working in partnership with the Chinese and other outside industry leaders is more than likely the next big step.

The need for targeted skills training in Africa, particularly from international sources, is a significant aspect of addressing the skill gaps and ensuring the upskilling of Africans. Despite considerable investment in public higher education by many African governments, there is often a mismatch between the skills taught in these institutions and those required by industries and sectors. This situation calls for a prioritisation of vocational education and skills-specific education, emphasising curricula that respond directly to market demand for labour. Furthermore, encouraging apprenticeships and integrating them into degree programmes is also recommended.

In response to these challenges, various initiatives and platforms are emerging to address the specific training needs in Africa. For example, Talstack is an all-in-one platform that helps African businesses upskill their employees with tailored and specific training programmes. This approach is essential because typical training methods, such as generic online courses from international platforms, may lack contextual relevance and fail to connect to specific growth or development outcomes in Africa.

Furthermore, partnerships like the one between I-Train Africa and UNLEASH Denmark aim to provide relevant soft skills training to over 50,000 African youths. This kind of targeted training addresses the critical need for literate African youths to understand the 'Whys before the Hows' in their academic and career pursuits.

The digital skills gap is another significant challenge. With about 87 per cent of African business leaders identifying digital skills development as a priority, there's a clear need for substantial investment in this area. The gap is stark, with African countries scoring much lower on the Digital Skills Gap Index compared to the global average. Effective interventions will require partnerships between local private sectors, global technology companies and educational institutions both within Africa and internationally.

To effectively upskill African youths, there is also a need to revamp the entire education sector, expand digital infrastructure and foster public-private partnerships. These efforts should aim to make digital and technical skills integral to the curriculum from primary levels onwards, ensuring that African youths are well equipped to compete globally.

Lastly, initiatives like AltSchool Africa, which has seen over 50,000 applications from various countries, are indicative of the demand for upskilling platforms that cater to the needs of African learners in various industries. Such platforms focus on providing skills that are directly relevant to the job market, emphasising the importance of practical and applicable training.

While there is a significant need for external training to upskill Africans within Africa, it is equally crucial that these training programmes are contextual, relevant and aligned with the specific needs of the African labour market. Collaboration between governments, private sectors and international partners plays a key role in achieving this objective.

I really do believe that this generation is ready NOW, and with smart funding to support these initiatives, the wheels on this global hub will begin to turn.

Africa is the future, and I encourage all readers to also listen to my SUSU (Start Up, Scale Up) podcasts with a range of entrepreneurs and thinkers, who believe the boom in the manufacturing sector is the next big thing in Nigeria and Africa.

I also encourage readers to look at the products and designs by up-and-coming young Nigerians. I guarantee you will be astonished by their skills and creativity. They are the truly meaningful future for our industry and economy.

Notes

1 http://lawsofsimplicity.com

2 https://konmari.com/

3 https://www.simplehuman.com/pages/trash-can

4 John Maeda. 2006. *The Laws of Simplicity*. Cambridge, Massachusetts Etc.: MIT Press. Page 1.

5 https://interestingliterature.com/2017/05/a-summary-and-analysis-of-goldilocks-and-the-three-bears/

6 Marie Kondo. 2014. *The Life-Changing Magic of Tidying Up*. Ten Speed Press.

7 John Maeda. 2006. *The Laws of Simplicity*. Cambridge, Massachusetts Etc.: MIT Press. Page 11.

8 https://www.flou.com/en/products/beds/nathalie_8

9 Ibid. Page 83

10 Ibid. Page 89

11 Ibid. Page 100.

12 https://www.linkedin.com/posts/demi-samande-7529a2187_tunde-onakoya-meeting-purpose-with-mindset-activity-7058447108336402433-ALPl

Communication and Storytelling

6

Where do you begin to tell your story and build your brand? There are many fabulous furniture brands all over the planet, but I would bet it would be difficult to name ten off the top of your head.

This brief exercise will demonstrate what I'm saying. On the left on a sheet of paper, make a list of the ten top furniture brands that you have encountered and perhaps appreciated over your life.

On the right, make another list of the kinds of furniture they make— tables, beds, mattresses, sofas, kitchen, chairs, etc. Then draw a line between the brands and the specific furniture.

Drawing that line between the brand and the product is essentially step one in creating a brand through storytelling. Literally by drawing the line, a storyline is created. We do this on a daily basis, making connections between all kinds of products, from shoes, makeup, hair and beauty items, jeans and furniture. But rarely do we realise that is how brands become indelible and thus more successful, because the storyline is direct and what we understand is simple—the products functional, beautiful and timeless.

Often, the thing that sets your product apart from another brand is *simply the story*. For instance, my sector is highly competitive, as many companies all over the globe manufacture well-designed and beautiful furniture.

The essential question becomes, what products or line of products do I design, and how will I make them stand out in a very crowded field? So, the storyline—the deep connection that consumers make between product and name—is as simple as drawing a line.

However, my story of how I built Majeurs Furniture from scratch in Nigeria is the storyline and the brand. That is why I put myself forward in so many public spaces—social media, podcasts, now books and public

DOI: 10.4324/9781003453994-6

speaking engagements. By retelling my story over and over, the storyline becomes indelible in the public's mind.

In fact, I would say that my overarching goal and brand is to be the new voice and face that advocates for the renewing and rebuilding of the Nigerian and African manufacturing sector.

If the general public one day can draw a straight line between my name and brand, then I know my hard work and the products I have designed and manufactured are making a connection.

The truth is, there is nothing really considered new anymore. Globalisation has made the world flat, and without getting into trade and politics, almost everything has mostly been done before. However, every now and then, we come across a new way of doing the same thing and are blown away by the authenticity, and that new way we can develop a cool X factor.

How then does the next generation of young designers and manufacturers tell their story and build their brand? These questions are often answered by how and where the furniture manufacturers are located, in Africa, Europe or China. The Chinese have built massive capacities, but is there a secret to their success? In October 2019, prior to the global Covid outbreak, I travelled to China for a month to really learn about how the Chinese were able to develop an industrial strategy and witness for my own eyes their economic miracle.

Here is what I discovered.

The Chinese Secret Sauce for Success

Before starting up my furniture manufacturing business in Nigeria, I visited various factories, walked the Great Wall of China, met with potential suppliers and did market research. My general goal was to try and learn the 'Chinese way' of doing business and find out if there was any secret sauce.

Here is what I learned on my one-month journey: the Chinese construct manufacturing using a specialised approach which I'll outline in more detail. Each manufacturer focuses on their contribution to a product and together they align communication and supply chain before coming together as a whole. This means that they can scale and create access to all components that are needed by the industry as a whole. They have a wonderful emphasis on scale and efficiency, breaking every job into tiny processes and steps. They are brilliant at leveraged economies of scale. The massive size of China's domestic market is coupled with huge investments by the central government in infrastructure which allow for unparalleled efficiency.

This is not just about low cost, it's about the speed at which they can go from raw materials to finished products.

Vertical Integration and Supply Chain Dominance

The Chinese model emphasises vertical integration.

China's vertical integration and supply chain dominance strategy involves a company controlling its supply chain, from raw materials to retail. This approach, evident in Chinese economic development, includes owning suppliers, manufacturers and distributors, leading to cost reduction, efficiency and market control. Particularly prominent in sectors like electronics, this strategy has positioned Chinese companies as global leaders.

Key to this model is state support and significant investment in infrastructure and logistics, exemplified by the Belt and Road Initiative. This not only enhances China's supply chain control but also extends its global influence. Such dominance impacts global markets, potentially affecting pricing and political dynamics.

For businesses focused on environmentally conscious manufacturing, adapting aspects of this model could mean enhanced control and efficiency. However, balancing this with flexibility, innovation and environmental sustainability is crucial. Integrating technology could streamline processes, ensuring efficiency and sustainability coexist. This approach offers lessons in efficiency and control, but adapting them to align with specific business models and values is essential.

Technological Adoption

The Chinese appreciate the importance of integrating technology in manufacturing. They also have been aggressive in cutting-edge technologies like robotics and want to push the boundaries of what's possible in manufacturing.

Agility and Responsiveness

China has built systems that are highly responsive to market demands. Once a design is shared anywhere in the world, they literally waste no time in adapting it to their collection. Quick changes to production lines, rapid prototyping and willingness to adapt have made Chinese manufacturing incredibly agile.

This is something that African manufacturing needs to follow up and we are teaching these methods at our training academy.

Intellectual Property

China has zero recognition or respect for intellectual property rights which I believe has aided in the rapid rise of their manufacturing.

Secret sauce, well there are many secret sauces, but the most incredible is that they are brilliant at rapid reverse engineering and adaptation of any product, though at the expense of the original.

IP holders. At my company in Lagos, we are aiming to make a big leap with AI-powered SaaS (software as a service) for furniture manufacturing—for our new Mande line. They've effectively reduced dependencies by controlling various stages of production. This not only cuts costs but also ensures excellent quality control.

The King and I...

What did it feel like to have the Prince of Wales and now King of England sit on one of my beautifully restored leather Chesterfields? That is what is called in storytelling a terrific parachute line. A prince walks into my shop and asks to sit on my leather Chesterfield sofa. We strike up a conversation, and in ten minutes I go from nobody to a minor celebrity. Now both can be described as oddly funny, charming and attention grabbing, and my story with the future King of England and David Cameron, the then Prime Minister, having a chat on my sofa. But the first storyline evokes an emotional response. How did I feel when His Majesty entered into the room, what did he say and what were my answers? A state secret, hardly, but I can tell you that he was not there to shop for a sofa for one of his castles.

The backstory is that Prince Charles is a big fan of restored leather furniture and in particular Chesterfields. I was asked by his team if HRH could be hosted at our London studio along with other startups with the goal of promoting the young enterprises rising in the UK. The Prince's Trust helps young people from disadvantaged communities and those facing the greatest adversity by supporting them to build the confidence and skills to live, learn and earn. To be asked to support this goal was an absolute privilege and honour. My work was recognised very early and that was enough to open my horizon to dreaming even bigger.

In essence, there were all the ingredients in place for a story and luck, timing, but also a lot of hours working mostly alone, repairing and restoring old furniture. There was also my own personal history growing up in a middle-class family in London with zero contact or interest in the royals. There were also a lot of hours traveling all over the UK in a van buying old pieces and delivering newly restored sofas and leather furniture. However cool that may be for some readers, and I'm not downplaying this incredible opportunity, and what small businessperson wouldn't turn it down, I knew that this was just one step forward and part of many more to come. This story is amongst many others that has become but one strand of the fuller story of Majeurs Chesterfields. What is critical for any young businessperson is to create your own story and develop three critical elements.

1. Centre Your Narrative on a Transformation

In Stanford University Professor J.D. Schramm's Book,[1] he is succinct:

> Every good story charts a change—even a subtle one—in the conditions, attitudes, actions or feelings of the characters.

If you break this down into smaller bitesize pieces of information, you could ask yourself, what was a small but transformative moment that began a change in my direction? Make a list and jot them down. Then rate them from one to five. I'm sure you will have a tough time deciding which one has the most impact on your decision to either start your own business, or a new journey in your life.

My story of having lunch in London with my brother-in-law is a perfect example. His impeccable thinking and timing to suggest to me that I should think about moving to Nigeria was transformative. Definitely outside of my thinking at the time. This story or journey has now become one of the many big, subtle, blockbuster or miniature stories that my company has built and incorporated into the company and our brand.

Your story may be as direct and humble as, 'My father toiled for many decades in building his business, and he has decided to retire. He has given me the keys to his shop and now I am the owner and operator of a small woodshop in Lagos.' That is a simple, direct narrative but the journey is implied, and the transformation to woodshop owner-operator is now part of your narrative.

2. Define the Impact by Telling Your Story

Then how do you build on that business journey story and build a bigger narrative to attract more customers, and investors, to scale up and possibly hire more employees?

Brian Moriarty, a Professor at the University of Virginia's Darden School, gives a good answer:[2]

> Define the impact you seek by telling your story. Then share an early draft with a friend or colleague. Their feedback will help you decide if your account provides too much detail or too little. Did your main message come through to your listener? Which part of your story had the most significant cognitive or emotional impact?

In essence, he suggests that you select what best makes an impact, and seek out listeners for your story. He also suggests that 'You may learn that rearranging or removing story elements will improve understanding or enhance the emotional impact.'

Own Your Story with Emotion

Good storytelling for your business relies on many factors, but to get to why we listen and appreciate these stories—it is because of the impact of emotions, and that we are hardwired as a species for stories.

Perhaps the woodworker was struggling in school, and had a tough life because they did not feel that they'd ever live up to their father's expectations. All these signify that the journey was not as simple and direct as originally written, and now the young woodworker has a story to tell his employees, potential investors and his customers who appreciate how he had to boot-strap his way up the ladder to success.

You will immediately know if your listeners are engaged. When I repeat the story about my famous lunch with Chinedu, my brother-in-law, or why I moved to Nigeria to start up a business, I often joke that it is his fault—if something goes wrong at least I can point a finger at him.

However, by owning my story, and stating clearly that while his suggestion was provocative, it was me who took a giant step, that was fraught with all kinds of potential for failure.

This is the same for the woodworker, who takes over his father's business, but then decides to transform it into a Chinese-style component business and decides the future for his company is to supply wooden legs to furniture manufacturers in Africa. Small legs, big legs, round and square legs and scale up to mass production, so a company like mine would never have to import Chinese furniture legs and components ever again.

This story can be repeated and further developed as other smaller one-man shops can scale up to meet the demand for larger supplies in the entire chain—I'm including this story not as some unique idea, but because I can see the immediate need for a small business to be developed using Chinese efficiency, reverse engineering, communication and date and supply chain logistics. That I definitely see as having an immediate effect both as a story and reality.

End with a Bang: Bang Your Own Drum

Stories that galvanise us and peak our imaginations create interest in the human story. I'd say this is even more true for young African entrepreneurs. My call to action is to the new generation of entrepreneurs. We want them to attend our academy where we can encourage them to make communication and a storytelling agenda a major part of any new startup in almost any sector.

These stories are what build and create your team, and how they describe where, what, why and how their company began.

African brands are the future, almost all economists are pointing to this fact, and many are on the cusp of big breakthroughs. I truly believe this is the way that African brands will penetrate the global market. We MUST NOT only tell our stories, but we must also curate them with the intention to package each story as the very product itself.

The woodworker I used as an example must break out of local regional mindset and economy and use all the tools, technology and social media to compete on a global scale. Then one day in the future, Nigerian-made chair legs will be exported to China and elsewhere to use in their furniture manufacturing.

★★★

Remember that a story is not always, 'I did this, then I did that, and by that date I managed to complete this and so on.' In fact, that narrative is quite boring, and your listeners and readers will switch off.

Instead, frame your narrative as a journey, and describe it in a few words. Where did it all start, where do you think it will end?

Stoke a memory in your listener, to stimulate and galvanise, and critically allow the listener into that memory. If someone is leaning in while you speak, their body language will speak volumes.

Fuel emotion: your story, however humble or subtle is always the starting ground. Bang the drum so that your listener will feel your confidence.

★★★

If we extend this narrative to the manufacturing sector in Africa, then as an industry what is the business plan, our narrative for Africa? The first step is we need to ask ourselves: how can we do it differently? How can we appeal to consumers in a unique way that resonates purely with them in a fresh way that reflects our culture and values?

My suggestion is creating a narrative about the individuals and success stories who are already competing in the global marketplace but also know the ground in Nigeria or Africa. Many of these topics I will explore later in the book.

Where do you begin your journey? A new language in a simple story that connects design and simplicity with our own uniqueness of living and working in Africa that cannot be replicated by another or in any other place. In later chapters I'll discuss and promote sustainable and green products, by businesses owned by African men and women, or products that are solving local problems that were deemed to be impossible in the past.

India's Moonshot: Africa's Challenge

In late August 2023, India successfully landed a spacecraft on the moon for the first time near its southern pole. Just consider that thought. Twenty years ago, India was listed as an overpopulated and chronically poor nation that struggled to feed itself. In fact, it needed to import food to prevent starvation. How did they get to this point? They developed a collective strategy.

With their moonshot, it has made a massive technological leap over many Western countries—including the UK, France, Italy and Canada. It proved the old idea that a moonshot is worth billions in investment, because if you can place a spaceship on the moon without crashing, then you can retrieve critical data on potential water on the moon to sustain life. For Indians this incredible leap into the future is inspirational, and shows the sky is the not just the limit.

My challenge to Nigerians and to Africa is this: who and where will we build the first rockets to reach the moon, either real or metaphorical. In a purely practical application, who will step up and build the first factory to manufacture wooden chair legs. The sky is the not the limit, and it will be our stories and our narrative that will get us there.

Notes

1 J.D. Schramm and Kara Levy. 2020. *Communicate with Mastery: How to Speak with Conviction and Write for Impact*. Hoboken, New Jersey: Wiley.

2 https://ideas.darden.virginia.edu/storytelling-in-business-engaging-stories

Lessons Learned   **7**

Relocating from London to Africa

Securing Funding

I could write an entire book on this topic, and perhaps that will be the next book so that new and young African entrepreneurs can secure funding to start up their businesses. This is the topic that keeps me up at night and most likely will be the biggest stressor for anyone considering a business startup. When I relocated from London to Lagos, I knew there was a lot of opportunity I was leaving behind, including a highly regarded reputation in leather furniture recovery, recycling and restoration.

The most important lesson I learned, and am still learning, is how to plan and mitigate funding problems well in advance. I'll readily admit that I learned this too late and as a certified and proven bootstrapper, this scenario works when the company is still in its infancy, and it really only relies on your own personal sweat, equity and commitment to see the vision come to fruition.

Everything changes when there are staff, workers, rent, electric bills and customers. Secure funding underlies every single decision that you will have to make, and it is often the make-or-break moment for any small startup.

This is the hard grind—the nitty-gritty, down in the dirt reality of starting up any company. It is the days and months spent attempting to raise money and it can wreck personal lives as well as professional lives, because these are the real hills in building a startup. One big lesson that I have learned is that there is never one golden pot of funding—there are hundreds if not thousands of small, medium and large funds that all need a specific pitch deck, for very specific kinds of funding.

If I had stayed in the UK, the options for funding a growing business were more readily available than in Nigeria. There are business-friendly

DOI: 10.4324/9781003453994-7

banks, hedge funds, business incubators, business zones and as a young Black female entrepreneur, in a field that has been traditionally dominated by white men, the opportunities were possibly even better, as the UK would like to promote and advance a diverse entrepreneurial class. In Nigeria, none of that exists, and I'll address this in a wish list at the end of this chapter.

As young entrepreneurs, it is very easy to get bogged down in day-to-day problem-solving, and trying to mitigate funding issues that I'll admit has been a big problem for me. In Africa, there is no source of data as to how and when to apply, or to whom, making for huge headaches. This is all part of the huge learning curve.

Lesson: You Cannot Do All of It on Your Own

Planning ahead is essential, and I believe that securing funding through family or personal connections at first will be the logical source. Unless your family's financial resources are bottomless, those funds will quickly dry up, and you must forward-plan to seek funding from other sources.

Do not wait to begin building your pitch deck and creating your financial plan. This deck or presentation to funders should be constantly upgraded and revised.

The pitch deck is the tool—with visuals and graphs—that funders review when making their decision to fund your company.

Unless you are that extremely rare startup that takes off immediately, called a unicorn, and you don't need external funding, then this is a major part of the ongoing daily work for entrepreneurs—writing and rewriting pitch decks for specific funders and their particular needs. In one year, if your company is active and looking to scale up, I'd suggest that a new and updated version is needed every quarter and possibly every month, particularly if you are looking for smaller investment funds.

Disclaimer: it took me several attempts to get my pitch deck to this stage and even now it still requires updates to keep it continuously fresh with up-to-date information.

Always Seek Professional Help When Developing Your Pitch Deck

No two are alike, and at first it will be a bewildering amount of data, both known and unknown that will keep you up all night developing your pitch deck. If you recall the previous chapter about storytelling, this is where a precise story of how and why you decided to start your company is crucial,

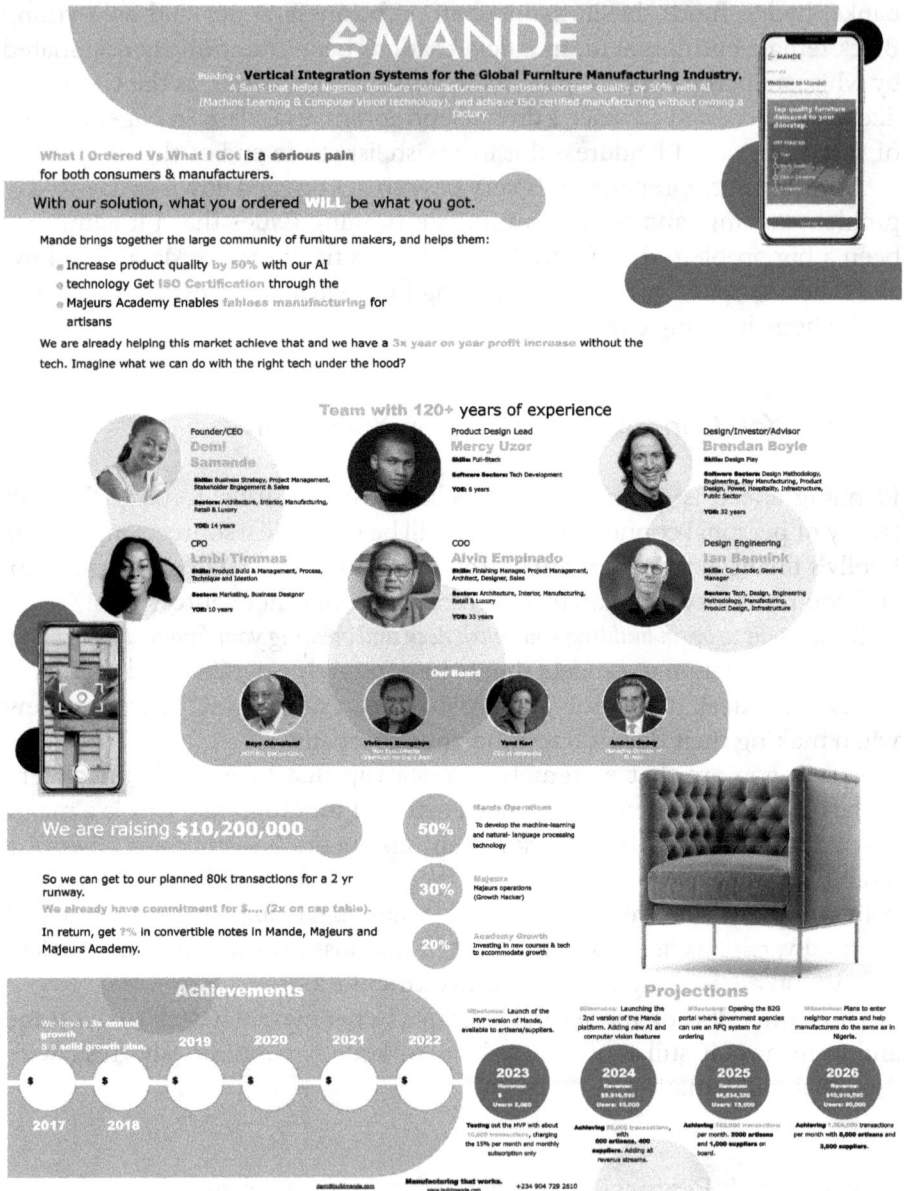

Figure 7.1 Modified pitch deck, 2024. Image courtesy of Majeurs Holdings.

as well as a vision of where it will be in one year, five years, ten years. This *story* that you need to hone and practice speaking out loud with confidence is an important part. So is your team, and their history of working with you. Remember, funders do not look only at your numbers, and although they are essential, they are interested in your personal and emotional decisions and what drives you to build a company from the ground up.

Be Prepared to Hear 'NO'

There will also be a lot of silence, and unreturned emails and phone calls. In my own experience of fundraising in both Africa, the UK and the USA, one thing is very clear: this process will be one of the most humbling, often embarrassing, humiliating things you do. I often make sure that I'm well caffeinated and prepared for almost any kind of question when I go into meetings, and I'm always prepped to answer any question that may come up, even the most innocuous.

My advice is to keep looking at the horizon, as often funding decisions are not made for many months after a meeting, and remember to keep your sense of humour with you.

In these funding meetings, I can recall the younger Demi, travelling in London on my scooter and bursting into hair salons announcing, 'Ladies, I have body shapers!' That confidence and sense of humour that I developed on the streets of London has helped me enormously, and I encourage all readers to always tap into that source of pride and self-confidence.

Lessons Learned 1: Externals Forces You Cannot Avoid

For instance, In Nigeria, the national currency, the naira, has lost enormous value against global currencies internationally and inflation is galloping. That means that everything purchased or ordered from outside of Nigeria costs even more. This precipitous drop makes my company and others gasp for air, because the outside forces in turn make the cost of doing business even more demanding. How does one mitigate against this? In some sense it is as serious as having a major fire on the premises, but as a businessperson, you must plan for all contingencies.

1. **Dollarization:** If appropriate, consider conducting business transactions in a more stable foreign currency, such as the US dollar, to minimise exposure to the fluctuating local currency.

2. **Efficiency and cost control:** Continuously assess your operational efficiency and identify cost-saving measures. This might involve optimising supply chain logistics, reducing waste or renegotiating contracts with suppliers.
3. **Hedging:** Explore hedging options to protect your business from currency fluctuations. This involves financial instruments like forward contracts that allow you to lock in exchange rates for future transactions, reducing the impact of currency devaluation.

Setting up a manufacturing business in Nigeria or Africa is high risk but has potential for high reward. What is important that your funders understand that the ROI may be slower—certainly, a crashing currency is not helpful to say the least.

Lessons Learned 2: HR and Other Obstacles

After finance, the next biggest challenge is finding and hiring management positions, designers, staff and craftspeople to work on the manufacturing floor. I'm sure it is obvious to readers that HR is always a big challenge for any small startup and I can clearly state that it is the second biggest issue that keeps me up at night. In a country like Nigeria that has a massive population of young people eager for work, you'd think you would be more or less choosing the best of the applicants. However, in Nigeria, and in fact all of Africa, it becomes more or less working from zero, as there is little or no data like job banks or websites. Thus, HR becomes a big task of searching for appropriate candidates, interviewing and working out all the complexities for commuting, then making sure your new staff member is actually trained and can do what they have told you in the interviews.

Have a very clear idea of who you need and when, and then develop your own HR plan. It is also essential in a company like Majeurs to plan ahead and mitigate for all the potential problems like worker engagement and retention. This will be a constant issue, as many of the workers might be coming from extremely long distances, and travelling across Lagos on a daily basis. There can be a mindboggling traffic jams of unbelievable proportions, many have never held a steady job and are often doing subsistence work, and more often than not many applicants have left school to work and help support their families.

It is a reality that I had to learn very quickly, and I believe has helped shape my gratitude for the small workforce—currently 30 employees—and their commitment to making the products.

Thus, the entire cycle of hiring to keeping your employees well paid, on the worksite and not late for work is a daily challenge. Every entrepreneur must practice patience and willingness to make it work for all the staff. Please see the websites below which detail our in-house HR practices and rules:

- The Little Book of Majeurs: http://tinyurl.com/3e4xucf7
- Code of Conduct: http://tinyurl.com/mrx3t8fm
- Culture Alignment Test: http://tinyurl.com/ye2y6z2j

Lessons Learned 3: Embracing Global Mindsets

In 2021, *Forbes* magazine[1] interviewed several young entrepreneurs and asked them what the major obstacles they were facing while attempting to start their new business, and some advice on how to overcome them. The article was US-based and therefore in a very different business environment, but there are some very global obstacles that I have learned about in Nigeria.

In many ways, I would think that as younger people are drawn into our academy, they bring their own experiences, culture, religion and desire to build something that will succeed and be sustainable. Like me, they will all have strengths and weaknesses that will be put to the test.

I have emphasised early on that you cannot do everything yourself, and always advise seeking help from professionals, particularly getting all the legal and compliance work done early. But in an African context, what if there are no professionals to help, whom do you turn to?

In the early stages, I was lucky to have the wisdom of my brother-in-law. However, not everyone has access to family advice.

One of the biggest lessons and obstacles I have encountered is limiting my mindset. My early goals were limited at first to focusing mostly on the Nigerian and African marketplace. Although the furniture was for sale on our website, which meant it was for sale anywhere in the world, I'll never forget the first time I received a call about my furniture being sold and shipped to Australia. Sydney is 9,700 miles away! I could not believe my ears. I immediately thought to myself, '*Would anyone go through the trouble of shipping my products that far? Surely they had very good furniture where they lived?*' However, it didn't take long for me to understand that I was thinking too small. Why not? It takes imagination and planning to realise that high-quality designer products built in small factories with skilled Nigerian craftspeople can also be packed and shipped all over the planet.

Flying Geese

You may be asking yourself at this point: with so many hurdles, why would I or anyone want to bootstrap it and then set up a manufacturing business in a poor economic climate that on first look seems very problematic?

> Manufacturing now accounts for only 13 percent of African GDP and 25 percent of its exports, both smaller shares than in any other region of the world save the oil rich Middle East.[2]

There are numerous old negative tropes to overcome, and I can attest that attracting investors is a constant stress. In later chapters of my book I'll go into depth about my experience and why I am not only bullish on Africa, but my belief that Africa is the future when it comes to manufacturing.

In Irene Yuan Sun's book,[3] she writes about massive Chinese investment in the manufacturing sector in Africa for many years, and why *flying geese* companies are migrating from China to Africa despite the obvious structural problems. Her argument holds water for all investors from a wide variety of nations. In Chapter Two she quotes Robert Lawrence, a Harvard University economist and South African by birth, who puts it this way:

> Globally as major countries like China move out of the bottom of the economic ladder, there are major opportunities for those countries still remaining at the bottom. It turns out that being at the bottom has its benefits—what economists have long identified as, 'the advantages of economic backwardness.'

Not exactly a flattering term for Africa to be relegated to the bottom, and labelled backward, but nevertheless, as Yuan Sun explains, there is attractiveness for investors who can see the long-term strategy succeeding, and I'm paraphrasing her quote for brevity:

> First low income countries are just that —low income, with wage rates cheaper than richer countries…Second, because poor countries still have the lions' share of their economic output in relatively low productivity types of agriculture, they have ample scope for productivity increases…

Third, instead of costly trial and error in developing high-productivity technologies, latecomer developing countries can adopt tried and true technologies and innovation from earlier, pathbreaking countries.[4]

I can break this down into two critical factors, as outlined above—structural and individual—and this is where potential funders usually lean in to really pay attention to my pitch.

There is an element of the Wild West, a new frontier in terms of manufacturing in Africa. Yuan Sun captures it perfectly when describing Lawrence Tung's (a Chinese businessman) massive investment in a new steel factory in Nigeria:

> How is it that they have suffered an oil crisis, a military dictatorship, a national bailout by the IMF an exchange rate that dropped like a stone and remain so optimistic about manufacturing in Nigeria?

It is a daunting list, and Nigeria is not a business environment for the weak of heart or stomach. However, there are so many incredible advantages that believe the rather unsubtle descriptions of being labelled a backward country. In fact, I've devoted three chapters to clearly outline the personal, the structural and where investment, both large and small, in Nigerian and African companies will power the next global manufacturing hub for the 21st century and beyond.

Yuan Sun concludes her thesis in a chapter aptly called, 'The Life, Death and Rebirth of Factories'. It cannot be stated better:

> That is not to say that structural explanations aren't valid, but instead to acknowledge that even the best of conditions require individuals willing to bet their livelihoods that they can make it work. *Progress results when individuals meet a context, act to change it, and are changed in the process.*

★★★

More than anything, I am continually amazed by the creative and industrious people who come to work for me every day. It is not just a distant feeling of success, but an acknowledgement that we are building the foundation for a sustainable company that literally sprung out of my mind (with huge assistance from my brother-in-law).

My personal commitment is to build from the ground up an ISO 21001-certified[5] and globally recognised furniture and design company, and alongside that a massive training and work development scheme through the Majeurs Academy all based here in Lagos, Nigeria and in Africa.

① IDEATION AND RESEARCH (WEEK 1-2)

The strategy involves conducting market research to understand the item's purpose and demand, particularly for eco-friendly sofas. User interviews are used to understand functional needs and gather feedback on desired features. The material sourcing is focused on choosing sustainable and reliable materials like recycled polyester and FSC-certified wood, aligning with the company's ethos.'

② DESIGN (WEEK 3-6)

The process involves several stages, including initial sketches, technical drawings, material sampling, prototyping, and final design approval. Initial sketches involve converting the conceptual idea into visual sketches using pencil sketches and CAD software. Technical drawings involve creating precise production drawings using 2D Drafting in AutoCAD and 3D modeling in Rhino or SketchUp. Material sampling involves testing materials for suitability, ensuring wood passes ISO 38200 standards and are properly dried.

Benefits for dry wood quality and longevity
Stability: less prone to changes in shape and size.
Strength: offers better structural integrity. Moisture weakens wood
Finish Quality: Finishes such as stains, paints, and varnishes adhere better
Prototyping involves creating a small-scale model or 3D rendering of the sofa, considering ergonomic aspects

③ FUNDING AND BUDGETING (WEEK 7)

Cost Estimation
Objective: Detail out the budget required for the project.
Components: Include raw materials, labor, and overheads.

Funding
Objective: Compute the cost implications of the manufacturing process.
Strategy: Establish your profit margin goal and ensure cost management is optimum keeping your eye on your profits

④ PRODUCTION (WEEK 8-16)

Raw Material Acquisition
Objective: Order materials.
Criteria: Ensure they meet your quality control standards, eco-friendly and ISO standards.

Cutting and Assembly
Objective: Produce the sofa frame.
Strategy: Use CNC machines for precision cutting.

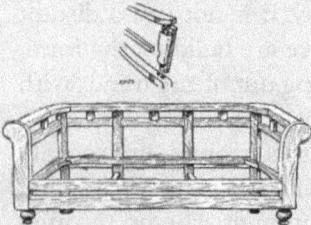

Upholstering
Objective: Attach cushioning and upholstery.
Details: Use high-density foam and chosen fabric or leather.

Quality Control
Objective: Ensure the product meets quality benchmarks.
Standards: Utilize your ISO requirements as a guideline.

CUSHION   MARKINGS

Figure 7.2 The odyssey of a sofa—a journey from conception to comfort.
Image designed by and courtesy of Majeurs Holdings.

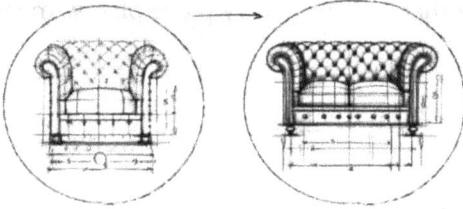

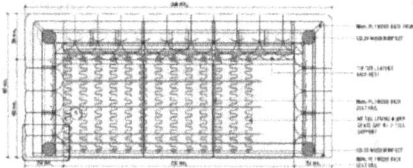

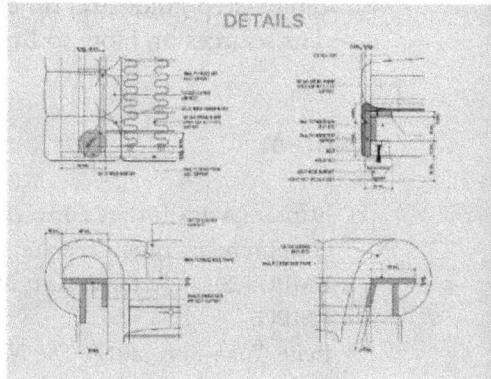

LEATHER

CUSHION

WOOD

DETAILS

5

FINISHING TOUCHES
(WEEK 17-18)

Paint and Polish
Objective: Finalize the sofa's appearance.
Materials: Use eco-friendly sealants and stains.

Final Inspection
Objective: Conduct a rigorous quality check.
Strategy: Ensure cohesiveness if the sofa is part of a larger collection.

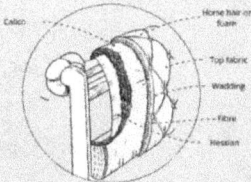

Photography and Marketing
Objective: Prepare for market launch.
Innovation: Consider using AI-based AR features for customers to visualize the sofa in their own space.

6

DISTRIBUTION
(WEEK 19 ONWARDS)

Inventory
Objective: Stock the finished products.
Strategy: Employ a well-organized warehouse system.

Shipping
Objective: Deliver products to customers.
Strategy: Utilize tech-driven logistics to ensure seamless delivery.

ROUTLEDGE

We have already begun—please follow the insert in Figure 7.2 which is a step-by-step guide and timeline that includes every piece of raw material and its sources on How to Build a Sofa in Africa.

Notes

1 https://www.forbes.com/sites/theyec/2021/04/20/eight-obstacles-young-entrepreneurs-often-face-and-how-to-overcome-them/?sh=3410f95630f5
2 KMPG. 2014. *Sector Report: Manufacturing in Africa.* Amstelveen, Netherlands: KMPG.
3 Irene Yuan Sun. 2017. *The Next Factory of the World: How Chinese Investment Is Reshaping Africa.* Boston, Massachusetts: Harvard Business Review Press. Page 45.
4 Erich Weede. 2007. *Economic Freedom and the Advantages of Backwardness.* Washington Cato Institute. http//www.cato.org/publicatins/economic-development-bulletin/economic-freedom-advantages-backwardness
5 https://www.siscertifications.com/iso-21001-certification-nigeria/

Why Africa?

8

The K Word: Kanju

The K Word: Kanju

In her terrific book, *Bright Continent*,[1] Dayo Olopade states: 'In Yoruba a language of Nigeria, kanju literally means, "to rush to or make haste"; in English we might say it is to "hustle", "strive", or "make do".'[2]

This may be one of the greatest lessons I've learned since moving to Africa. Understanding the power of *Kanju*, and then how to tap into that phenomenal well of creativity. For someone who was raised and educated entirely outside of Africa, I can relate to this desire for creative hustle that was instilled in me by my mother. In my experience, since moving to Nigeria, Kanju is not a theory, nor is it something to be taken for granted, it is an experience lived by everyone I've encountered. Anyone who travels to Africa for business or like me has the ambition to set up a manufacturing company and training academy must be able to recognise that daily struggle for basics of housing, clean water and food is a reality for many Africans.

However, given opportunities for further training and good employment, I am literally gobsmacked by this deep well of Kanju, and creative hustle. I have witnessed and felt this collective energy every day at the academy and on the manufacturing shop floor where my team must do many workarounds to deal with supply chain shortages, power blackouts and the daily problems of moving about the city, and the daily grind of dealing with a litany of difficult decisions that I must make.

The core argument for my book is to point to the massive manufacturing opportunities that Africa presents and they are almost endless. The following three chapters of the book could be described as my lessons learned about a people and culture that is both foreign and familiar.

DOI: 10.4324/9781003453994-8

Building a sustainable manufacturing business in Africa is not an easy task, and I'm in no way sugarcoating my pitch to readers or potential investors and entrepreneurs. But investing in people and their further training, providing steady employment like manufacturing jobs and thus improving lives is possibly one of the most gratifying business and life decisions I have made. I've seen on a daily basis how very small decisions inspire ingenuity and tap into the staff's Kanju, creative hustle and problem-solving. In fact, the entire work culture in Africa is creative hustle.

Political scientist Joel Migdal calls Kanju logic, 'strategies for survival–blueprints for action and belief in a world that hovers on the brink of a Hobbesian state of nature.'

Olopade cleverly encapsulates her thinking: 'Africa's kanju culture is more Darwin than Degas, less about subjective beauty, than about practical solutions, and doing far more with far less.'

That is a natural resource that runs deep in almost every person I've met. It's a huge lesson to be learned and relearned. There are so many examples that I've personally come across that completely reverse any preconceived perceptions about the African workforce. For instance, on one of my birthdays my staff decided to give me a gift. But like many artisans, they always have more bills than resources for extra gifts. My staff raided the

Figure 8.1 Demi with the very first sofa built in Nigeria by Majeurs.
Image courtesy of Majeurs Holdings.

factory floor wastebins and decided collectively that 'madam loved handbags' and they would make me a beautiful handbag with all the whistles (with a metal clutch that ensured my belongings did not fall out). I was blown away by their ability to put a smile on my face while also being sustainable in their approach and create something from nothing. This after all is the Majeurs way. They embodied this and I couldn't have been more proud.

When I walk the streets of Lagos I see examples of Kanju at every turn. Young boys playing football with makeshift abandoned tyres marking the parameters of goal posts as they kick balls on quiet streets. Young girls and boys trying to keep up with the trends of the world with their fashion choices. No matter the financial condition they will always look good, from their head to toes.

I am amazed by my staff, who given the demand of a client or a project would do what it takes to ensure it is completed come rain or shine. As I write this chapter at 20:37 p.m., I have just got off a call about two armchairs that I rejected this afternoon before leaving the factory. Jude, my trusted helper in ensuring that our production team finished the work to the standard that I have held my team to, called to inform me that he would personally cover the cost of the labour for work not done to the specific quality we aim for. As a result of the time and wastage of materials, the budget has been affected.

> Demi, Ola has just arrived at the factory, I have spoken with him to continue the work not executed by the other upholsterer. I will be paying the difference in the cost myself, do not worry about it, the item will be ready within a day and a half, I assure you.

As manufacturers we often go through a myriad of problems with staff, but if there is one thing that I know about these people is once they have invested in your success, they would move mountains to ensure that you win. My biggest goal as the leader of my organisation is to ensure that I find people who are vested in my success by making it their success. I cannot pretend to have got there but what I do know is that each day I must kill the ego a little more to ensure that I do. God help me because 'good people are hard to reveal'.

Olopade writes in an interview with Mohammed Ibrahim, the Sudanese-born billionaire of an international telecommunications company, Celtel:

> I always say Africans are the greatest entrepreneurs...many people wake up in the morning not knowing what they're going to do—but they have to make some money, so they do what is needed. If it is raining, you'll sell an umbrella. If it's hot, you sell ice or some Coke. People try to find ways to make a living, and there's a great energy.

In my view, Kanju, or creative hustle or entrepreneurship and all its international variants, have a connection to making a better life for yourself, adding value, being of use to your family and for future generations.

I'm not fooling anyone that by building a relatively small furniture manufacturing business in Lagos, Nigeria will change the world. However, the African ground is ripe to make a massive transformative impact and make Africa the next global manufacturing hub. We will need to tap into that powerful Kanju to deal with the myriad of obstacles that on first look may seem unsurmountable, and I can offer up my lessons with Majeurs Furniture as a working prototype.

The E Word: Electrical Grid

The big issue confronting any new entrepreneur starting a business in Africa is infrastructure, particularly the electrical grid, which at its best is tenuous. While I'm writing this book in September 2023, the power was shut down to the entire nation on 13 September. Again! Imagine a country with a population of 223 million citizens suddenly plunged into total darkness for an indefinite time period.

Dayo Olopade[3] wrote in 2014 about the energy poverty that has truly stunted growth, and rather go into my litany of complaints, her description which is almost ten years old is almost the same story today. It raises a lot of questions about government and corruption, and I'll address this big issue in the final chapter of the book. However, the energy poverty must be addressed before any large- or small-scale business can begin. For a continent with spectacular resources of sustainable energy—including sun, wind and hydroelectric power—Africa is woefully underserved, and the electrification of Africa needs big thinking and even bigger solutions. Why cannot governments and electronic utilities companies think and behave more like cell phone companies and the massive investment in undersea cables that they made, thus making a gigantic leap in global communications in less than a decade.

In many respects not much has changed since Olopade[4] wrote so compellingly:

> Unfortunately, national governments have failed to pass on the benefits of energy wealth. Monopolistic utilities don't provide electricity. Decades of power sector subsidies have gone to the wealthiest and best connected, (literally) without making light more affordable. Crude-rich Nigeria still imports refined petroleum. In the DRC

(Democratic Republic of Congo), half the year is spent in darkness. In Guinea-Bissau, it's the equivalent of one in three days. In Tanzania, which has a projected $150 billion in natural gas reserves, 86 percent of residents have absolutely no access to electricity.

As a manufacturing business, we have developed a number a creative workarounds, like just about everyone, but I believe the moonshot of electrifying the African continent with sustainable energy would be one of the biggest economic boons and multiplier effects, like the cell phone leapfrogging explosion that has transformed the African workplace, family life and connected every place to the globe.

Olopade also made it clear that it is just not families and small businesses that suffer:

> The power pinch affects big businesses, too: manufacturing plants with machinery or ordinary businesses with IT equipment suffer from electricity failures. Mobile networks gnash their teeth at the cost of maintaining power to the wireless towers that connect their exploding customer base… MTN [Nigerian cellular phone company] spends $5.5 million a month powering six thousand base stations for nineteen hours a day—in Nigeria alone.

At Majeurs Furniture, manufacturing our solutions cost us dearly. For instance, we have recently been told we need to spend $171,301.36 to take our production off grid and rely on 80% solar, with no guarantees. We must still have an inverter backup then a diesel generator backup. I almost cried when I got the bill amidst us sitting in the factory with no light. I did cry out of frustration. The tears fell, not because I was not able to afford the quotation in front of me, but because I was in the middle of a crisis—production had halted and I felt so alone. Nobody was coming to my rescue. I had late deliveries, staff idle because without light they couldn't work, and glaring at me was such a large quotation. They often say that entrepreneurship is lonely but I would say that entrepreneurship in Africa at times feels like you are lost in space with no idea where to turn, it's total darkness and your feet have no ground to stand on.

In a September 2023 news report posted on *Reuters*,[5] 'Nigeria's electricity distribution companies reported "a total system collapse" on Thursday after a fire on a major transmission line, causing widespread blackouts across Africa's biggest economy, before power slowly started to return. Adebayo Adelabu, minister for power, said fire had caused an explosion on a transmission line connecting the Kainji and Jebba power plants in north central Niger state, tripping the grid.'

Figure 8.2 Demi working on one of her pieces. Image courtesy of Majeurs Holdings.

The solutions and workarounds are very costly, and at my factory we have installed diesel-powered generators for when the inevitable daily blackouts happen. These expensive standalone solutions don't address the root problems for a factory such as ours or the growing list of tech companies setting up business in Nigeria.

Nigeria is one of the biggest global players in exporting oil, however, the electrical grid is tenuous at best. The *Reuters* article describes clearly what I and other business owners must face, and frankly the sad facts, 'Grid power is erratic in Nigeria, a major oil and gas producer, forcing households and businesses including oil firms and manufacturers to resort to diesel and petrol generators.'

'The cost of fueling a generator is eating into our finances and, as a tech business that relies on power, this is a heavy burden to bear,' said Dickcion Bolodeku, an executive at technology firm Bayelsa Tech Hub in the southern oil-producing Bayelsa state, noting that President Bola Tinubu removed a subsidy on fuel in May. In Lagos, despite enduring power cuts on an almost daily basis, some people were surprised at the nationwide blackout.

On a final note on electrical infrastructure, Nigeria has already built existing capability to increase power supply that would be consistent with anywhere on the globe. Perhaps by naming the culprits in this book, and by a motivated consortium of business leaders, we can finally convince the politicians and energy companies to complete and fulfil all the power grid requirements, and make blackouts and power shortages a thing of the past, rather than part of what *Reuters* reported:

> Lagos-based Eko Electricity Distribution Company, one of the biggest, said grid power was being restored. The grid collapsed at least four times in 2022, which authorities blamed on technical problems. Nigeria has 12,500 MW of installed capacity but produces about a quarter of that.

In a nutshell, that is the massive issue that must be addressed—underdeveloped electrical capacity, and there is an obvious investment needed to the electrical grid infrastructure, and it must be completed to attract and sustain more manufacturing and tech companies in Nigeria and Africa.

If we as small businesses are to get our footing, there must be solutions that play to where we are in our journeys to growth. Gas as a solution in business districts that attract SMEs like my own are a great solution to better energy options. I once enquired about gas power solutions and I was told that unless I have a large enough organisation I simply could not access the service. Can we build business districts for SMEs where there is already a gas supply for units that we can share?

Solar Power

Why it works: With abundant sunshine almost year-round, Nigeria has a high potential for solar energy generation.
Cost: The cost of solar panels has dropped dramatically in recent years.
Government's role: Subsidies or low-interest loans for the installation of solar panels can make them more accessible for SMEs.
Statistics: According to a World Bank report, Nigeria has the potential to generate up to 427,000 MW of solar power.

Mini Hydroelectric Power Plants

Why it works: Unlike large-scale hydro projects, mini hydro plants can be constructed on small rivers and waterways.

Cost: The construction cost is relatively lower, and operational costs are minimal.

Government's role: Local governments can invest in these projects and sell electricity at subsidised rates to SMEs.

Statistics: As per International Energy Agency, small hydro has the potential to contribute 3.1 GW of power in Nigeria.

CNG (Compressed Natural Gas) Plants

Why it works: CNG provides a cleaner alternative to conventional fossil fuels, reducing carbon emissions and enhancing energy security.

Cost: The construction of a small CNG plant can be cost-effective, especially when considering long-term savings from lower fuel costs.

Government's role: The government can offer grants, subsidies, or tax incentives to businesses that adopt CNG as an energy solution.

Statistics: According to a study published in the Renewable Energy Journal, Nigeria produces over 227,500 tons of waste daily, much of which can be converted into CNG production. Greatly reducing reliance on imported fuels.

Wind Energy

Why it works: Coastal and some northern regions in Nigeria have suitable wind speeds for energy production.

Cost: Initial set up costs can be high but can be offset by long-term gains.

Government's role: Encourage R&D in this sector and provide incentives to businesses that install wind turbines.

Statistics: There is significant potential for wind energy in Nigeria, especially in Northern states and offshore areas like Lagos through Ondo, Delta, Rivers, Bayelsa, and Akwa Ibom states. The first wind farm in Nigeria is situated in Rimi village, 25km south of Katsina City. It is the largest in West Africa and designed to provide power for over 2,200 homes and consists of 37 turbines, each with a capacity of 275 kW.

The L Word: Labour Shortages

There is much work to be done to build the groundwork and infrastructure, then lay the foundations for the expected growth. The top challenge currently facing furniture manufacturers are skilled-labour shortages. I'll also discuss shared issues on how to begin solving this number one problem; most manufacturers report that their greatest obstacles in 2019 were finding and training skilled workers.

My experience is that finding and training skilled workers is initially very difficult. In a country that has many skilled carpenters, and streetside furniture repair workshops, it is quite difficult to find skilled workers with any experience in end-to-end manufacturing, from raw materials to finished products. There have been some surprises, but in general, a big part of me and my staff's work was initially finding, training and retaining workers for the factory floor. That is why in part I knew I had to build a complete skills and training academy to fulfil our growing needs, for workers to operate complicated machinery and also learn all the safety protocols when working in my manufacturing business or for others. This investment is to mitigate the potential for labour shortages, which have plagued many small manufacturers.

It is an ongoing challenge, but with a constant intake of new students, we are slowly chipping away at the problem.

I'll mention Kanju here again, because it is a common difficulty and really an African problem. Using a practical training system, I believe this labour issue can be addressed so that manufacturers, big and small, have committed, trained and skilled operators and are not faced with essential assembly line stoppages.

***

Over the last 100 years, the hub of furniture manufacturing has migrated across the globe. Many of the first professional commercial cabinet and chair makers were found in the USA. However, when production and labour costs ballooned, the manufacturing industry shifted to Taiwan and then to China.

Currently there are over 50,000 furniture manufacturers in China (a staggering number) and 4000 in the USA vs. the recorded 400 in Nigeria (although data in Nigeria does not account for the millions of roadside artisans doing small-scale furniture repair and manufacturing). With the industry's need for constantly lower production and labour costs, it is no secret that Africa will be the next hub for manufacturing in the near future.

Why is Nigeria particularly primed to be the next centre of manufacturing? Key factors such as a long history of design and quality, coupled with Nigeria's manufacturing costs which are very low.

The advantages are huge—when building factories in Nigeria, for example, building space costs per square foot are about 1/20 of those in the USA and 1/10 of China. The cost of workers' wages is even less than that, and the low labour costs justify simple single-purpose machinery, which is cheaper and more efficient to operate.

For a relatively new furniture manufacturing business, I've discovered that there is one thing that Africa can offer over the Chinese juggernaut: the ability to train a motivated and highly skilled workforce, and pay competitive wages, because the average cost of living is still far lower in Africa than China.

Besides low labour costs, the biggest advantage Africa has over China is its proximity to raw materials. One challenge faced by China's furniture industry is the pressure of raw material shortages, such as in the production of mahogany furniture. This is due to the protection of tropical forest resources. It also has limited forest resources relative to its manufacturing needs. Therefore, it heavily imports various types of wood, including hardwoods and softwoods, from countries like the United States, Russia and countries in Southeast Asia. It also imports wet blue leather from Brazil and Australia, and a variety of textiles, cotton, wool and synthetic fibres.

Why does this matter, I hear you ask me? It matters because easy access to timber and other raw materials like metals, textiles and leather is crucial, and many nations go to great lengths to bridge the shortage of these resources.

Given Africa's abundant natural resources, sourcing local materials can substantially reduce both the cost and the carbon footprint of production. Africa accounts for about 17% of the world's forests, according to the Food and Agriculture Organization (FAO) of the United Nations.

The B Word: Bottlenecks

There are many bottlenecks in the supply chain that make it almost impossible to build non-consumer goods that are affordable to the mass market. I'll describe the headaches that businesses like mine suffer and the number one problem of finding quality, skilled labour.

- Power supply: Unreliable electricity leads to frequent outages and high production costs due to reliance on diesel. We often spend more on power solutions than on raw materials.
- Road network: Poor road conditions make transportation inefficient and risky. I resorted to shipping my items by air when we experienced far too many damaged items in transit.
- Port delays: Inadequate port facilities can result in long waiting times for imported production materials or components.
- High import duties: Make imported raw materials more expensive.
- High interest rates: Make borrowing expensive for SMEs. Our last loan cost us 26% interest. Banks are no longer an option for us.
- Skill gap: A lack of adequately trained personnel can affect productivity.

- Logistics: Difficulty in accessing markets due to poor local distribution networks.
- Multiple agencies: Dealing with various regulatory bodies can be time-consuming and intimidating.
- Corruption: Navigating through corrupt practices to get things done. I call this the cost of doing business.
- It is not for the faint of heart, and readers will have many takeaways and discussion points.

The C Word: Corruption

In Irene Yuan Sun's book, *The Next Factory of the World*, she gives an honest appraisal and diverse accounts of what African companies face on a day-to-day basis. Surprisingly like me she also believes that these issues are worth it and believes that we are on track to change the continent.

For young entrepreneurs, investors, professionals and academics, I'm being ruthlessly honest about the cold hard facts: there are enormous challenges to overcome, particularly corruption.

I recently had a run-in with a corrupt official at customs while trying to export my furniture. We produced a beautiful leather set which was gloriously wrapped and ready to set sail to London, and an impressive fabric set for California. On getting the quotation we had agreed on the price of the items which was communicated to our customers before they were delivered to the customs office for checking. On arrival, my staff called me in a panic informing me that the agent had given him another bill and we were expected to pay it with urgency. It was three times what we had agreed to pay. We were told that if we did not pay, our items would not leave the shores of Nigeria.

I asked for the items to be retrieved at which point I was informed that we would only be refunded part of our payment, our payment would be short by a whopping $600. Needless to say, I was livid. Was this really the cost of doing business in Nigeria? And was this price too high? I believe so. When we talk of export we are filled with pride that we have created value-added products to serve the world, but at whose cost and who is picking up that bill? What we save in production and low labour costs is being consumed by customs who I believe should be rejoicing with us as the products leave Nigeria. We are bringing in the much-needed dollars that Nigeria desperately needs to earn.

The government talks about promoting the export sector—on paper they give concessions on the cost to manufacturers yet, in reality, these so-called concessions do not exist. I begrudgingly had no choice but to forfeit part of our profit to the official. It was a bitter pill to swallow. For African manufacturing to succeed, old school and corrupt officials need to be weeded out. All businesses big and small should get tougher and demand easier restrictions so we can grow and prevail. Yes, there can be a tax on export, but it can be moderate for all who are involved.

In my experience I would say that you should use a reputable company who can pick your item up from you directly and ship it to your customer's doorstep in whatever country they reside. With my bad experience I called on my network and was saved from the wrath of the customs officials, short of $600 but a hard but important lesson learnt.

A quick tip: if you want to ship furniture out of Nigeria, make it flat pack! unless your client is Bill Gates and can afford it.

The F Word: Fear

Despite the setbacks, and obvious fixes like a steady power grid, the potential for young entrepreneurs means that in many sectors of manufacturing, that the ground is truly ripe in Africa.

In Olopade's must-read book, she provocatively points to the multiple layers of what she ironically calls poverty porn, that 'reinforce that there's no money in Africa, economists engage with the continent from the top down, focusing on the dispiriting macroeconomic factors such as GDP per capita, fluctuating interest rates, and donor funded government budgets'.

If only faced with these numbers, both investors and entrepreneurs will normally balk at the cold, hard facts, but the reality is in fact the inverse—street-smart, rule-bending, Kanju-driven Africans are building new businesses while making do with a lot less. I am proud to be a part of the new wave of dynamic and young entrepreneurs who are rapidly changing the business landscape:

- Odunayo Eweniyi: Piggyvest online savings and investment platform
- Jumoke Dada: Taellio, a furniture manufacturer aimed at the mass market
- Louisa Kinoshi: Founder of BeautyRevNG
- Damilola Solesi: Founder of Smids Animation Studios
- Damilola Teidi: CEO of GoDo Hub, a tech hub in Lagos aimed at fostering innovation in software and hardware tech
- Dele Bakare: Founder of Findworka, a marketplace for elite software developers and tech talent in Africa
- Bilikiss Adebiyi-Abiola: Founder of Wecyclers, a Lagos-based company focused on recycling and waste management tech solutions

***

A culture of fear, and yes, ignorance can permeate funding decisions that can be made thousands of miles away. I can point to my furniture manufacturing business success and growth that I hope is a prototype that can be repeated all over the continent. Believe me, I have run into many of the above preconceptions in funding presentations, because there is still prejudice. Dayo Olopade nails it when she describes Ugandan businessman CEO Andrew Rugasira of Good African Coffee, who was pitching investment and distribution in the UK, 'People were expecting Idi Amin…No one makes any distinction between older generations of African businessmen and the new generation.'

The negative tropes about the African workforce and description just don't fit anymore, a middle class has been well established. Talented, inventive and skilled workers are filling positions, but training in manufacturing on a large scale and making the leap to scale up is really the next big step.

However, investors also need education, and reminders like the global boom in Afrobeat music are at least a starting point because the artists are played and enjoyed all over the planet. So, then, my question and point of frustration is, what is the essentially the problem?

I agree with Dayo Olopade, when she states:

> Fear of what is known euphemistically as 'political risk' is overstated: The World Bank's Multilateral Investment Guarantee Agency compensates investors in case of coups, expropriations, and other externalities in developing countries, has paid out only six times in the past twenty-five years—and only twice in Africa…international institutions and investors miss the simpler story: commercial activity is a powerful, shovel-ready network in Africa.[6]

I argue that for investors, both institutional and private, it is with education, persistence and energy that some of the investment class will slowly come to understand that the culture, the people and the economic outlook for Africa are ready to make the next big leap in manufacturing. There are many difficult obstacles that I've outlined in this chapter, however, the positives, energy and demographics certainly outweigh the so-called negatives.

Godwin's Journey: From Caretaker to Craftsman

When Godwin first walked through the doors of Majeurs, he was a young man burdened with the weight of limited opportunities and a 30,000 naira monthly salary, which is approximately $30.00. As a caretaker, his role was rudimentary—cleaning, upkeep and errands. He was energetic, yes, but his potential remained veiled under the mundane tasks he performed daily.

But Godwin had something that couldn't be ignored: an insatiable curiosity and a keen eye for detail. This didn't go unnoticed, especially by our expatriate craftspeople in the upholstery section. Seeing his potential, we decided to give Godwin a shot at something more aligned with his unspoken aspirations. With some initial training, Godwin transitioned from a caretaker to working along-side our expat team, learning the intricate art of quality furniture making.

Today, he's not just earning a paycheque; he's learning a skill, a craft that can sustain him for a lifetime. But we didn't stop there. Recognising his quick growth and unquenchable thirst for learning, we enrolled him in our recently launched academy. Godwin is now honing his skills in a formal setting, an experience that's not only improving his craft but also his future earning potential.

The Big Picture

Now, let's zoom out. Imagine hundreds of Godwins. Imagine the change in the narrative around manufacturing in Africa. The story of Godwin isn't just an isolated feel-good anecdote; it's proof of the untapped potential residing in Africa. It's the embodiment of why investors—whether institutional or private—should be looking at Africa, and particularly its booming youth demographic, as a fertile ground for the next manufacturing revolution.

I argue that it's not just the physical resources but human capital like Godwin that make Africa ripe for the next big leap in manufacturing. Yes, there are challenges, as outlined in this chapter, but the enthusiasm, the ingenuity and the unbridled energy present here cannot be ignored. It's time for investment classes, bankers and decision-makers globally to recognise this and be part of Africa's transformative journey in manufacturing. I'm in clear agreement with Olopade's view:

> When it comes to human development, African commerce has three built in advantages. In the first place, commerce is common—both widespread and shared. Even the least well-off can join in the supply and demand for goods and services. Second, commerce is account-able, in every sense of the word. Parties to even the smallest roadside transaction agree to specific terms for which both are responsible. It's a banal fact but, in the context of distortionary charity flows, important to recognise. Last commerce is a proven tool to create jobs and dis-tribute goods in Africa—including 'development.' [7]

I'll add my list of advantages, because this is really an essential lesson for investors to understand. My manufacturing company and other young entrepreneurs are in fact light years beyond the ancient and tired rhetoric around the words 'African development'. My company has created and employed at its current point, 30 staff members. What drew them to train, upskill and then find steady employment? Not development, or charity, but the fact that their investment in a commercial enterprise is not unlike any other startup all over the globe. They are fearless, by taking a risk in a small company that is starting up from scratch. Their lessons, and Kanju, are what is driving the new African business, and in meetings with investors, podcasts, talks and this book, I'll always say this: when it comes to African business investment, the time has come to get over your fear.

Other direct advantages are covered in the sections that follow.

The Ultimate Untapped Markets

Africa is a continent of 1.3 billion people, with a median age of around 19.7 years according to the UN's 2019 data. This represents a massive, youthful consumer base that's largely untapped, presenting entrepreneurs with an opportunity for market penetration that's unprecedented on a global scale.

Challenges as Opportunities

Though the startup environment comes with its challenges, including access to capital, market readiness and infrastructural constraints, each obstacle presents an opportunity for innovation. Africa is in need of those who have the appetite for great businesses, with both feet in. In recent years I have seen the greatest entrepreneurs step into Africa with more than curiosity. There is a reason far deeper than mere interest. The chessboard has already been played.

I conclude this section with a longish quote by Dayo Olopade, where she makes a second provocative and eye-opening statement. It deserves to be highlighted, and it should be part of every pitch from young entrepreneurs, who are pitching their ideas for a business startup to institutions and private investors:

> African [investment] provides a higher rate of return than any other developing region of the world—including the celebrated 'BRIC' nations of Brazil, Russia, India and China. Seven of the ten fastest growing economies in the world are African…It's members are not oil barons or oligarchs.

> These are the people who have steady jobs, who own property, perhaps even a car...health emergencies don't knock them to the mat. They indulge in tiny luxuries in the form of a movie ticket, imported sweets or a fancier mobile phone and make larger investments in cable television, home computers, or a decent private education for their children.[8]

I can also proudly add that they also buy well-designed furniture made in Nigeria and they make sophisticated choices about design, colour, texture that help drive my business and its growth. Therefore, Kanju thinking, Kanju manufacturing that is building sustainable, commercial enterprises is in fact the way to develop and change perceptions about Africa and get past the old perceptions and ghosts of colonial past.

Olopade concludes with this intriguing statement:

> As Africa's commercial century continues, fewer good ideas will die for lack of finance, ventures of all sizes and persuasions will continue to experiment with funding and small business models unique to Africa's challenges. They may not fit our existing labels—private-public partnerships, IPOs, or impact investing—but are more exciting for their novelty.[9]

From my vantage point, two stories resonate deeply with me as they embody for me the African stories where excellence meets vision. Those who dared to dream and won. As we proceed at Majeurs the future I envisage is that which merges manufacturing with tech.

The Aliko Dangote Story: Cementing a Legacy

In a continent often celebrated for its abundant natural resources, Aliko Dangote saw an opportunity that many overlooked: manufacturing. Born into a business-oriented family in Kano, Nigeria, Dangote displayed entrepreneurial flair from a young age. But it was in the realm of manufacturing that he would leave an indelible mark.

Dangote's journey into manufacturing began in earnest in 1999 with the establishment of Obajana Cement Plant, which later became part of Dangote Cement. The goal was audacious yet simple: to produce high-quality cement at a scale that could meet Nigeria's rapidly growing demand for infrastructure. Before Dangote Cement, Nigeria was importing a significant amount of its cement. According to data from the World Bank, Nigeria's cement imports in the late 1990s were as high as 3 million metric tons per year.

With significant investment in state-of-the-art technology and an unyielding commitment to quality, Dangote's venture turned the tables. By 2015, Nigeria was not just self-sufficient in cement production but it became an exporter, a significant economic turnaround. Dangote Cement, according to its 2019 annual report, now has a production capacity of over 45.6 million metric tons per annum across its African operations.

But Dangote's impact isn't limited to the cement industry. He has diversified into other sectors of manufacturing, including food processing, with his sugar and pasta factories, and even oil refining. His under-construction refinery in Lagos is projected to be one of the world's largest and aims to turn Nigeria into a petroleum exporter.

In terms of numbers, the Dangote Group's economic contribution is staggering. According to a 2021 report, Dangote Cement alone accounts for about 1% of Nigeria's GDP.[10] But more important than numbers is the narrative that Dangote embodies—a narrative of possibility, resilience and transformative impact.

Dangote is not just a manufacturer; he's a nation-builder who understands that manufacturing is integral to Africa's economic independence. His ventures have created thousands of jobs and stimulated ancillary industries, becoming a focal point in the broader narrative of Africa's industrialisation.

The story of Aliko Dangote serves as a testament to the transformative power of manufacturing in Africa. His journey is a rallying cry for entrepreneurs, showing that manufacturing—when done right and at scale—can be a cornerstone for economic development and empowerment.

African Advantages that Make Investors Excited

In a world increasingly seeking diversity and dynamism in its investment portfolios, Africa stands out as a land of unparalleled potential and promise. This continent, rich in resources and brimming with talent, offers a unique tableau for investors looking beyond traditional markets. Africa's allure lies not just in its vast natural resources or its growing consumer market, but in the resilient spirit of its people and their innovative approach to problem-solving.

Resilience and Innovation

Entrepreneurs in Africa are often tackling unique, localised challenges, which breeds an exceptional level of innovation and resilience. The startup ecosystem is not just mimicking Silicon Valley; it's generating solutions

Figure 8.3 Demi with Tony Elumelu, Chairperson of Heirs Holdings, Transcorp, United Bank for Africa (UBA) and the founder of The Tony Elumelu Foundation. Image courtesy of Majeurs Holdings.

tailored to the African context. Companies like Zipline in Rwanda, which uses drones to deliver medical supplies, highlight this fact.

The Imperative of Due Diligence and Calculated Risks

While it's crucial to shift perceptions about investing in Africa, it's equally important to stress the need for due diligence—just as one would exercise in any other part of the world. The risks associated with investments aren't unique to Africa, but the methodologies to mitigate those risks should be universally applied.

Vetting and Verification

Investors must create robust vetting systems to sift through the noise and identify genuine opportunities. This is not just about eliminating fraudulent ventures but also about identifying those startups that offer true promise and a clear roadmap for sustainable growth.

Seek Local Insights

For authentic, on-the-ground information, look no further than local experts like me and the various successful founders discussed in this book. We can offer critical insights into market dynamics, business culture and the genuine opportunities that abound here. Trust that in Africa, like anywhere else, the cream does rise to the top—but you must be willing to pour into the cup of investment to see that happen.

Calculated Risks: Win Some, Learn Some

Let's be frank: business is all about risk, but what sets a successful venture apart is calculated risk-taking. As the saying goes, 'Some we win, and some we learn.' Each investment opportunity should be viewed through the lens of both its potential reward and the wisdom it imparts, irrespective of the outcome. This is a universal principle, as true in Lagos as it is in London or Los Angeles.

Iyinoluwa Aboyeji: Shaping Africa's Tech Future

In the ever-evolving tech landscape of Africa, one name stands out for its association with multiple groundbreaking initiatives: Iyinoluwa Aboyeji. A graduate of the University of Waterloo in Canada, Iyinoluwa returned to Nigeria to co-found Andela in 2014. The company's aim was audacious but crystal clear: identify and train software developers in Africa and place them in companies around the world.

At first glance, the idea might have seemed lofty, especially in a continent grappling with myriad social and economic challenges. But the brilliance of Andela was in turning a challenge often seen as a liability—Africa's burgeoning youth population—into an asset. According to data from the African Development Bank, Africa is home to 200 million people aged between 15 and 24, a number projected to double by 2045. Andela leveraged this untapped human resource to fill the global tech talent gap.

Andela's impact was both immediate and far-reaching. By 2019, the company had secured $100 million in Series D funding, according to Crunchbase, and had placed thousands of developers in over 200 companies globally. But Iyinoluwa wasn't content with just this success.

He went on to co-found Flutterwave, a payments technology company that aimed to simplify the fragmented payment systems across Africa.

According to a 2021 report from the company, Flutterwave had processed over 140 million transactions worth over $9 billion. This success earned Flutterwave a valuation of more than $1 billion, making it one of Africa's few unicorns.

Iyinoluwa's ventures have made him a key figure in Africa's tech ecosystem, shaping conversations around innovation, investment and the role of tech in Africa's economic transformation. Yet, his impact goes beyond numbers. Iyinoluwa has become a beacon of what African entrepreneurs can achieve with the right mix of vision, grit and an unswerving commitment to transforming challenges into opportunities.

As we turn the last page of this chapter, the story of Iyinoluwa Aboyeji serves as a compelling testament to the potential that lies within Africa's entrepreneurial landscape. It is a vivid reminder that African startups, bolstered by ingenuity and an indefatigable spirit, are not merely participants in the global tech race—they are contenders for its leadership.

Notes

1 Dayo Olopade. 2015. *The Bright Continent: Breaking Rules & Making Change in Modern Africa*. Mariner Books.
2 Ibid.
3 Ibid.
4 Ibid.
5 https://www.reuters.com/world/africa/nigeria-power-grid-collapse-causes-nationwide-blackouts-2023-09-14/
6 Dayo Olopade. 2015. *The Bright Continent: Breaking Rules & Making Change in Modern Africa*. Mariner Books.
7 Ibid.
8 Ibid.
9 Ibid.
10 https://www.dangotecement.com

Buying African

9

If I gave a child in Lagos 50 naira (64 cents at the current exchange rate) to buy something sweet, what would be the trickle-down effect of this microeconomic decision? With the coins burning in their pocket, they would race to the nearest shop and stare at the vast selection of choices. Following cultural and social imperatives for most kids in Lagos, they could choose a Cadbury Lunch Bar, which is by far one of the most popular snack chocolates—with crisped rice, wafer, peanuts, caramel and of course delicious chocolate. The bright blue, yellow and red packaging is always front and centre of any shop and the child would be playing a small part in supporting the Nigerian economy, which is the fourth-largest grower and exporter of cocoa.

Not So Sweet

However, like so many things in Nigeria, the chocolate bar is imported from elsewhere, in this case, South Africa. Thus, a large portion of the cost goes on importation fees, and manufacturing profits of the famous lunch bar go to South Africa and the UK where the parent company, Cadbury, is making sure that the key ingredient, Nigerian-grown cocoa, is kept at a very low price. The question is, where does the money circulate on to once the child pays for the lunch bar?

If the child was educated in buying African, they would buy locally made Chin Chin, kuli kuli or fried plantain chips, and the 50 naira would circulate and multiply in the local economy without having to import finished products to Nigeria, while exporting valuable commodities.

DOI: 10.4324/9781003453994-9

This rather simple story illustrates that 'Buying African' has a huge *trickle-down* effect. It actually is visible and tangible and creates wealth and a way out of the endemic cycles of generational poverty.

Buying African-designed and made products and services makes a real impact. Currently in the Majeurs Furniture factory, the Buying African challenge is certainly working on every level.

All our products are tagged 'Proudly Made in Africa'.

Ethos

One of the cornerstones of Majeurs' commitment to fostering talent and contributing to sustainable economic development in Africa is our recently launched Majeurs Academy. Initiated in January 2023, the academy serves as an educational arm of our manufacturing business, targeted at teaching furniture manufacturing and empowering young people.

Every graduate from Majeurs Academy becomes an ambassador of our 'Proudly Made in Africa' ethos, going out into the world with the skills and the consciousness to produce quality, sustainable products.

By investing in people through Majeurs Academy, we're not merely producing furniture; we're building futures, uplifting communities and contributing to the broader agenda of economic empowerment in Africa.

Curriculum and Skill Development

The academy offers a comprehensive curriculum that covers everything from the basics of woodworking and upholstery to advanced techniques in sustainable manufacturing. This structured learning environment ensures that the participants don't just become proficient at tasks but master a craft that has both local and global demand.

Mentorship and Job Placement

Beyond the skills, the academy also incorporates a strong mentorship component, aligning students with experienced artisans and even expatriates in our team. This offers a well-rounded education, exposing them to international best practices. Following their training, graduates are either absorbed into Majeurs or assisted with job placements in other companies, thereby directly contributing to reducing unemployment.

Sustainable Practices

In line with our ethos of environmentally conscious manufacturing, the academy also has modules that focus on sustainable practices. This ensures that our graduates not only enter the workforce with skills but also with a mindset that prioritises sustainability.

Community Partnerships

We're also looking to establish partnerships with local communities and educational institutions to make the academy more accessible. The idea is to scale this model and potentially collaborate with governments and NGOs, aiming to impact more lives positively through integration into work.

Take Godwin, for example, who we spoke about in the previous chapter. Godwin started as a caretaker earning a modest salary. Within a year at Majeurs Academy, he moved to working in the upholstery section alongside our expatriate experts. Now, he's becoming proficient in high-quality furniture making. His life is a testament to what targeted skill development can achieve, and he's just one of the many we aim to empower.

The Story of Ben: Transformative Power of Exposure and Skill

In 2018 a young, hard-working guy called Ben, after working with me for two or three years in sales and marketing, decided to move to the US with his young wife. Often in our day-to-day interactions I brought Ben into tasks such as managing a CRM software, something he initially hesitated from, both for not recognising the importance of us using it as an organisation and the complexity it presented to him. I often say that the biggest problem we have in Africa is exposure. Like many Africans who leave the shores, we are exposed to the innovations of the world.

The day I got the call from Ben updating me about his new life in the United States, I was elated to hear from him. He was among my first hires at Majeurs in 2017 and one of my favourite workers. He was incredibly reliable and exhibited the right attitude that any startup requires for growth. Ben was now working for a hospital and was thrown immediately into a CRM system, and to his own surprise took to it like fish in water. His new employer could not be more happy with him.

Although I am not advocating for people to leave the shores of Nigeria (we all know the extent of which this is robbing Nigeria every day) I am convinced that our problem can be improved by exposing our people to the technology of the world and in doing so position them to compete on a global level. This is happening, but I would love to see it happen with more intentionality and speed.

Ben excelled in his time with me, and we talked extensively about his future plans, his dreams and his fears. I saw him grow through the months and develop the confidence that he needed to dream even bigger. My strength I believe as a founder and entrepreneur is my ability to impart the challenge in others to dream bigger. I want to be fortunate enough to continue doing this through my life's work, through this book, through my podcast, through every piece of furniture that we produce.

The Story of Phillip: A Lesson in Perseverance and Transformation

In 2018, Phillip, a father of three, approached me with a resumé that mirrored the struggles of many Nigerians desperate for economic stability. He had dabbled in almost every kind of business imaginable, but couldn't seem to find his footing. What struck me was not his list of failed enterprises but his indomitable spirit—his eyes still sparkled with the same hunger that I've often noticed in the scores of individuals desperate for a stable income and a brighter future for their children.

I decided to take a chance on Phillip, despite his lack of experience in manufacturing. And why? Because at Majeurs, we believe that the right attitude is often more valuable than years of experience. I introduced him to our rigorous training programme, focusing on the nuances of quality finishing in furniture manufacturing, and customer-interaction skills aimed at building long-term relationships through value addition.

The transformation was remarkable. Phillip soaked up the training like a sponge. He wasn't just learning a trade, he was absorbing a future, a promise of stability where he could provide for his family. His performance caught the attention of everyone on the team; he quickly became an integral part of Majeurs, embodying our core values of quality, service and sustainability.

Fast-forward to today, Phillip has opened his own factory in Lagos, specialising in furniture manufacturing. His journey is a living testament to the sheer transformative power of opportunity, skill and relentless perseverance. As long as Phillip continues to uphold these values, I am confident that he will not only provide for his family but offer them a stepping stone to even greater opportunities.

Phillip's story doesn't just affirm the life-changing impact of manufacturing in Africa; it embodies Majeurs' mission to uplift lives by investing in human capital. This tale is a beacon, illuminating the path for others to follow, proving that manufacturing isn't just about producing goods but about creating futures.

The Story of Baba: A Legacy of Craftsmanship and Mentorship

In 2019, Baba walked through the doors of Majeurs. His posture may have been slightly hunched due to his years, but his eyes were bright and alert, as if challenging us to overlook him due to his age. He was in his late 60s, a master carpenter by trade but with no steady income to sustain himself in his later years.

The first question that came to our mind was a practical one: could Baba, at his age, still perform to our standards? We had reservations, but Baba was steadfast. He insisted on being put to the test. So, we gave him a chance. What we discovered was nothing short of astounding.

Baba was a gem from an older generation of artisans who approached woodworking as an art, not just a trade. He crafted chairs with the kind of elegance and finesse that can't be learned overnight—it was the culmination of years of experience, the sort of craftsmanship that we aspire to at Majeurs. These weren't just chairs; they were international-standard pieces of art.

But Baba's contribution didn't stop at his skills; he became the wise elder of our community, a mentor to the younger craftsmen who looked up to him. Baba once confided that work was what kept him going; he had dedicated his entire life to carpentry and wasn't about to stop. He trained, mentored and instilled a sense of excellence in all of us until his very last day. When Baba passed away, it wasn't just a personal loss, it felt as though a library had burnt down. A wellspring of knowledge and skill had left us, and the entire team was submerged in a profound sense of loss.

Baba's story exemplifies the ethos we aim to build at Majeurs: a place where experience meets enthusiasm, where young apprentices can benefit from the wisdom of seasoned artisans and where everyone has a chance to contribute, regardless of their age. Baba didn't just make furniture; he built a legacy, enriching our community with his skills and wisdom, and reminding us that real talent has no expiration date.

★★★

Previously, I mapped out the journey of the construction of a sofa from idea to final packaging and shipping. You'll notice a lot of raw materials that must be outsourced, because as yet these finished goods cannot be located anywhere in Africa.

This is a big challenge and a difficult and expensive business decision. I'm challenging students of the academy to look at one piece of the supply chain to see if they can come up with one part of the manufacturing process, like metal legs. Africa's long history exporting raw materials and importing finished manufactured goods must begin to turn, and thus the multiplier effect of money circulating in the economy can truly make an impact.

What is profoundly clear to me are the human success stories of my current and future employees that are directly influenced by every piece of furniture purchased from my business. It is the circulation of money from my workers to my suppliers to my contractors that's making a direct impact in Africa by simply owning a business that employs local artisans and using local contractors.

That tangible circulation of money to their families, of paid rent, groceries bought and education for the children jump-starts their lives, and in time they can afford to buy small luxury items, and necessities like motorbikes, and even cars. This statement is not some pamphlet about how workers can improve their lives, but how commerce really does change lives for the better.

★★★

These stories I am deeply proud of, and they point to the advantages of how commerce and training is transforming the African workplace. However, in the manufacturing sector there are major issues facing African companies, and below I've set out a wish list of things I'd like to change.

Like my initial story to begin this chapter—of the child buying the lunch bar—a lot of my profits are rolled back into importing 70% of my raw materials from outside of Nigeria. That is a big number, and until the issue is resolved, and more local solutions are found, i.e. high quality, made in Nigeria, then it is part of the cost of setting up the business.

I'd prefer to source from Africa. I'm actively encouraging the students at the academy to seriously look into developing supply chain companies, metal, leather, cloth for furniture and upholstery, so that we and other furniture manufacturers don't need to outsource raw materials that are paid often in prohibitively expensive foreign currencies. When I moved to Nigeria in 2011, the dollar was worth N350, today it is as high as N1,150 and rising. Importation of any material is now detrimental to businesses.

***

As mentioned in previous chapters, the most urgent and greatest need is to build a bigger and more skilled workforce of finished leather manufacturers, accessory fabricators, metal fabricators and fabric manufacturers. Top of this list are skilled labourers who are willing and able to teach their skills.

The question is will Nigeria and Africa be forever like the Cadbury Lunch Bar? Growing cocoa and exporting it to South Africa and other locations, and then importing the chocolate-covered candy bar at a phenomenal markup? Or will it begin investing and scaling local industries, that source and use skilled workers to create stable manufacturing jobs, that provide manufacturers with precisely the right product on time?

At the academy, it is critical for the young entrepreneurs in training to understand that money in constant circulation is critical to a community's potential for economic mobility. More money in circulation means higher financial stability and potential for economic growth. It is one of the things that has contributed to the growth of all established countries. There are phenomenal bright spots, and certainly the explosion of cell phones and now smartphones in Africa has created the long overdue leapfrog for fast transactions in money.

A basic case in point is Vodaphone/Safaricom's M-Pesa[1] (Swahili for money). This allows the Kenyan Online Connectivity system that disrupted how ordinary Kenyans are able to now circulate money to function.

Interestingly, both Dayo Olopade and Irene Yuan Sun comment on this tech-driven revolution that has unleashed a whole range of unprecedented innovation, but at the root of its success is how money circulates, and unburdens Africans from the fear of constantly dealing with hiding their money.

Olopade states,[2] 'The idea is simple, customers deposit cash onto their mobile phones at one of 37,000 official M-Pesa kiosks in Kenya. By producing identification, and a PIN code, they can withdraw it at another kiosk, perhaps hundreds of kilometers away.'

If you consider that before this revolution most Africans hid their money under mattresses or in boreholes, thus risking theft, and required a hypervigilance of minding physical cash, which in many areas is very risky, particularly for girls and women. This fintech connectivity has created an entirely new way for millions of Africans to move money, considering that in most countries in sub-Saharan Africa, up to 80 per cent or more are considered unbanked. Now money is circulating, and moving across borders, where before, theft by corrupt border officials was commonplace.

Olopade adds:

> M-Pesa enables a range of financial services. In the event of an emergency, funds can be wired to relatives or friends by simply using their phone number. Payment and collection of debts do not require face-to-face interactions. Many users 'store' funds electronically in their Safaricom accounts—a kind of rudimentary savings scheme.

Now, companies like MTN and Orange, along with Nigerian unicorn startups such as Flutterwave, Jumia, and Interswitch, are experiencing remarkable growth. The numbers are booming, especially with the rise of online payments through platforms like PalmPay and others.

Mobile money is now more commonplace than cash, and this revolution is driven in large by a massive demographic—half the population is under 19, and 65 per cent of the population is under 35 years of age.

If you consider that Nigeria has a population of over 233 million and the city of Lagos is home to 20 million, and a majority do not have access to banking, even though some of the most established banks in Africa have long been in existence, the generational leapfrogging using mobile connectivity has reshaped and exploded all the boundaries, and products for sale.

Olopade states without irony:

> In Somaliland, the ZAAD Money transfer system deploys the vast network of retailers of *khat*.[3] In 2010 a study of M-Pesa found that users tend to strengthen and consolidate extended networks beyond immediate relatives. The technology turns phone contacts into potential lenders, borrowers, or collaborators in financial activity.

In the ever-evolving landscape of African fintech, platforms like M-Pesa and Flutterwave have undeniably rewritten the rulebook. They've democratised finance, bringing banking right to the palm of your hand and empowering communities often bypassed by traditional banks. But let's hit the pause button for a second and ponder: are these platforms equipped to fuel the kind of large-scale, sustainable business growth that sectors like manufacturing desperately need?

See, here's the deal. M-Pesa's genius lies in its simplicity and accessibility—facilitating microfinancing and peer-to-peer transactions. It's groundbreaking for daily commerce and small businesses, no doubt. But what about ventures like mine at Majeurs, where we're leveraging AI-powered tech to reshape the furniture manufacturing industry? The type of capital we're talking about isn't something you can ping across a phone line, at least not yet.

I'm in the business of long-term, scalable growth. At Majeurs, we're not just churning out ecofriendly furniture; we're also uplifting artisans by boosting their quality and output. What we're building here isn't a gig, it's a sustainable ecosystem. This isn't money under the mattress; it's investment in machinery, skilled labour and next-level tech.

Now, imagine a world where the artisan, who's been able to save a bit thanks to platforms like M-Pesa, can reinvest those savings into a bigger venture through Majeurs. Suddenly, we're not talking micro; we're talking macro. We're talking about transforming micro-opportunities into macro-achievements. That's where the real magic happens, and it's precisely what I think should be the next step for African finance.

I'm simply suggesting a transformative scenario where financial technologies like M-Pesa aren't just endpoints for savings but are stepping stones to more significant investment opportunities. In simple terms, we're talking about moving from merely saving money to meaningfully investing it.

Let's Break It Down

Micro-opportunities: With platforms like M-Pesa, artisans and small-scale entrepreneurs have the tools to save money and engage in microfinancing. This is fantastic for day-to-day sustenance and small-scale growth.

Macro-achievements: Now, imagine if these same artisans could take their savings and invest them into a platform like Majeurs. Here, we're not just selling furniture; we're a full-scale ecosystem that employs artisans, promotes ecofriendly practices and even educates young people through our academy.

Return on investment (ROI): When artisans invest in Majeurs, they're not merely placing their money into a business. They're buying into a scalable, sustainable model. Their investment could lead to better machinery, higher-quality products or even more training programmes. As Majeurs grows, so would the value of their investment, yielding a higher ROI than if their money sat idle or was used in lower-impact ventures.

Community impact: Moreover, their investment doesn't just yield financial returns. It creates jobs, promotes sustainable practices and educates the next generation of artisans—multiplying the impact of every dollar invested.

So, when I say we're talking about transforming micro-opportunities into macro-achievements, I mean that we can use the foundational saving and transactional abilities of platforms like M-Pesa as a springboard to more considerable, more impactful financial ventures. We're essentially elevating the game from just saving and spending to investing and growing, both individually and as a community.

***

As raw materials still flow out of Africa, and not enough finished products are being made in Africa, the lunch bar chocolate economics lesson is still true.

For entrepreneurs of startups who are attempting to set up manufacturing, the lesson in basic economics is important to understand, because currently in Africa much of the investment money, i.e. capital, doesn't circulate locally at all—stifling taxes, red tape and corruption are all holding back progress and innovation. As entrepreneurs in a variety of spaces, we are not making enough and whatever money we do make is losing out to imported goods and services, meaning that our money is leaving our shores on a daily basis, and this results in the weakening of our currency.

This lesson about Buying African maybe difficult to grasp, but if I can return briefly to the child buying the lunch bar. If as I've suggested, they are educated that instead of spending money on imported goods that cost a lot more money, investing the micro sum on local foods, or local products like furniture that are manufactured by local artisans, designers, creates a stronger local, regional and national economy and social bonds.

My argument is not some kind of Eurocentric or nationalistic of only Buying African scheme, but I believe that educating young entrepreneurs about the big picture of the lack of money and capital circulation in their attempts to obtain financing. Getting a grasp of potential problems is an essential first step for new entrepreneurs to understand *before* starting up a new business.

For instance, it is a lesson not often talked about enough. Our collective buying power vs. money circulation is something most of us have not come to fully grasp. Although Africa has more buying power than ever before, our economic prosperity is still very limited. Buying power—or the amount of income that someone has to spend—does not directly equate to general economic growth. I argue that *governments do not build economies or a country's wealth, only businesses can do that, and only businesses that are creating products and services that are being purchased locally or exported in exchange for foreign exchange.*

The challenges of today should not be the reason why we sell out our economic futures that continue to enrich other nations. Buying African and instilling these ideas in a culture is crucial, where it is implicitly understood that if it comes from elsewhere, it must be a vastly better product. I and my team at Majeurs Furniture are setting out to disprove this false notion, one leather sofa at a time.

I once stumbled across a study carried out in America[4] that proves that money circulates *one time* in African-American communities, and *nine times* in Asian communities.[5] In white communities, money circulates *nearly an unlimited number of times*. In part, this explains the wealth gap for African and Asian nations globally.

The velocity of money within a community directly correlates with that community's ability to self-fund new businesses, invest in community services and build generational wealth. In the context of my business, Majeurs, and other entrepreneurial ventures, understanding these dynamics can guide us on how best to foster community development and financial literacy, keeping the bigger picture in mind.

The Nigerian Context

Now these studies may be leaning in American environs but let's not forget that our culture and approach to wealth as Black people can be not only intergenerational but also cuts across cultures. Lest look at a study recently done in Nigeria.

Low savings rate: With only 1.4 million people holding over 500,000 naira in their bank accounts, it becomes clear that the majority of Nigerians don't have significant savings. This affects their purchasing power and potential for long-term investment.

Impact on SMEs: Small and medium-sized enterprises (SMEs), which form the backbone of the Nigerian economy, also feel the pinch when consumer spending power is limited. This is particularly significant for my venture, Majeurs, as it underscores the need for making products more accessible and affordable for the average Nigerian.

Role of fintech: Despite the dire savings scenario, the fintech revolution in Nigeria is noteworthy. Platforms like Flutterwave, Jumia and Interswitch are making it easier for people to manage money, make payments and potentially save better.

★★★

I see Africa as an extension of this huge money-circulation gap. We invested heavily in the very things that rob us of our wealth, we import far more goods and services than we export.

There is also a common belief—or magical thinking—that somebody else will come along to save us. From my point of view, the realities have never been clearer: nobody is coming!

Dayo Olopade strikes to the heart of the problem for young entrepreneurs when she states:

> Among the unbanked populations in Africa, it's nearly impossible to rely on [backstop savings and personal loans]. Without credit cards to max out on or relatives to shake down, African entrepreneurs begin business with one hand tied behind their backs. Moses Mwaura, who works for Enablis, an advisory network for small businesses around the world, says that he was shocked to realise that even small businesses that are structured, with an office with three or four people, can also be in subsistence mode.[6]

Mwaura astutely notes:

> Unfortunately, informal finance can't stretch as far as it needs to, in part because African lenders and borrowers are still poor. Even when a better off, 'uncle' serves as an angel investor, small firms don't have a growth vision…your nieces grow up and you employ them in the business. You humble along and bumble along. That's a big problem.[7]

In my own business venture, which has managed to humble and bumble, I was able to secure outside capital.

★★★

Mwaura's observation strikes a chord that resonates deeply within the African entrepreneurial ecosystem, and it's a tune I'm all too familiar with. Informal financing has its limitations, and when it comes to scaling a venture, the informal 'uncle and auntie' investments often don't cut it. Let me paint you a picture of my experience in raising capital within Nigeria.

I'd liken my journey to secure funding to a labyrinth—confounding and often discouraging. Despite being fully vested in my business and showing evident growth and potential, the initial rounds of talks with local VCs and angel investors were less than promising. Imagine pitching to over 50 potential investors and most of them either undervaluing your life's work or setting unattainable milestones before they even consider opening their chequebooks. Some even had the audacity to propose taking nearly half of my company for a cheque that was far from equitable.

The phrase 'early-stage investment' became a term that lost its essence. It felt like these investors didn't understand the concept of risk-taking, of believing in a vision before it becomes a full-fledged reality. I often found myself spending countless nights sifting through databases, curating lists of potential investors who I hoped would see the vision and value of Majeurs. Hours turned into days, days into weeks and weeks into months. I scoured LinkedIn, meticulously filled out investment applications and paid for services that promised investor leads. More often than not, these attempts either fell on deaf ears or led to disappointing outcomes.

I even expanded my search for capital globally, attending pitch events outside Nigeria. This wasn't just emotionally draining but financially taxing as well, given the costs involved in travelling and the countless hours spent on preparations. Scheduled meetings would be inexplicably cancelled, calls unattended and promises unfulfilled. The boat didn't just sail; it felt like it never intended to dock at my harbour.

However, amidst these setbacks, there was a glimmer of hope: an angel investor who, within minutes of my pitch, handed me a cheque. This experience became my beacon, reminding me that not all was bleak. But the journey has taught me that securing working capital in Africa is a colossal task riddled with challenges, from misaligned expectations to the lack of a mature investment culture.

This is why platforms like Majeurs are pivotal. They're not just businesses; they're ecosystems that can potentially change the way capital flows, bringing a formal structure to what has traditionally been an informal, inefficient market. And as we've managed to 'humble and bumble' and secure external capital, the dream is to pave the way for other African entrepreneurs to do the same, but with less friction.

That brings me to a crucial revelation that fundamentally changed my approach to fundraising: the power of introductions. If I had realised this sooner, I would have saved myself many nights of futile labour.

Here's the nugget of wisdom I offer to you, dear reader: do not underestimate the value of your existing network when seeking investment. Lean into it as early as possible in your fundraising journey.

Let me give you a real-life example that drove this point home for me. I once meticulously crafted a cold email to a potential investor. I spent days tweaking every word, ensuring that it was compelling yet concise. And after hitting send? Radio silence. It was disheartening, to say the least.

However, upon realising that a friend of mine was connected to someone who could potentially introduce me to this investor, I swallowed my hesitation and asked for that introduction. You wouldn't believe how quickly things can move when a warm intro is made. Within 45 minutes, my friend was sitting in my living room, crafting an introductory email on my behalf. The result? I got the meeting, and I made the pitch.

Had I known this 'hack' from the get-go, I would have spent months not just refining my business model and deck but also meticulously nurturing my network for these all-important introductions. If you're navigating the often-choppy waters of fundraising, especially in a landscape as challenging as Africa, my advice is this:

> Invest as much in your network as you do in your venture. Aim to cultivate relationships that can connect you to the right people—those who not only have the capital but also share your vision and can add significant value to your journey.

In a world where 'it's not what you know, but who you know' holds an overwhelming amount of truth, mastering the art of the warm introduction can make all the difference. And remember, while the financial capital is important, the human capital—those connections that open doors you didn't even know existed—can be just as valuable.

★★★

Dayo Olopade sees the problem and advantages as clearly as I do:

> The lack of capital put to work in Africa is surprising. After all, the marginal dollar goes much farther in the region, where there is low hanging investment opportunity. Rents, wages, and other labor inputs are much lower, and the markets are less saturated with competition.

She continues:

> We are busy discussing 2018, when developing countries are discussing 2080. No nation is built by accident. This disparity in focus highlights a

crucial gap in long-term planning and vision, underlining the need for developing countries like Nigeria to adopt forward-thinking strategies to ensure sustainable growth and development.

Olopade underscores the importance of future-oriented policies and planning for nation-building.

Olopade concludes this paragraph with perhaps the most prosaic question in her book: 'So what's the hold up?'

The future of global manufacturing is on the march to Africa. The advantages I've pointed out in previous chapters are numerous, plus population demographics literally speak volumes, as the current manufacturing hubs in China, Japan, Korea, Europe and North America are all in various stages of aging and population decline and with a low replacement (some may even call it a death spiral).

Manufacturing in Africa and the Global South is emerging, despite all the infrastructure, social and political obstacles, but access to capital that blocks new ventures is a growing problem, so much so that Kanju-style investment solutions such as leveraging African diaspora savings are estimated by the World Bank to be worth more than $52 billion annually!

Could this be the next frontier of diaspora bonds and access to necessary capital for the young entrepreneurs locked out from conventional finance?'

It is more than clear to me that Africans must learn to create our own 'magic' in being self-sufficient, wisely utilise our abundant natural resources, then ramp up and manufacture well-made goods, create, innovate and export around the globe.

The question then becomes, are we ready for this challenge? In the next chapter I argue that only the next generation of trained, informed and savvy Africa-based entrepreneurs can drive innovation and make this leap into the future.

Notes

1 https://www.vodafone.com/news/inclusion/mpesa-marks-15-years
2 Ibid.
3 https://hightimes.com/guides/what-is-khat/
4 https://www.congress.gov/116/crec/2020/12/09/modified/CREC-2020-12-09-pt1-PgH7056-2.htm
5 https://detroitmi.gov/sites/detroitmi.localhost/files/2023-05/CAY%20Gen%20wealth%20draft%20ek.pdf
6 Ibid.
7 Ibid.

Our Africa

10

The Coming Industrial Revolution 4.0

Colonialism bred an innate arrogance, but when you undertake that sort of imperial adventure, that arrogance gives way to a feeling of accommodativeness. You take pride in your openness.

A tiger does not shout its tigritude, it leaps on its prey and devours it.

—Nigerian Nobel Laureate, Professor Wole Soyinka

Africa's future is a fight between the Hippos—complacent, greedy bureaucrats, wallowing in the muck and the Cheetahs—the fast moving, entrepreneurial leaders and citizens who will rebuild Africa.

—Ghanian economist and author, George Ayittey

The Nigerian playwright, teacher, novelist and 1986 Nobel Prize winner for literature, Wole Soyinka, wrote his stunning canon of literature as part of a massive African diaspora that mostly went to the UK. His plays were performed all over the globe and revealed that the struggle to become African and be heard as authentic African voices might be better said and received outside the shores of our continent. Certainly, with the murderous regimes, genocides and military coups that nearly brought Nigeria and other postcolonial African nations to their knees. My parents' generation knew instinctively they had to leave Nigeria in order to build a better future for their children.

As a daughter born to parents from the Nigerian diaspora, it was *only 15 years ago* that we would demand hip hop in predominantly African clubs. Yes, we always had Afrobeat (musicians like FelaKuti and Sunny Ade) but these were the sounds of our parents' generation, as well as the plays and then novels of Wole Soyinka. We only paid attention to this music at weddings,

DOI: 10.4324/9781003453994-10

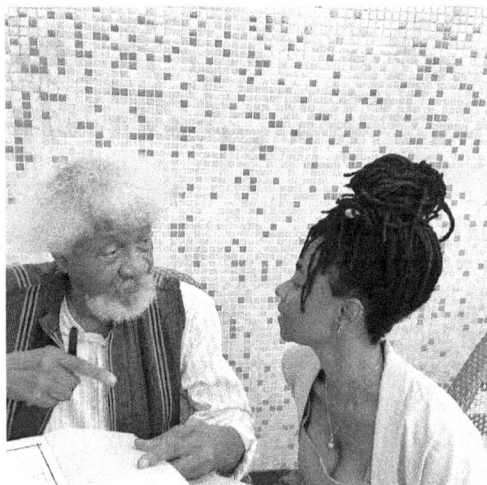

Figure 10.1 Demi in conversation with Professor Wole Soyinka. Image courtesy of Majeurs Holdings.

birthday parties or when we accompanied our parents to traditional or cultural occasions. To be perfectly frank, our generation, those who were born and raised in the UK diaspora or elsewhere, were simply not interested in historical and cultural occasions, and in fact, were embarrassed by it.

It was not cool—we were dialled into the imported sounds of American and British pop, that spoke to us because we grew up by in large in those cultures and more often than not, felt disconnected and disinterested to Africa or Nigeria.

In recent years that is no longer the case, as we have found our sound that speaks directly to our generation. The likes of Davido, Wizkid and yes, I'll begrudgingly add Burna Boy to the list, have manufactured and transformed the sound of Afrobeat, packaging it for a young generation globally. Our African music has not only transformed us, but it is also transforming the world—cutting across race, communities and diverse demographics. We are the Cheetah Generation who will actually rebuild Africa, as the great Ghanian economist George Ayittey proclaimed in his blistering TED Talk in 2007[1] and in his provocative and essential book, *Africa Unchained.*[2]

Wole Soyinka's quote about accommodations now seems slightly antiquated for the fact that for Africans, who do not have that lived experience of family, cultural and physical disruption, the world for my generation and my world view is in fact in a very different place.

As a returnee from the diaspora to Africa, I rapidly gleaned that Nigerians are striving for success built from within, and not necessarily imported wisdom from the diaspora. Their pride is not about making accommodations, and getting bogged down with the Hippos, but attaining very practical goals: getting upskilled or trained, starting and building new businesses and commercial enterprises on a scale that are both profitable and sustainable. Not only is it a young, hungry generation, they have what Professor Soyinka would call 'tigritude' by the bushel.

To bend the Top Cat metaphor a little further, the Cheetahs have seen the wasteland of the Hippos and what they have wrought for Africa, and are pushing hard and fast to leap over that generation.

The question, therefore, is what is driving this new thinking and a growing feeling that the next economic boom will be in Africa? Since arriving in Nigeria in the past eight years, I can state for the record that African tigritude is deep, wide and in fact has already begun.

It could be described as the Industrial Revolution 4.0. This is born out with historical shifts in economies, and a workforce ready and willing to work. First: England and America (18th and 19th centuries); Second: Japan, Germany and South Korea (post WW2); Third: China and India (late 20th and early 21st century); and now, Africa (21st century).

The other massive advantage is that because of rapid digitisation and the flattening of the world, a consumer in Perth, Australia can use their phone and buy a handmade leather sofa manufactured in Nigeria and have it shipped to them, with the entire transaction completed on a smartphone, and electronic payment completed in less than five minutes.

In Dayo Olopade's[3] book she describes the uptake of cell phones and digitisation in Africa in a very clear image: 'Cell phone adoption in Africa is best described by thinking like a hockey stick—the shape of the graph plotting the sharp increase in new users over the last decade…'

The numbers are in fact staggering, and now the rise of 'smartphones' vs. the older Nokia 'dumbphones' is also rapidly taking over. Her supplemental quote states, 'Over the course of writing this book, I have had to revise that statistic multiple times. There will be a projected 525 million smartphones online in Africa by 2020.'

At the writing of this book in 2023, smartphone adoption has gone off the charts, where in Nigeria alone,, post-pandemic it has surged to more than 64 per cent of the population.[4]

Thus, the African digital revolution when the SECOM's 10,000-mile-long fibre-optic cable under the Indian Ocean is already changing livelihoods, travel and access to consumer goods, and creating a massive array of opportunities.

Industrial Revolution 4.0: Culture and Commerce

What I mean by cultural and economic revolutions is that as African entrepreneurs, we must also learn from our deep well and long history of contemporary poets, writers, musicians and artists—who are creating with passion by entertaining and educating their massive fanbases that announces to the world that Africa is cool, and open for business.

In two recent art exhibits at New York's Museum of Modern Art[5] and the Brooklyn Museum of Art,[6] African and Nigerian fashion designers, artists, textile designers, photographers are not only getting noticed but are also celebrated and garner press and direct attention to the creatives living and working in the sub-Sahara. This soft marketing will in turn encourage consumers to fall in love with African-made products and then export them to the globe with pride.

We must see the beauty and power in reaping our own fruit on a global stage and hold ourselves accountable for sustainable, stable and long-term growth.

What is central to the cultural and economic tigritude is that we must 'act' promptly to seek new investors within and without Africa and champion the creativity, in all sectors and that includes the manufacturing sector.

In a recent article published in the blog 'South African Engineers', the post-pandemic outlook for the manufacturing sector looks incredibly strong, even the author states:

> The world is changing at an unprecedented rate in terms of innovative technologies, shifting customer expectations, as well as increasing social awareness of gender equality and restoration of previously marginalised communities. These major shifts have a considerable impact on the future of Africa's manufacturing sectors. If African manufacturers can efficiently balance a combination of efficient economics of production and supply chains; strong and reputable products; loyal customers, an established logistics network as well as reliable online business elements, they will be well positioned in the future industrial marketplace.[7]

The quote covers a lot of territories that I've continued to talk about with young entrepreneurs that I champion. To attain many of these lofty but necessary goals, the groundwork must be accomplished, and as I've written in previous chapters and will speak about in the next part of the book, is really about taking action and what are the necessary steps.

***

Smartphones and digitisation are rapidly making innovation and customer expectations shift, but so is addressing the dire need for stable infrastructure of clean water, a reliable electrical grid and an all-hands-on-deck approach to routing out corruption, and yes, the recognition and restoration of previously marginalised communities.

Table 4: African countries among the top 20 contributors to global population growth by 2050

Country	2019 pop estimate (million)	2050 medium-variant projection (million)	Additional population 2019–50 (million)	Ranking in global growth tables, numbers added 2019–50*
Nigeria	201	401	200	2
DRC	67	194	127	4
Ethiopia	112	205	93	5
Tanzania	58	129	71	6
Egypt	100	160	60	8
Angola	31	77	46	10
Uganda	44	89	45	11
Niger	23	67	44	12
Kenya	52	91	39	13
Sudan	42	81	39	14
Mozambique	30	65	35	16
Madagascar	26	54	28	20
Total	786	1613	827	

*The eight non-African countries in the top 20 are India (1), Pakistan (3), Indonesia (7), USA (9), Philippines (15), Iraq (17), Bangladesh (18) and Mexico (19).   Source: UNPD, *World Population Prospects: The 2019 Revision – Highlights*, p. 13.

Figure 10.2 Table from UNPD, World Population Prospects: 2019 Revision – Highlights, Pg. 13. Reprinted in: Edward Paice and Africa Research Institute. 2021. *Youth Quake: Why African Demographics Matter.* Head Of Zeus Publishers Ltd. Page 22.

The numbers are staggering, and in the blog below, I believe the author is being conservative in their projections. I'm including this quote, because it truly does back up what I'm seeing and experiencing as a manufacturer in Nigeria, of what could be deemed luxury goods that the one per cent of the one per cent consume. This I believe because of the projections that the population in Africa will double in the next decades, and a growing middle class with the majority of them employed in the commercial, tech and manufacturing sectors will drive the Industrial Revolution 4.0. The middle class will have better pay, safer working conditions, in less hazardous conditions.

> Experts purport that Africa conveys a positive economic growth trajectory, deeming it a feasible alternative to other markets. Africa is regarded as the world's fastest-growing continental economy, and its business-to-business market is fundamental to this boom. B2B expenditure in the continent's manufacturing is projected to reach $666.3 billion by 2030, $201.28 billion more than it did four years ago. As the buying power of Africa's middle class continues to rise, demand for products and services across the continent subsequently increases, thereby enabling sustainable economic growth and much-needed integration amongst regions.[8]

Africa is not by any stretch of the imagination totally free of postcolonial traumas and fears. At the time of writing of this book, Niger and Mali are again roiling under military takeovers which add to the painful reminders that political control and relative peace is short-lived. Political corruption and personal safety are obvious topics in Africa and I'll address this reality in the concluding chapter.

★★★

There are many examples of this African Economic Tiger, some that I've been lucky enough to interview on my blog, SUSU, as outlined in the sections that follow.

Bankole Bernard

Bankole Bernard is the GMD and CEO of Finchglow Holdings, a conglomerate of multi-award-winning subsidiaries. He started his career in the banking sector and worked for Ecobank, and the now defunct Metropolitan and First Atlantic banks.

In 2006, he left and started a travel agency, Finchglow Travels Limited. Through his marketing genius, radical creativity and transformational leadership, he's grown the company to a top three in the industry in Nigeria with eight thriving subsidiaries.

Tara Fela-Durotoye

Tara Fela-Durotoye is a trailblazer in Nigeria's beauty industry, known for pioneering the bridal makeup profession. In 1999, she launched Nigeria's first bridal directory and set up world-class makeup studios and the country's first makeup school. As the founder and former CEO of House of Tara International, she created renowned beauty products like Tara Orekelewa and Inspired Perfume. By 2019, House of Tara boasted 270 products, 23 stores, 14 beauty schools and 10,000 representatives across Africa. She received the Africa SMME Award in 2007, was listed among Forbes' 20 Young Power Women in Africa in 2013, and featured in Forbes' 50 Most Powerful Women in Africa in 2020.

Steve Babaeko

Steve Babaeko is a Nigerian advertising and music executive, public advocate and founder of X3M Ideas, a Lagos-based digital advertising agency that was described in 2017 as 'one of Nigeria's fastest growing communication agencies'. He is also the founder/CEO of X3M Music, a record label that has as its marquee act, among others, Nigerian singer-songwriter Simi. He was on the 2018 jury of the New York Advertising Festival.

Nkemdilim Uwaje Begho

Nkemdilim Uwaje Begho is an entrepreneurial and strategically driven executive with experience as a CEO, founder and non-executive director of private, listed and public sector organisations.

Nkemdilim is a seasoned IT professional with over 15 years of cross-sector industry experience in Nigeria, Africa's largest emerging economy. She combines strategic, digital technology and operational experience with a deep understanding of business transformation, change leadership and risk oversight.

Onyeka Akumah

Onyeka Akumah is a technology entrepreneur with a focus on transportation, agriculture, real estate and media sectors. He is popularly known as the founder of Treepz Inc. Prior to founding his company in 2019, Onyeka Akumah was the CEO of Farmcrowdy. He is credited with having been involved in the success of various tech and e-commerce companies in Africa where he held positions and contributed to their growth.

Africa Can Be Ours, Truly Ours!

> WB Yeats wrote in his stark but prescient poem, 'The Second Coming'[9] that the 'centre cannot hold.' Across Africa, it turns out that the center never was. And only when the dust from the half-century of inauthentic failed states clears will a dynamic, assured, post-national public shine through.[10]
>
> —Dayo Olopade

Africa is truly for the taking. There has never truly been a social, political and economic leap in Africa like the 21st century. The old Hippo class is dying off, or escaping the continent with their ill-gotten gains, like bandits. The Cheetah generation, unencumbered by postcolonial trauma, is poised to become stewards of our own political and economic power. Leaders such as:

- **Ngozi Okonjo-Iweala:** Nigerian economist and international development expert, currently serving as the Director-General of the World Trade Organization.
- **Aliko Dangote:** Nigerian business magnate, the wealthiest person in Africa, known for his significant contributions to the continent's development through the Dangote Group.
- **Mo Ibrahim:** Sudanese-British billionaire, known for his work in telecommunications and the Mo Ibrahim Foundation, which focuses on the importance of governance and leadership in Africa.
- **Ellen Johnson Sirleaf:** Former president of Liberia and Nobel Peace Prize laureate, known for her leadership and efforts in rebuilding Liberia post-conflict.
- **Strive Masiyiwa:** Zimbabwean businessman and philanthropist, founder of Econet Global, contributing significantly to African telecoms.

- **Kumi Naidoo:** South African human rights activist, known for his leadership roles in international organisations like Greenpeace and Amnesty International.
- **H.E. Mrs. Graça Machel:** An esteemed African stateswoman with a deep-rooted professional and public life dedicated to Mozambique's self-rule and international advocacy for women and children's rights. Her notable contributions include producing a groundbreaking UNICEF report on the impact of armed conflict on children, significantly influencing the UN's response in conflict zones. She is a founding member of The Elders, a key figure in establishing Girls Not Brides and participates in the UN Secretary-General's Sustainable Development Goals Advocacy Group.

Africans need only to look at their recent history, and success stories in both commerce and global cultural power, and realise that the facts are clear. In the 1960s and early 1970s, Nigeria's export of wood products and agricultural commodities provided more than 70% of the gross domestic product (GDP) for the country. There is plenty of historical proof that we can do this because we once did.

The economist and public intellectual George Ayittey, in his provocative 2007 TED Talk 'Hippos vs Cheetahs', asks his audience directly, 'to consider that in the last fifty years there's have been over 200 leaders in Africa'. He then asks them to name 20 leaders who have lifted their people up for the common good. He mentions two, Mandela and Kenyatta, and even ironically mentions the Ugandan terror monger, Idi Amin.

The flight of capital from Africa from the mostly criminal Hippo class must be stanched. Once that begins in earnest, the next generation of builders, entrepreneurs and leaders will have access to capital, investments and become empowered to become what I provocatively stated: Africa will be ours, truly ours for the taking.

The question, therefore, for Africans is where are the models of success to emulate, that are not imported or imposed from outside of the continent of Africa?

In my opinion, we have in Africa one example of an actual rebirth of a nation and that is Rwanda. Most readers will recall the bloody genocide between the Tutsi and Hutu tribes that literally, metaphorically, figuratively, brutally hacked apart the landlocked nation.

In a starkly written paragraph about Rwanda's trauma, Dayo Olopade writes:

> Ten percent of the population was killed in the genocide, hundreds of thousands more people were forced to live in refugee camps, and

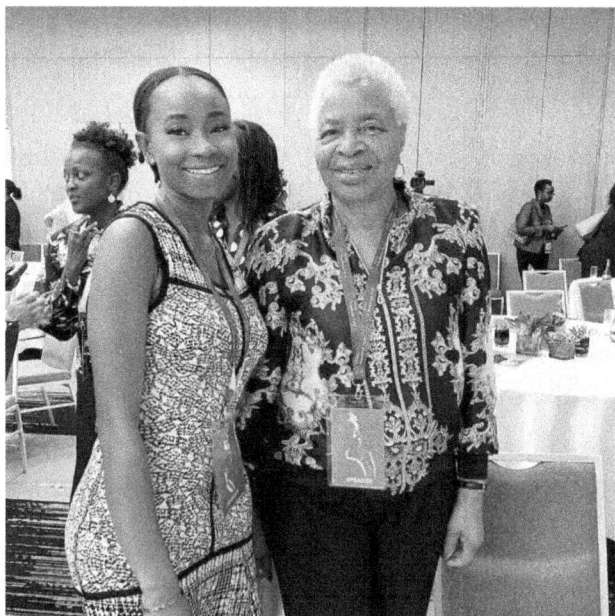

Figure 10.3 Demi with H.E. Graca Machel in Rwanda. Image courtesy of Majeurs Holdings.

Figure 10.4 Demi with the Governor of Lagos State—Babajide Sanwo-Olu. Image courtesy of Demi Samande.

those who were left were barely alive. There was no central bank, no auditor general, and no school syllabus, archives and documents were destroyed, and there was no institutional memory.

If there was one nation in Africa that was on a rapid downward spiral to a failed state, or even worse a petri dish and homeland for terror and chaos, it was Rwanda.

Stephen Kinzer's *A Thousand Hills*[11] gives a vigorous examination of the Rwandan genocide, and its rebirth through leadership.

Leadership, Innovation

Paul Kagame and the Rwandan population has in some ways engineered a remarkable turnaround, that frankly no one thought was possible. Although not without its imperfections, I believe it is also important to recognize the significant strides the country has made in various areas since the genocide. Many countries who went through similar have not recovered, such as Sudan.

However, they have made an incredible leapfrog forward, using innovation and yes, somewhat audacious reforms, as Dayo Olopade states:

> A push to integrate the nation into the global economy, the official language of business was changed from French to English, children are required to attend three additional years of school, and a universal health insurance scheme is in its first stages.[12]

Now, under Paul Kagame's leadership, Rwanda is one of the easiest nations in Africa to start up a business, and their economy 'is growing at rapid place—about 7.5 percent in 2010—2 percent higher than the East African Community and more than the Sub Saharan Africa at large'. Rwanda's GDP growth rate reached 10.9% in 2021 before declining to 8.2% due to climate shocks on domestic food production, high energy, food and fertilizer prices, and weak external demand on exports. [13]

Another surprising but necessary form of leadership in Rwanda has emerged out of the ashes of genocide and devastation, and that is women entering into business and politics, which in the past were controlled by men. In Rwanda and elsewhere, female entrepreneurs are driving the new economy and are now accepted and entering the formerly closed political realm as well.

In Rwanda in particular, as Dayo Olopade writes,

> For several years running…the country has had the highest proportion of female lawmakers in the world. Women have run the ministries of

foreign affairs, agriculture and health. The same goes for the speaker of the Parliament, the vice president of the Senate, and the president's chief of staff.

This takeover by women was also driven by the grim reality that 'after the genocide, female survivors found themselves alone, with a country to rebuild—and skill to contribute'.[14]

'That's the secret of nation building in Rwanda, it's the women, it's the youth, it's the marginalised groups,' stated the former Minister for Reconciliation and Gender, Aloisia Inyumba.[15]

These are words and actions by outstanding women and certainly resonate with me, and I've dedicated the next chapter to highlighting and promoting this next generation of female Cheetahs. I'm also convinced that with more women owning and operating businesses, being responsible for HR, upskilling of their staff, scaling their operations, they will be a huge part of the cultural and economic shift. They must also confront and push accountability for those who continue to act as corrupt Hippos. I'm also convinced that that this powerful group of women will insist on the necessary and social changes that will be as profound as Rwanda's but without having to lose life and limb.

These women's stories offer inspiration but also highlight their creativity, passion and determination to rebuild their infrastructure, family bonds, education, health systems, as well commercial and profitable businesses. In Rwanda and elsewhere in the Sub-Saharan States, like Ghana and Nigeria, women are rebuilding and tapping into 21st century technology, connectivity and distribution.

I'm bullish that with women in the driver's seat, CEOs, COOs, managerial and operations, in many sectors of business including light and heavy manufacturing, technology, mobility and communications, the lives of Africans and their economies will certainly achieve far more than the former years that were beholden to colonial masters and then to autocrats, military juntas and bad actors.

I realise that this chapter may sound like I'm standing on a ladder in Hyde Park Corner, but women do have an innate and deep understanding of business. My mother was a perfect example, and her creative hustle, and desire to make sure that her family had everything we needed, including extra school trips and cash on hand for any emergency. Her small-scale enterprise was in essence my MBA field research. I lived it, and participated in it, although at times with childish reluctance. All that was missing was how to scale it, and where to look for and access capital to fund her dreams.

Capital Conundrum

This issue of finding access to secure capital and scaling a business is in fact exactly the same issue I and many other entrepreneurs in Africa are currently facing. The classic and tired excuses from the investor class—some of whom I'll admit are reformed Hippos—who need to constantly be reminded that profits from all investment dollars into African-owned companies tend to remain and circulate back into the community, with salaries, food and social improvements like health and safety for workers, and a general sense of betterment for family through education, and a possibility of upward mobility.

Rwanda is certainly not the perfect model for grand reinvention, and although Paul Kagame is considered an energetic mixture of right-wing authoritarian with a grand dream to lift Rwandans from generational poverty and of course unspeakable acts of violence. As a case study, it provides other Africans a deeper understanding of how to reinvent and create a mostly corruption free nation—where taxes are paid on time, but also the benefits are returned such as governmental transparency, health services and education in a digitally connected society. There is now the orderly circulation of money, combined with straightforward and easy structures to set up and grow a business, that is actually working, and is available to all despite historical tribal conflicts.

The essential dilemma that is reiterated in hundreds of studies, by economists, NGOs, the World Bank, is how can we as entrepreneurs help kickstart the next Industrial and Cultural Revolution in Africa? I have no doubt that the Cheetahs are going to make it happen. There is so much commercial activity and powerful voices starting to emerge, many that I've pointed to, and another generation ready to actually become the trained and skilled workforce that powers the Next Factory of the World, by making Africa the next global manufacturing hub.

However, without capital, or smart capital, or soft capital—early capital that funds commercial growth—then so many incredible ideas will be left on the vine to die and whither.

Dayo Olopade concludes her magisterial study of Africa with a warning about the lack of capital. Her actionable words bear repeating:

> In modern Africa, scale is everything, …Good ideas that languish in local clinics or tech hubs will never reach their generative potential.

These ideas are born along diverse and complementary vectors: family, technology, commerce, nature, and youth.

It is a collective demand and acknowledgement that the next generation is poised to take over and with capital and proper levels of investment they will pounce.

★★★

On an average morning in Lagos, I walk through my furniture manufacturing business, that only ten years ago was a very lofty dream of a rather idealistic young woman in London. The workers are slowly moving into their positions, looking over their plans for the day, whether it is cutting wood for the inner frames of the furniture, or beginning to stretch and prepare the leather for the tufted upholstery, or nailing the final finishing nails on a classic Chesterfield sofa. I also see the team in the packaging and shipping department, that were living hand to mouth just a few years ago. Now with fulltime employment they can actually afford a scooter to come to work rather than deal with the insane and dysfunctional public transport system in Lagos. I can see the concentration on their faces as they ready themselves to fulfil their work goals for the day. I also revel in their Lagosian humour, expressed in many languages and facial expressions, and the smiles on their faces are worth a million pounds. I appreciate their skills and commitment to manufacture a truly wonderful piece of furniture for my company. I recognise that these craftspeople are also raising families, and literally putting food on the table, that otherwise would be a massive daily grind and struggle.

I ask myself often, is this the prototype for the Next Factory of the World where culture and design thinking come together? I'm not alone, as you will read in the next chapter. A wave of young entrepreneurs will start factories, such as Majeurs, and then they will have the same satisfaction as I do every morning. The quiet satisfaction that despite all the headaches and challenges and obstacles, I am literally changing the lives of my employees.

This is not Africa of old, with its dirty hands begging for food or inundated by foreign aid after yet another crisis, but driven by commerce and the practical goals of scaling a modern business that will meet the needs of consumers all over the globe.

My generation of businesspeople are definitely bucking conventional wisdom, and whether we call it *Kanju* economics, or *Cheetahs vs. Hippos*, or *Tigritude*, what is clear—and I can see it every morning on the factory floor of my business and training academy—is the joy, creativity, the hard work and collective power of Africa and its youthful energy and *relentless optimism*.

This optimism feeds directly into my thinking as the CEO and it gives me a very clear mission: I intend to, along with long list of Cheetah-generation entrepreneurs, designers, artists and creatives, continually persuade, cajole and convince investors that this entirely new generation of entrepreneurs are leap-frogging over many of the old problems through innovation, design thinking, by creating strategic partnerships, with secure investments, combined with hard work and determination. The future is Africa—it can be ours, truly ours!

Notes

1 https://www.ted.com/speakers/george_ayittey
2 George B.N. Ayittey. 2006. *Africa Unchained: The Blueprint for Africa's Future.* Basingstoke: Palgrave Macmillan.
3 Dayo Olopade. 2014. *The Bright Continent.* Houghton Mifflin Harcourt. Page 92.
4 https://furtherafrica.com/2022/07/19/african-countries-with-the-highest-number-of-mobile-phones/
5 https://www.nytimes.com/2023/06/09/arts/design/lagos-nigeria-moma-photography.html
6 https://www.brooklynmuseum.org/exhibitions/africa_fashion
7 https://www.engineeringnews.co.za/article/the-future-of-african-manufacturing-making-things-in-a-changing-world-2023-09-13
8 Ibid.
9 https://www.poetryfoundation.org/poems/43290/the-second-coming
10 Dayo Olopade. 2014. *The Bright Continent.* Houghton Mifflin Harcourt. Page 235.
11 Stephen Kinzer. 2008. *A Thousand Hills.* John Wiley & Sons.
12 Ibid.
13 https://www. afdb.org (see: Rwanda Economic Outlook)
14 Ibid.
15 https://en.wikipedia.org/wiki/Aloisea_Inyumba

Cheetahs, Titans, and Movers and Shakers

11

Start Up, Scale Up. That is precisely what I was doing. I was making the scary and precarious leap from a small furniture and design company to a larger scale manufacturing company. There were so many unknowns and no one I encountered had any answers to my questions. My answer was to start a business and podcast with Nigerians in the manufacturing and tech sectors that delved into the topics that so many new entrepreneurs struggle to find answers to. Covid expedited that vision, because I had plenty of time to spare. Thus in May 2020, I created the SUSU (Start Up, Scale Up) podcast, that allowed me to speak to a wide range of business entrepreneurs, in Nigeria and elsewhere. I was definitely a newbie to Africa and although my own story was not unique, as the daughter of parents who were part of the diaspora, I felt I needed to reach out beyond my comfort zone. I didn't want to be pigeon-holed as a returnee, which can be emotionally tiring.

I've always felt that conversation and verbal communication was my strong suit, and the format of the podcast was the ideal format to introduce myself to a wide variety of Nigerian Movers and Shakers, Cheetahs and the new giants in the tech, manufacturing, design and creative spaces. What started as essentially an audio business promotional vehicle has now become a much bigger thing, and although all the conversations with guests have expanded, at the root is the central argument about how my guests started, and through trial, error and failure, began to build businesses that are well established and provide Nigerians with employment and better yet, hope for the future. My initial goals for the podcast were straightforward. Promote my own company, which was a completely new entity in Nigeria that was starting from scratch. I knew that I could learn from the most prominent entrepreneurs, creatives and tech companies who also had found

DOI: 10.4324/9781003453994-11

their ground over the years. Our conversations were always focused on how Nigeria and indeed Africa was on the cusp of a major breakthrough in tech, manufacturing, design and where they also saw the shifts and changes in the economy.

I didn't want guests to be all like-minded, nor did I want them to be didactic, or a just become a forum for complaining about government regulations and corruption. I wanted the SUSU podcast and now this book, which is a logical outgrowth, to first and foremost educate, enlighten and stir the pot for young entrepreneurs to understand that there is a long history of companies in Nigeria, and multiple pathways to build manufacturing companies. I've always encouraged this kind of debate and exchange of ideas on the SUSU podcast, to challenge my preconceptions and thinking, but also it acts as an informal place for the builders to express their views that may not align with my ideas.

In fact, for anyone intrigued about what is happening in Lagos, Nigeria and Africa without the filter of traditional media, I highly recommend listening to the SUSU podcast. I hope you find our 'virtual roundtable' as lively and engaging as the podcast.

I've chosen to highlight three very different people for this chapter, and although their own stories are divergent, one is a true 'Cheetah' in the children's design, manufacturing and retailing space, another is a mover and shaker in the rapidly growing tech sector, and one is a senior C-suite member of one of the 'Titans' in Nigerian manufacturing.

Figure 11.1 Demi with Adenike Ogunlesi. Image courtesy of Demi Samande.

The members of my roundtable are first, **Adenike Ogunlesi**, one of Africa's foremost children's fashion and retail entrepreneurs. She is a Nigerian businesswoman and part of the Cheetah class who began her business selling high-quality children's clothes, Ruff 'n' Tumble, literally from the boot of her car.

Second is **Iyinoluwa Aboyej**, the former co-founder of Flutterwave and Andela, and now CEO of Future Africa. I've mentioned his impressive bio in an earlier chapter.

And last is **Folascope (Fola) Aiyesiomju**, GMD/CEO of UAC, The United Africa Company. UAC is truly a Titan in Nigerian and African manufacturing across several sectors: real estate, logistics, animal feeds and now paint. Founded in 1886 by Queen Victoria under a Royal Charter, The Royal Niger Company, RNC, the trading company at one point was one of the largest trading and private land holders in Africa.

All three guests spoke with me individually, and I've edited our conversations for brevity and clarity and written it as a virtual roundtable.

The full interviews are available on the SUSU podcast here: https://www.youtube.com/@SUSU-PODCAST/videos

Figure 11.2 Iyinoluwa Aboyej. Image by Godson Ukaegbu: https://thewilldowntown.com/iyinoluwa-aboyeji-your-friendly-neighbourhood-fintech-and-startups-guru/

Figure 11.3 Folascope (Fola) Aiyesiomju. https://www.uacnplc.com/
uac-nigeria-appoints-aiyesimoju-group-md-ceo-2/

Demi: Mrs O, you started very humbly and bootstrapped for a long time, what can young entrepreneurs glean from your experience?

Adenike: I learned how to take one naira and make it ten. I learned how to take ten naira and make it a hundred. You need skills to do that. You need focus. You need mental resilience. You need discipline. In fact, you need laser focus. You need discipline, mental discipline, physical discipline to be able to achieve some of those things a clear plan. I have my list of C's. You need to know what you want. Clarity, Commitment, Consistency: I always say that, look, the first C is commitment. So, are you just interested or are you committing to something? If you're committing to it, okay. Then you need to be consistent. Commitment will get you started. Your consistency is what is going to keep you going, because you're putting one brick on top of the other, on top of the other until you have a six-foot wall. Then you have commitment, your consistency. I have to go back to the top all the time. You then have to learn and have the ability to cooperate with different people. When you build a team that you can cooperate to achieve a result and achieve a project, you now have to learn to collaborate with external parties. And what drives all of this? Communication. Communication. Communication. That's what drives all of it.

Demi: You mentioned technology. When you began in 1996, how often have you moved with the technology age over the years?

Adenike: I was very pro-technology from very early on. The idea of people writing out receipts by hand when somebody buys ten dresses and then somebody is sitting there and writing out every single item on an invoice or a receipt drove me absolutely nuts. [..] Ruff 'n' Tumble is very tech enabled. The entire business is sitting on technology, from our support centre, we can receive the data about every last sale from the furthest store in Kano, in Abuja and Port Harcourt in our support centre. We can see every last sale in the last ten minutes, then in five minutes and we can see into the stores. And we also have connection of cameras that we see from, that we watch from the support centre. We have them because it is there to drive compliance.

Demi: Technology is wonderful for businesses in terms of automating your systems and making you derive the right data from this, from your transactions. I'm in the midst of developing technology and data, to help my company resolve consistency errors and partially make decisions about the manufacturing process to aid waste reduction, create better working conditions, and a database that looks at marketing and development. I asked Iyinoluwa, who is really embedded in the burgeoning tech sector, how do you see technology help make small businesses like mine succeed and build tech capacity?

Iyinoluwa: I used to think that it made sense to try to solve what I now call problems at the margin. But we had to do something, you know, something that made you look cool. If you're really serious about building a business in Nigeria, you go after the fundamental problems that people have and that they believe they can't solve. My first foray into that was Andela. Because with Andela [a tech training and hiring platform] the problems and solutions were clear: there was 40% youth unemployment in Nigeria. There were no jobs, there was very little growth, and the harsh reality was people just couldn't afford to pay any more with rising costs. The Nigerian currency had just crashed and we needed something for what people needed to survive and we thought, okay, what happens if we can divorce your job from your geographic location? Then essentially build a remote work industry on the back of that. I think the biggest lesson for me in building Andela was just realising that it doesn't really take a lot of money to solve huge problems. You just have to have the right kind of systems thinking to take on something small, because we started with four people, trained four people on how to build JavaScript, and we put them on a freelance sites. Before you know it, we are training 20 people, and then training 20 more people every two weeks. Then were training three times 20 people every three weeks before you knew it. We had skilled the whole country and now we're doing all the training of flying into another 22 states and in small communities.

Demi: Incredible. So, similar to Adenike's problems of creating a better experience in her shops with tech, her fundamental problems was, how do you do quicker and more efficient check out and stock accounting? What about [the] rapidly growing tech sector and compare that to manufacturing?

Iyinoluwa: If you think about it from a systems level, you can solve a big problem with it or not. The problem we're trying to really solve is that our laws as a country are not representative of the reality of our economy, which is that over the last 40 years, 55% of our country's economy is now services.

When you think about it and you say, okay, where are the country's incentives? All that is going to manufacturing and trade. That's what all these [tax] free zones are for. Well, if you are now as a country that is a 55% service economy, it's only a matter of time before you realise that you have to incentivise people to bring service companies to Nigeria and then export services to the rest of the world.

If you think about what we do in Africa, for example, like our banking services are some of the best in the Africa[n] financial-services industry. Are we intentionally exporting that globally? You think about our professional services. You know, some of the best people who work for KPMG, McKinsey and PwC are now leaving Nigeria because they are excellent. Are we intentionally exporting that talent globally?

I'm not talking just about call centres, I'm talking about anything that anybody can do a service. If you combine the fact that anything can be called a service, you can do it via the internet. So, what does that look like? I was talking with a friend this morning about design, outsourcing. We have all these CAD-trained engineers. Is it possible for us to put them on the platform and get them to, like, design things remotely for other people to manufacture elsewhere?

Demi: I am a manufacturer myself. That's where my passion lies. When you think about services and tech, how do you envisage that merging with the manufacturing space? Because as much as yes, 55% is services, Africa needs manufacturing. Whether we like it or not, Africa needs to be able to position itself to utilise its full resources and create value-added products to export to other places, because that creates a huge opportunity in creating other industries and services that support that work. If you really want to tackle the massive unemployment issues, how do we possibly begin to do that without manufacturing?

Iyinoluwa: I think we really have to ask ourselves what are the competitive ones, and are there certain parts of the manufacturing value chain that are not competitive purely because we don't have a dependable electrical grid? Whenever somebody comes to me, I say, okay, how much power do you actually need? And they tell me, well a lot. I tell them, then don't do it. You can never be able to compete because at the end of the day, the customer's only better off if they get the cheapest price. On the other hand, if electricity was very cheap, so there are parts of the manufacturing value chain where you can get a lot more value by doing it here than in Nigeria than anywhere else in the world.

I actually did not agree with Iyinoluwa's assessment that we as Africans need not bother with manufacturing because we cannot compete. He states that we should simply accept that manufacturing is not one our strengths. My argument is that he is a manufacturing sceptic and I believe that there is nothing that Africans cannot do given the right tools and the system to support it. There was a time when technology was not an African strength. People like Iyinoluwa and Adenike have proven that not to be true with companies like Ruff 'n' Tumble and Andela. We are silencing the critics just as China did. What we ask is that the tech world, and people like Iyinoluwa, support the manufacturing sector with technology, we need them to lean into manufacturing spaces and help with tech solutions.

I'll readily agree that the problems with [the] electrical grid sometimes can feel insurmountable, but manufacturing companies have a very long history in Nigeria.

★★★

I've invited **Folascope (Fola) Aiyesiomju** *who is the GMD/CEO of UAC, The United Africa Company, that has roots in Nigeria that go back to 1866. I asked him his thoughts on how to succeed and thrive in Nigeria, and the role of planning, longevity and leadership.*

Fola: Well, the [UAC] company goes back to the 1800s, so I think anyone who says that it was all planned out has the most optimistic views of planning. There have been two World Wars and the Nigerian Civil War. What I will say is that UAC has reasonable longevity because of leadership. I would say that each leadership change brings with it some deliberate planning and therefore a tweak in the approach. Presumably, each of these leaders would assess what the environment is like at the time of taking the helm, craft their plan and then tweak the company. It's not random, but I would say it's more in cycles and phases than one long plan from the beginning.

Demi: What were challenges that you faced historically and today?

Fola: I would say there are probably three types of challenges that have shaped the group to where it is today. The first is macro. I think my view is that Nigeria is going through some of the worst macroeconomic times its ever experienced. But when you've been around for as long as UAC, you've seen this before. The late '80s were probably a lost decade, probably as bad. Then I think when you've been around for as long as UAC, you stop participating in discussions with people saying, 'Oh, this thing can never happen,' because you've seen these things happen. You've seen the naira go from 1 to a dollar to 1,200 to a dollar. I guess it's good and bad, however, the UAC group is very conservative. We don't take excessive risk because we've seen what can happen in an economy like Nigeria. Second, we very much would set ourselves up to be in line with the macro. A UAC company would almost never take negative foreign exchange risk, borrowing in dollars or relying on imports, because of what we've seen. Or maybe I can just put all this into good risk management and [being] very conservative, which has its pros and its cons. Being mindful of our exposure to currency volatility. Because if we are not so conservative, we may grow a lot faster or we may also not be around. That's one. The second is if you look at UAC's journey over the last 30 years, it's slimmed down and slimmed down and slimmed down. In the past we were 30 or 40 divisions in the '80s and it's kept coming down. The realisation that running a super-diverse and complicated business in Nigeria is incredibly difficult. The degree of control you need to put in place, the standards you need to maintain are so high or so difficult that then we simplify, simplify, simplify to where we are today. I think the final thing I would mention is that we've come to realize that in our industries you can build very, very interesting businesses and there are two key impediments. Third, by far the biggest one we think is people. It's just finding enough talented managers to run your businesses. And the second is capital and I'll say people before capital. Again, it's our view to streamline, streamline, stream-line the group further.

Demi: A universal theme our roundtable is currently facing is an exceedingly bad economy in Nigeria. This fact plus the diffi-culty of attracting talent, plus training and holding on to work and staff. My question to Adenike is then, is [being] entrepre-neurial [about] guidepost resilience?

Adenike: You have to be mentally strong to be an entrepreneur. And I'm not talking about getting a 5 billion naira contract from the government. No, I'm talking about making and creating. I'm talking about creating, birthing something, growing something from nothing, putting all the different bits together, and then it becomes something that's a gift.

Demi: Is that the part of your journey and your work that you love the most?

Adenike: Somebody said to me yesterday or the day before yesterday, every time you come into this factory, you smile. But there were days when I went into the factory and cried. Well, now I smile because I've got some great people on my team. They understand the vision. They're running with the vision, and I'm just grateful to be in that space and in that place.

Demi: How much sacrifice do you think you've made to get to that point where you found your tribe, your business tribe, as I like to call it, because I know there's some stories behind that.

Adenike: As I said to somebody once, I kissed many frogs who didn't turn into Prince Charming. But I finally found my tribe. But I kissed many frogs.

Demi: How many years did it take?

Adenike: I started when I turned 50. I wanted to build a business that would outlive me. And I realised that I needed to bring in a different kind of person. I felt I had done as much as I could do at the time with what I knew, even though for me. Continuous learning. It's a lifestyle. It's not I've learned this, I know how to do this, and I stop. It's I'm constantly learning. I'm learning how to manage my emotions, how to manage, how to interact with people, how to deal with difficult people, how to sell a new product, anything. Just keep learning something. First of all, it makes you interesting. You know, and that it's nice when you're interesting and it's nice when people sit with you and they learn something from you, you know, it makes you feel purposeful and useful, you know? It's good to always learn.

I can also see that continuity is an essential ingredient for survival and growth. Both Adenike and Fola spoke about the fact that while the Nigerian economy may have tanked globally, there is a vast domestic market to tap into. Along with UAC, which is a true Nigerian titan founded in 1886 and is now a major company with portfolios in animal feeds, real estate, paint, trucking and distribution. How do you reach that level with all the challenges of doing business in Africa? How do you get to the point where you're not only sustainable but also able to secure funding and build your own eco-system in an environment where many have sworn is impossible to do?

The clear response from all my roundtable guests was that the glue binding all this activity is the commitment to making it work in Africa, despite all the struggles and endemic corruption. Once a company achieves scale, it can make powerful and audacious moves, such as building factories, homes for workers, hospitals, and schools that drive the local economy.

I asked Adenike about her current thoughts on the manufacturing and tech spaces, and she was actually quite upbeat about how she views the future.

Demi: What do you think of Nigeria when you consider the future of manufacturing, threefold? And when you think about the future, taking the lessons you've learned along the way and the contributions you've made to the industry, where do you see Nigeria and Africa in terms of manufacturing in the near future? Let's say, over the next 50 years?

Adenike: You know, I think there's a huge opportunity ahead of us. I'm not a doom and gloom kind of soul. I'm an eternal optimist.

Demi: Do you know any entrepreneurs who are doom and gloom that have succeeded?

Adenike: No I don't. Besides which, I wouldn't hang out with low-energy people. I don't hang out with low-energy people. I like people who, you know, they see the possibilities. They see the opportunities. They have a can-do spirit, and they have that mindset that is expansive. Once you sit with people who are moaning and complaining all the time, it's contagious. It's a disease.

Demi: In some instances, maybe the way they describe Africans now.

Adenike: What has happened is the systematic breakdown of the educational system of Nigeria which has been a disservice to the young people of this country, a complete disservice. But you have the internet, you have access. There is nothing that should stop you. If you want to learn something, you will learn that thing and you will stand out with it. You don't need to learn it in a classroom.

All my guests were extremely concerned about finding skilled employees that would avoid bringing in expats to work. I questioned Folascope about how UAC sought out and retained talent.

Demi: What's your approach to talent? Is it we're bringing in the best from a global market or we are actively trying to breed and nurture local talent? What is UAC's standpoint on talent acquisition as a model for great business?

Fola: I would again say that it has changed over time with various CEOs, and I tried to run through things that I felt were consistent and not just relevant in the time I run the business. If I go back 40 years ago, UAC's approach was to go out and find the brightest young Nigerians. We had a huge training school and we would train these people and then put them into our businesses. It was taking very young talent and growing them. It was a very GE [General Electric] type of approach where you train people through their careers. You keep coming back and being trained and you're placed in roles across the group. Very centralised HR and organic talent development.

Demi: What year was that, would you say?

Fola: At least in the '80s, and it probably continued until the... it continued with increasing dilution until the mid...It's like 2013, '14, '15, but with increasing dilution. Because it's quite an expensive...it requires major infrastructure to keep that going. Then we went through an approach where we...as that got diluted, we went through this mismatch where you combine, you build some of your own talents and also you try and recruit where you can. But we were never the best payers. The best [salary] payers in Nigeria were always the banks, the management consulting firms. I would argue that that impacted our ability to attract tier-one talent. Then most recently in 2018, we went through quite meaningful management turnover. What we did was just go on a safe external recruitment drive to fill the gaps and then in parallel, just launch graduate trainee schemes to bring through our own talent. We found that...We almost went back to the core, went back to the core of the business, which is growing your own talent. But the difference here was that we don't do it centrally. Each of our businesses runs their own schemes because the culture, the idea that you need to produce and sell paints, animal feeds and so on and so forth. This is by far from a group perspective, there are very few things that we get involved. But hiring talent is one of the ones where we get involved. Talent is number one. We have a group head of turn strategy where we coordinate the approach to attracting and retaining talent. We get involved in what we call reviews of talent to make sure that we know who the best people in the company across the group are, we know who the worst people across the group are. We understand how our managers were launching an effective manager series to coach managers on doing reviews, giving talent opportunities, and that. We provide the tools and the quality assurance talent strategy for the operating companies execute.

Demi: Mrs O, we're at this inflection point where we are asking ourselves many questions such as, how do we sustain ourselves in the near future? What is your vision for Nigeria and Africa as a whole in terms of the training manufacturing skills? What do you imagine for Nigeria and Africa moving forward? And how do you think the skilled labour journey needs to be mapped out in order for it to be successful?

Adenike: I think the quality of the training in some cases, is not as good as it should be because, you know, everybody falls into this bandwagon of, I want to train, I want to train. What we do at Ruff 'n' Tumble is we bring 50 people in, we pay for their transport to come every day and we give them a food allowance. Of those 50 people, maybe we will shortlist only ten people that we can add to the to the pool. We're doing this throughout the year. It's not only about them having the skill. The technical skill is three things. It's also having a good character.

Demi: Every so often I worry about the ways in which we are exporting our raw materials out of Nigeria. If I were speaking to multinationals about the possibilities of them buying our raw materials I would make it mandatory that in exchange for that they would open their factories here, hire our locals and export their finished products from Nigeria.

Adenike: That's what I told one company who came to us and said, oh, they usually give it to people who can make it in Turkey. They go and make it. Do I know where my resources go? Yes, I know where my resources go. I make it emotional. You are a big enough company that should have a social conscience and recognise that you are actually robbing Nigeria of those jobs. And if you are robbing Nigeria of those jobs, what is the social implication of that? Young people all over the place with no work, nothing to do.

Demi: There is a high level of importation across [the] economy that we bring into Nigeria every day. Do you believe that our young people can provide services to these manufacturing industries easily?

Adenike: It will take time to get them because it's taken us time. It's taken me bringing in technical managers from Bangladesh, from all over the place to, to train our people because you pay $6,000 for a machine that is just doing one part of a shirt. It's that you actually have the skill and if you go in anyway, you can add value. And because you can add value, you will always receive value, that's what we do. For me Africa has to wake up. It is. The dawn is now. We have to wake up from slumber. We have to rescue our continent.

I definitely share the point of view of Adenike, and I believe the manufacturing sector must also awaken and then make a bigger statement about its successes and how we can be a massive job generator. The cost of importing expats becomes unsustainable, and just as the Lee Group representative pointed out, and if Africa is your home, [you are] more committed to working through all the issues and making it work. The tech sector, music sector are all seeing a big increase in employment, and I asked Iyinoluwa about his investment issues with his new group called Future Africa.

Demi: Iyinoluwa, what does the next ten, twenty years look like for you? Now you're taking on real challenges. What does it look like for you in the next few years? How do you feel that those decisions for you are going to play into Africa overall?

Iyinoluwa: It's very hard to talk about the next ten, twenty years. The reality of the last ten years is I feel like God was really preparing us. It's like a demo, you know, it's like a demo tape. Everyone's hailing you for your demo tape, LP, I think you call it an EP. You know, I feel like we just released an EP album, you know, and everyone's like, 'Oh wow, that's such a brand-new sound.' Now that we have quite a number of things that are falling into place, we can do the work now to build things at scale, you know what I mean? We have a very supportive leader of the ecosystem, I mean, in the government. We have a country that is poised to grow. We have an economic situation where all the things we've been saying for the last ten years are now gospel, truth. We need to focus on talent. Productivity is the way to go. Connectivity needs to be cheaper. We need to be more productive on food supply and on things outside of just software. Everything we've been saying for the last ten years is almost now true as of right now. So, the question that we, I, ask myself all the time is, given that reality, what should we do? I think it's the question we have to answer over the next ten years. How do we take the things that we've built and try and get them to national scale?

Demi: Absolutely. I think I always ask myself this question every day, is how do you get people to work? How do you get them work and how do you get them productive? You know, we can't teach everybody to be developers. Everybody can't be a developer where there are so many skills in so many sectors required for collective growth.

Iyinoluwa: I think it's to show people where they can work.

Demi: Where do you see Nigeria going in the next ten years, possibly in terms of other industries? What are the industries you think we could create?

Iyinoluwa: We've got a lot of room. You know a lot of what's happened over the last five years is that a lot of the barriers to productivity in a lot of industries have come down. So, you know, I'd love to see more Nigerian companies tap into that space.

Demi: Which particular space?

Iyinoluwa: The space of many spaces. But let me be more specific. You think about things like healthcare. What can technology help us do to reduce the cost of healthcare? You think about education. What can technology help us do to reduce the costs and increase the outcomes with education? We think about things like renewable energy, agriculture, and how we make our food, like transport. Each of these pieces you can identify very useful innovations that have transformed that space that just need to be scaled across the continent.

Demi: Folascope. We are now in 2024, I imagine that [at] UAC, with any other organisation who is very intentional about their growth and their business, direction is something that you guys are always reviewing and taking stock of. What do you hope to still achieve with everything that you guys have done since the 1800s? Where is the hunger for you guys now and what's fuelling that hunger?

Fola: The hunger for us, I'd say, is growth, where next year we're gearing up for it to be a mouse to the ear for us who want to grow. We want to aggressively scale the business. And it comes from I would say a number of places. One is there's the legacy. We're custodians of a 100-plus-year-old business, and so one of the things we try to do is to ensure 100 years from now, the company is still there and we have one small chapter in the company story. We don't want to be the management team that ended the company. It happens very often. That's one. Second is we feel that Nigeria is, but we know, Nigeria is extremely difficult. The way we describe it internally is that if you're on the tracks and there's a moving train, you have two options: outsprint the train or jump off the track. Let's say we're not doing Nigeria again and we're selling and moving to I don't know where, but as long as we're here, we think we need to grow aggressively. The third is that we have a very high-quality team and a very ambitious bunch of people. They're one of the surest ingredients to retain and keeping those people happy is growing the business. Those are the fuels.

The opportunities are there because its got companies like UAC that have really stuck through the test of time and they're doing well. Is it funding? Is it a network? Is it a system? What is it? I've interviewed a series of people for my book and I'm trying to gain from them just nuggets that have just contributed to their success…

There is so much to chew on and I hope these brief sections for full interviews allow the reader some valuable insights into exactly what is happening on the ground, in Nigeria and in Africa. The future? I loved Iyinoluwa's description, 'the space of many spaces', and given the explosive population demographics in Africa and in particular, Nigeria, this fact compounds the problems, with more and more people chasing for scarcer resources, but it also creates a potential for a gigantic local marketplace that must be tapped into. I've suggested throughout my book, entrepreneurs must lead the way in job training and development.

To close this chapter, I'm giving the last word to Adenike, who I feel has built a classic bootstrapping company from scratch, in the children's clothing and manufacturing space. Self- taught and self-made, she is always looking forward, but with her feet firmly planted in African soil.

Demi: Mrs O, what are your thoughts on Nigeria's and Africa's future?

Adenike: If you look into the whole wide world, Nigerians are doing some of the most amazing things all over the world in science, in agriculture, in medicine, in banking, in technology; name an industry there is a Nigerian in their top ten. He or she is there. And some of them went to university in Nigeria, by the way. Some of them went to University of Lagos. What went wrong? We've all been driven to be in survival mode. People are trying to survive. And when people are trying to survive, there's very little innovation that can come out of that space. But if you think about some of the things that are coming out of Nigeria at this point in time. Music, fashion, technology, fintech, the movies, the content, the things people are building.

Demi: But a lot of people are almost brain-dead from the hardship of daily survival and they can't take on anything else because all they just want to do is survive. When people start fainting on the road because they ate two days ago, that's a bad sign. We need to put money into things that serve the people. Things that are in the best interest of the majority of the people, not a few. And we need to get to that place really quickly. We need to awaken the consciousness, the thinking.

Adenike: My generation is responsible. We were all in survival mode and got into businesses and left a whole different set of people to go into politics, forgetting that they would, in fact turn round to make the choices and decisions that would affect our lives. So, I feel we have a warped system and I feel like our system isn't working. I feel that as a people we are incredible. We are a cocktail of many colourful cultures, from all the different parts of Nigeria. This is my country. This is the country that has blessed me. This is the country that made me who I am. I can never curse it. You get more of what you say. Remember the power of the spoken word. What are you speaking into existence in your life? When you sit down and curse the country that you are in? How will it bless you?

Demi: By creating a new narrative?

Adenike: Yes, why don't we create a new narrative? For a powerful, colourful, cultural Nigeria and the young people who are doing it. And that's why I love the young people, they're doing [it] in fashion, furniture, music. You can go to a nightclub anywhere in the world and you hear Nigerian music, even in hotel lobbies. They play Nigerian music in restaurants. What does that mean? What does that say about who we are? We have so much we can export.

Demi: We have a captivated global audience. What do we do with that?

Adenike: The potential and the possibilities of this country are limitless. You need to be able to see beyond. You have to elevate your thinking and elevate your consciousness into a place where it can create. As opposed to a place where nothing is good.

***

I want to personally thank Mrs O, Folascope, Iyinoluwa for coming forward and discussing their successes, struggles and how they see the future of not only manufacturing in Africa, but as Mrs O so eloquently said, we need to create a new narrative for a new generation of Cheetahs, Titans, Movers and Shakers.

As I've mentioned at the top of this chapter, the full interviews are available on the website and SUSU podcast on YouTube, and I urge all readers to listen to their compelling voices.

'Majeurs' Lessons   12

To learn from failure, however, you have to 'own' it. You have to figure out what went wrong and what to do better next time. If you don't, you're liable to repeat your errors in the future.

—Tom Kelley and David Kelley, authors of *Creative Confidence*

Well, you've got a very unique business. You know Nigeria is the type of market where these things don't exist, and there are people looking for it every day. You might just find that Nigeria just might be the break that you need—and a new start—a new opportunity. Have you ever thought about taking your business to Nigeria?

—Chinedu Igbokwe

Failure, Fear and Family

Many people I've encountered over the years, funders, friends and family, have asked me:

Demi, why on earth did you leave London—you were building a tidy business with a steady clientele, and had become a minor celebrity? You've chatted to the now King of England as he sat on one of your Chesterfields. You were asked by former Prime Minister David Cameron to restore a leather chair that belonged to Winston Churchill at 10 Downing Street. Why would you pack all this up to move to Nigeria?

DOI: 10.4324/9781003453994-12

For many young entrepreneurs with this burst of energy would take this as a literal launching pad to commercial success in an extremely difficult market. If I had followed that path, I'm sure I would be a major player in furniture, design and restoration in the UK. Access to capital, emergency funding, relatively inexpensive workshop space and a trained labour force would make everyday operations and high-level business decisions easier.

You see, staying in the UK after all that attention and success could have opened up a world of opportunities for my career in furniture manufacturing and restoration. The access to talent, although expensive, would have been unparalleled. I could have easily tapped into the best minds and skilled artisans in the industry, right at my fingertips.

In the UK, I would have been in an environment where excellence was not just encouraged, but expected. It's a place where craftsmanship is highly valued, and I would have been challenged to continuously improve and deepen my knowledge. Unlike Nigeria, where I sometimes felt like an expert in a sea of mediocrity, in the UK, I would have had to remain focused in my pursuit of excellence.

I believe that if I had stayed in the UK, my skill set would have expanded significantly within these last seven years, and I would have learned at an accelerated pace because of the significant number of hours I have dedicated to my work non-stop. However, whether the UK would have given me more in return is a question that's harder to answer. The UK market is undoubtedly competitive, but with the right talent and resources, I could have continued to make a name for myself and my business, possibly positioning myself as more of a designer than a manufacturer. It's a path not taken, but one that I occasionally wonder about, as I continue my work here in Nigeria, teaching others what I have been fortunate enough to learn in the last 14 years of my journey.

In many ways, I had all the pieces fall my way. There was interest and intrigue in my choices, and being in demand and having that X-factor with clients, media and friends is certainly nothing to sneeze at. I was able to make a very feisty little company in a very niche market work for me and my partner.

The company had a name, a business account and full legal status— Majeurs Chesterfield (as we were formally known). I, along with my partner, poured in buckets of sweat equity, literally hauling old wrecks up the stairs to our studio and showroom, and spent thousands of hours rebuilding and reupholstering sofas and leather chairs. We had become one of the successful startups. We had bought, sold, restored and resold, a lot of great furniture pieces.

Don't get me wrong, I am not one to complain, but I believe that every entrepreneur needs to clearly understand this lesson, that failure, and failing, is perhaps one of the greatest fears we face and this can act as a personal weight, particularly if it is not confronted early on.

Five important and difficult lessons to consider:

- First and foremost, you don't need to be an expert to be an entrepreneur.
- When possible, find other people with expertise—professionals, like accountants, lawyers or other competent and *trusted* family, friends or colleagues who know what they are doing.
- Perfection is not your friend, in fact, it can hinder you from moving forward.
- One of the hardest lessons I've learned is to let things go and embrace iterations as you grow. I can state this fact with confidence, *nobody starts out on the top of their game.*
- Always seek advice. I cannot emphasise this enough. There are always other people, sometimes family members or even distant relatives or colleagues, who can offer their thoughts and guidance. Don't let fear of failure take hold, because a good advisor or friend will offer plenty of options that you can choose from.

There are literally hundreds of books about entrepreneurship that focus on how to be a success, and how to attain a successful career. However, these books rarely teach the most critical aspect of building a new business, and that should be one of the first lessons. What is your exit plan? In fact, it was a lesson that I had to confront in my own career as an entrepreneur.

The following short story illustrates many of these hard lessons learned and the big reason why I decided to relocate my business to Nigeria. It is also a deeply personal story but sets out clearly for readers about seeking and listening to advice and also having an exit plan.

Leaving London and Finding Nigeria: A Short Story

It was a cold day in November. It felt as though summer was years ago. I've been sitting here for hours, the heating just never seemed to be hot enough. What the hell am I doing? What is this? Constantly struggling with this business, and no idea how I got to this point. No more staff, no more work coming in, yet I'm swamped with work. This contract I collected a couple of months ago is still on my case. I'm still putting in hours through the night to finish these pieces of furniture. I've already spent the money. No new work coming in and I still have to deliver on the work. It's been months since I've had a very strong contract come in, and I think I've lost my mojo.

'What am I doing?' I keep asking myself over and over again. It's the dead of the night. I'm in a studio all by myself. In the middle of covering this chair I just burst out crying—confused, lonely, tired. [Sigh] *Should I just give up? Should I just call it a day...?*

My partner left me—well, we shouldn't say he left me. He left the business...I guess we did break up after all. We'd started the business together and here I am by myself—doing this all on my own. He'd been doing the heavy lifting between the two of us. I've been struggling for eight months now, carrying these things by myself. I do wonder if I took him for granted when he'd carry these heavy pieces of furniture up these stairs. It wasn't as though I didn't help, of course I did. But with him carrying the bulk of it, I just didn't realise how heavy these things were until he left.

God it's cold in here. Who do I call? These days it seems like my friends are not reachable anymore. Well, I only have myself to blame, because for so many years I was unreachable. Now they've gotten into the habit of not hearing from me, so why should I be surprised by not hearing from them. [Long sigh] *This is so frustrating. Should I go home?* Probably not because I've got to be here early in the morning again. If I drive all the way home again, by the time I get to sleep, I'll only get about five hours of sleep, and I have to come straight back. I guess it's going to be another night spent in the studio.

I close my laptop and I go lay down—I've got a large piece of furniture in the showroom that I usually take a nap on. I cry myself to sleep.

The following day I get a call. It's barely 9:30 in the morning. Uncle Chinedu is calling me.

Why is Uncle Chinedu is calling me? Why is he calling so early? I hope nothing has happened? Are the kids OK? Is he OK, he never calls this early. What's going on?

He was married to my sister who passed away several years prior. It seems that since she died we've gotten so much closer. Maybe because of my business. He is the person I usually go to cry, and moan and complain, and financially he's just been a godsend. The last dry spell we had in business, he lent me £5000 and just told me to take it in my stride and not to put much pressure on myself. I'd gone crying to him, lamenting how difficult things have been, and why I started this business. I didn't want to give up then...I just needed a little help. And he did—he really helped. He saved me with the £5000 and told me if I needed anything to not hesitate to come back.

This morning he is calling me. I hesitate to answer initially and then as the phone stops ringing, I tell myself to immediately call him back just in case there was an emergency. Why am I scared? Surely the sooner I find out the better off.

I call him back immediately. My voice is hesitant, but also very anxious.

'Uncle Chinedu', I say, 'Good morning, Is everything OK?'

'Oh yes, yes, yes, of course everything is fine. I'm just checking in on you. You know the last time I spoke with you—you seemed quite down. Is everything OK with you? How's everything going, I take it you're at work already?'

'Oh, yes I'm here.'

I didn't tell him that I'd spent the night here again. I think he could hear in my voice that something was wrong, yet again.

'Demi, you're OK?, I hope you're not working too hard again. I told you just take your time. Take each day at a time. Business is not easy.'

'But really Uncle Chinedu, I'm trying. I really am trying, but sometimes I just don't know what to do…'

He cuts me off mid-sentence.

'Are you free tomorrow, shall we meet for lunch?'

I was so broke these days and lunch with him was rather fancy most times—I didn't hesitate to say, 'Of course, what time?'

'Well just meet me at work, at twelve noon.'

'Yeah, sure, see you then. '

The very next day I don't hesitate. I start working a little earlier in the morning. I grab my things and I jump on the nearest train. I make my way to London Bridge. Uncle Chinedu worked for the government—he worked for the mayor's office which for me was huge. After all, how many people did I know who worked for the government and for that matter in the mayor's office? I was so impressed every time I went there.

I waited outside for him and called to let him know that I was here. I sat on the nearest bench and I saw him walk out of the building. I just looked him and thought to myself, *Wow*. We weren't this close when my sister was still alive, but I really appreciate having him in my corner. I really do.

Every time I told him about business, I knew he wasn't necessarily a businessman himself, but he seemed to want to understand. I could tell him anything—any struggle, any worry, any self-doubt. He always set me back on the straight and narrow. I was hoping today wasn't going to be any different.

As he approached, I tried to put on a brave face. He didn't buy it. He just hugged me and just gestured that we go to the nearest restaurant. As I walked by his side, hands in my pockets, clearly cold, because by this time of the year the UK weather had gotten into my bones…I was just sick and tired. I didn't know what I was more tired of, business in terms of state of affairs or the British weather. It just seemed to be getting worse for me year by year.

I'd always lived here, I grew up here. Why was the weather so difficult for me to just acclimatise to? I've always hated winter, and every winter I despised it a little bit more.

We get into the restaurant and I sigh out of relief. It's warm in there. I immediately move to where the sunlight is, because with sunlight I get a little bit of heat. I gestured for Uncle Chinedu to sit on the shady side. I think he appreciated that.

As we sat down and went through the menu, I found him staring at me.

He began by asking me questions:

'What's going on? Why do you look like this? Are you sleeping, are you resting?'

I try to put on a brave face and just pretend, 'Oh no, no, no, I just didn't get enough hours last night.'

He knew I was lying. I'd been putting in long nights back-to-back, and he knew it. As I began lamenting to him yet again about how things were getting more and more confusing for me.

He cut straight to the chase, 'Is it because Toks has left?'

I looked at him a little bit shocked and tried to fight back the tears. I knew he was right. There was a part of me that missed him. I missed him dreadfully, not just because the relationship over the last eight years had come to an end, but because I no longer had the help with the business I used to have…

I was now all on my own, and the reality had set in. It's difficult running a business. I needed a partner in crime. Somebody who you can always turn to, who stood right beside you. To now finding yourself alone. Having nobody to rely on but yourself. And then the hours, those long hours. My companion was gone. All on my own, I couldn't just help the weight, the responsibility, all on my shoulders.

I told him, 'I don't know…I don't know if it's because Toks is gone…well I guess I'm sad that he's gone, but at the same time, I feel as if I've lost my mojo, my drive, the thing that pushed me every day…the passion for this…I still love what I do, of course but something is different…I just don't feel content anymore.'

Before I could utter my next set of words, he said to me, 'Have you ever thought about going to Nigeria?'

I looked at him a little bit shocked, 'Nigeria, for what?'

'Well, you've got a very unique business. You know Nigeria has a type of market where these things don't exist, and there are people looking for them every day. You might find that Nigeria could be the break that you need—and a new start—a new opportunity. Have you ever thought about taking your business to Nigeria?'

I believe it was the first time he said those words aloud to himself, and from the look on his face, he also looked like he was shocked by his own words.

Hmm, Nigeria, I was a bit confused... *Does this man understand a word about what I'm saying?*

Did I think he was sympathising with me, but really deep down he wasn't really listening.

What on earth does Nigeria have to do with what we're discussing, my mind told me.

With confusion and a hint of annoyance at his lack of understanding of my frustration I said, 'Nigeria is the last place on my mind, Uncle Chinedu. I have no history there. I have no understanding, the last time I was in Nigeria I hated it.'

'Hated it?' he said.

'Yes, I hated it, all we kept doing was going from one auntie's house to [one] uncle's house, to church—to one boring event after another. Nothing fun. Nigeria is dead, there is nothing there, and furthermore, what on earth would I do in Nigeria. I don't know anybody. All my extended family that I met there practically all live in the UK now. Nigeria is not really for me.'

'Hmm, you're probably speaking to soon. Have you ever experienced Nigeria as an adult? You know it's very different,' he said.

'Oh really?' I said. 'Oh maybe, maybe one day, but for now I really need to focus on my business.'

We proceed to order and eat, and it was a fantastic meal. I felt a little more relief having spent the afternoon with him. But something in my brain was dreading that I'd have to go straight back to work. After all, I still had a deadline to meet.

I gave him a hug and I left.

★★★

I felt better as I jumped back on the train, and still felt better when I got back to the workshop. I just continued, working, working and working for the next three days.

But something in my mind kept going back to that idea of Nigeria. Nigeria! What could I possibly do in Nigeria? *What could Nigeria possibly offer me,* my mind kept asking? Eventually that thought disappeared and I was back focused on what I was doing again.

★★★

Until that day…that day, when my heater broke. I was doing a long day again in the workshop. Wearing several layers just to get by. The heater was on and I felt relatively comfortable, until all of a sudden the cold hit me again. I turned around. The heater was plugged in, but for some strange reason it was blowing cold air? I should check the socket.

I made a sound of frustration and I went over to find out what was wrong with this bloody heater. I bend down, I turn off, I turn on…nothing happened. On turning it back on it's still blowing cold air.

After five minutes of it being ON, I'm frustrated, I'm angry and I kick the bloody thing out of anger. I sit back at my desk, pulling at my jacket and my layers to stay as warm as possible. I try and find another heater that I may have that I didn't know about. I'm clearly going crazy, because I knew very well that I only had one heater, but the frustration was getting the better of me.

I sat at my desk and I began to cry. It didn't last very much this time though…

Then it came again…Nigeria.

Nigeria's hot, isn't it, my mind said.

Surely, I wouldn't have to deal with this cold for a couple of weeks, if I do as Chinedu said.

If I went to Nigeria, it would be to investigate of course. It's not a holiday. I'm strictly going for business opportunities. I want to go and understand what he meant by my products would do well in Nigeria.

I sat with that thought longer this time, my mind calculating, how and when. Will I even have the opportunity to leave this freezing studio?

By the end of that day, I had decided yes, I am indeed going to Nigeria, but first I must finish this set of deliveries.

I apply myself. I buckle down. After five days I made the delivery to the client.

I got another call for another job, but I quickly said to them that delivery time right now is a little bit extended. They said that they were in no hurry. That meant that I could go to Nigeria and come back and still have plenty of time to complete the job.

I take the order, I take the deposit and begin to make my plans to go to Nigeria.

★★★

The takeaways from my story are numerous, and I would hope they pro-voke plenty of questions, but offer the central idea that often gets glossed over. I cannot emphasise this fact strongly enough. If there is someone close to you who has a far better idea of how to structure your life, listen and accept that they may be totally right.

I was obviously at a very low point in my life, despite the appearance of success, without getting into a territory that I have no expertise in and that is, how do you gauge your own happiness? If your choices and work are not fulfilling and you lose your mojo to begin each and every day, then you must make hard choices. I was privileged to have had a very attentive family member, who was able to admit the truth, and although it landed like a bombshell at the time, this famous lunch with my brother-in-law Uncle Chinedun is the turning point in my life.

Exit Plans, Failing Again and Again, Until...

Uncle Chinedu's wisdom and deep pockets helped facilitate my eventual move to Nigeria. I in fact didn't drop everything like a lightning bolt had struck me, but allowed the idea to percolate and grow on me.

It was obvious to me that if I moved to Nigeria and brought my business with me as Chinedun had suggested, it would take some time and I needed to really find out if there was real opportunity there, and who would have better information about what was actually happening on the ground in terms of furniture manufacturing, design.

It is hard to believe as I write these words, but it has in fact been seven years since I moved to a new continent and culture to build my own factory with a dedicated team of 30 male and female employees. Where has the time gone? We have directly trained 96 people, hired over 125 individuals over the years and learned some hard lessons. As I write this the hard lessons are still in the making.

I can't say that Nigeria feels completely like home yet, but it certainly feels closer to home than London. There are moments where I feel that, *If not Nigeria then where else?*

If truth be told, I still have the feeling like I am not fully settled because in the last seven years I have simply not had a moment to stop and immerse myself into the 'being present' phase. I have been fighting for survival in a culture that doesn't want me to remain the way I arrived (foreign). Nigeria has a way of consuming you, invading your identity, urging and insisting on you relinquishing everything you once knew to assume a new identity. I have not.

Since relocating to Lagos, I frequently shifted from one workshop to another, and I'll openly admit that I've made costly mistakes along the way. By 'iterations,' I mean that I've made multiple attempts and adjustments, often leading to unnecessary expenses. Moving itself is expensive, and the costs extend beyond mere financial transactions.

These expenses encompass various aspects, such as the downtime in production, unforeseen variables causing disruptions, disorganisation during transitions and the need for people to resettle in new environments. All these factors add up to lost funds and excessive spending.

There have been instances when we've had to redo tasks two or three times because we initially lacked a complete understanding of the complexities involved. We've made hiring decisions that didn't align with our needs, made regrettable investments and spent money on items that, in hindsight, were not essential. These experiences have taught us valuable lessons.

As a result, today our approach revolves around meticulous review and careful consideration of every decision. We weigh the pros and cons thoroughly, questioning whether there are more cost-effective alternatives available. We ask ourselves, 'Are there better, less expensive options?' and explore different approaches to problem-solving. It's a conscious effort to avoid simply throwing money at every challenge we encounter.

However, the one thing I have done extremely well is continually getting better year after year. The lesson learned from running a business in London, is certainly being nimble, and always having a plan and a budget for contingencies.

My biggest takeaways: listen and heed to the advice when it is offered. You cannot bootstrap forever, unless you don't need or want a personal life.

My Uncle Chinedu's advice was right on the money, 'I told you just take your time. Take each day at a time. Business is not easy.'

HR and Making It Work

I made one of my initial mistakes by not hiring HR personnel sooner. Looking back, if I were to start the business anew, my approach would be different. I would prioritise hiring HR and accounting professionals, and perhaps even a Chief of Staff. I used to believe I had to do everything on my own—manage the staff, build the product—but 've learned that building a strong team is fundamental to success.

In hindsight, my first moves were instrumental in shaping the business. My very first hire was a seasoned carpenter. With the assistance of my uncle, I located a workshop in the heart of Surulere. Fortunately, the workshop was next door to an old building undergoing renovation and available for rent. I quickly secured it, even in its unfinished state, and established it as my live-in office and workshop.

I assembled a team for sales and marketing, and together, we began seeking potential clients. My living quarters transitioned from my bedroom to the living room, which was adjacent to the office. This small two-bedroom house became the epicentre of my business operations. In many ways, it was akin to a neighbourhood where I lived and worked.

This location was far from glamorous—a smelly gutter ran in front of my driveway, there was no gate and no security. However, to me, the workshop was a gift. It allowed me to be both at home and oversee all the work happening in one place, all while avoiding the notorious Lagos traffic each day.

During those early months in the workshop, I was still in the process of training the carpenters on how I wanted the work to be executed. This setup afforded me the ability to demonstrate and instruct without the constant back-and-forth of site visits. It was during this time that their respect for me solidified. They came to understand that I knew precisely what I was talking about and doing.

These humble beginnings and the time spent in that workshop played a crucial role in building a strong foundation for my business and fostering a sense of mutual respect and understanding among the team. In the midst of all this chaos, our very first sofa emerged—a classic three-seater brown tweed sofa with traditional Chesterfield scroll arms, made especially for my cousin.

Looking back at that initial year in the Surulere ghetto, I can't help but think how different things might have been with the support of an HR professional and an accountant by my side.

Having a dedicated HR personnel and a financial expert would have significantly reduced the stress of managing our rapidly growing team. It would have spared me from the countless emotional breakdowns I experienced while trying to navigate the vast landscape of things I simply didn't know. I persisted, relying on my resilience, and stood firm when my staff suggested that an item was 'good enough' for delivery, insisting that my standards couldn't be compromised.

The frustration of not being understood by them and struggling to understand them, in turn, often left me in tears and restless nights. I needed structure, systems and assistance to bridge the communication gap and ensure that our shared vision and standards were upheld.

***

A major topic for entrepreneurs is hiring. It sounds simple but it is actually quite complex. My advice: *hire with care*. When I wanted to hire, I began by taking on a carpenter. I took to the streets for several weeks before landing on my first carpenter. Mr. Afisiru, a middle-aged Muslim man who was introduced to me by a man whom I met through my uncle. My uncle had dabbled in furniture making several years back and still stayed in contact with his old furniture maker friends. On hearing that I had moved to Nigeria to build my own furniture brand he had much to say by way of advice, and made some introductions. He was intrigued by my interest but couldn't understand why I would leave England to pursue something as demeaning to him as carpentry.

Nonetheless, he supported me and made the introductions. One thing I have learned about Nigeria is that there is immense value in introductions. This cultural and business lesson of being able to hold people accountable by the relationships that connected you to them.

> My advice: lean heavy on introductions in all areas of your start up when it comes to hiring, it goes a long way at the beginning and throughout. Whether you are introduced through your personal network or through an agency, always take the time to put the right people together to hire and access talent.

After several introductions, I finally settled for the carpenter who I could trace back to others. He treated me immediately like family and was willing to work with me on my terms. Through him we hired several more carpenters and thus my first team of six staff was made.

After all, I am in the furniture business, and what better way than to find the skilled hands that make everything come together...right?

Well, HR and hiring, it always sounds easier than you think, and in my case I was somewhat naïve, but here are some basic starter questions that you must consider either asking a potential candidate or should form part of an application form. These questions of course shift between positions, like management and workforce, but nevertheless these can act as a basic guide. Some of these are more Lagos- and Nigeria-specific, as cultural and real-world issues also must be discussed and contended with.

I can almost guarantee that you will make mistakes, but if you heed my note about hiring with care, then you can always say to yourself after, well at least I was warned.

Top Ten Questions to Ask Your Candidates

Over the years I have discovered that our culture must be intentional and we must hire to fit that culture. So here are some culture-fit questions I ask all new hires before they join us.

Customer Obsession & Ownership and Accountability

Scenario: You have just finished a high-priority project for a valued customer. However, you realise there's a minor flaw in the finished product that the customer is unlikely to notice immediately. What would you do?

Simplify and Innovate & Bias for Action

Scenario: Your team is using an outdated process that is reliable but time-consuming. A new software solution could simplify this but comes with some risks. Your manager is on vacation. What do you do?

Strive to Be Earth's Steward & Document and Demonstrate Contribution

Scenario: You notice that the team is using materials that are not eco-friendly, though they are cost-effective. You also realise this could be documented for future sustainability reports. What's your approach?

Professional Communication

Scenario: Imagine you're writing an email to a vendor, and they have repeatedly failed to meet delivery timelines. How would you address this issue in the email?

Willingness to Assist Coworkers

Scenario: A coworker asks for your help on a project that's not part of your job description but aligns with your skills. You have a tight deadline on your own project. What do you do?

Timeliness

Scenario: You're stuck in Lagos traffic and realise you will be late for an important meeting. What would be your course of action?

Office Gossip

Scenario: You overhear colleagues gossiping about a manager's alleged favouritism. What would you do?

Adaptability

Scenario: Your manager assigns you a task that requires you to stay late, disrupting your personal plans. How would you handle this?

Openness to New Challenges

Scenario: You're offered a new assignment that you've never done before. You feel a bit out of your depth. What would be your reaction?

Professional Appearance

Scenario: It's your first week at the job. How would you choose your attire?

Approach to Mistakes

Scenario: You've made an error in a client project that has caused a delay. How would you handle it?

Teamwork in Production

Scenario: Your production team is falling behind schedule. The team lead asks for suggestions to improve efficiency. What would you do?

Team-building and Chemistry

Easy to write but difficult to do for most first-time entrepreneurs. In an ideal scenario, my first thought. I might agree that the first person to hire would be a trained and expertly skilled HR person, who can carry out your hiring plans. However, for first-time small entrepreneurs, who are just starting to scale up their business, normally you want a workforce to build the product or create the service that will be generate positive income. So that the all-important positive cash flow is in fact doing that—starting to flow. Therefore, the first hire in my case was a skilled carpenter.

I also remind entrepreneurs to resist the urge to leap in. Focus on the structure in order for the flow to be smooth and consistent moving forward. Think of your HR and accounts as your partners in crime from the outset. If the budget is not there, then HR must have an accountant or bookkeeper that can be outsourced.

In a massive jump I went from a one person company to two, and often the first hire will set the tone for the following hire as your company grows.

Expectations

I firmly believe that expectations should be stated from the very beginning, so that your potential hire is fully informed, and that there is implicit agreement that the candidate can understand every request and in turn abide by the company HR rules. I've included the webpage where you can find "The Little Book of Majeurs" which focuses on our company culture. Perhaps it will inspire you to create your own: www.demisamande.com/books/the-little-book-of-majeurs.

These expectations, values and rules can be adapted to various industries, but I believe that they clearly lay out expectations, communications, between the team and management, and more critically what is the work culture.

I later learned that in order to build a team, it helps to establish expectations and *set goals for the entire team*. I needed to learn how to create specific tasks and then learn how they are to be managed. I was a rookie, but always willing to learn, adjust and adapt. The most vital lesson that I will discuss in this chapter is how clarity and direct approaches to employees will help a great deal.

Employee engagement is essential and it is something I've strived to improve on every day as my business in Lagos has expanded to 30 employees.

Please note that this book would never have been possible to write without the entire team who has worked with us over the years. We are eternally grateful to every individual who has contributed to our growth. Those who have taught me extremely difficult lessons in leadership and helped me to improve my Yoruba from comprehension to conversational level.

This booklet is given to every employee, and it has course evolved over the years, but the basic premise is laid out for everyone to respond to: clear expectations, plus bold communication, plus respect, plus dynamic human-centred company culture equals a strong and dynamic team and a successful commercial enterprise. You will note that it is also full of humour and good-will, which at this company is essential to get through the day, with the umpteenth power blackout.

The Academy and Looking Forward

13

The Future is Africa. This bold statement reflects what I actually see on the ground, and the energy of youth and desire to use their hands and minds and really transform the continent into a global manufacturing hub.

The biggest advantage for anyone considering building a factory in Africa is the abundance of low-cost labour. However, our workforce is generally lacking in skills and, therefore, efficiency. This central issue is the number one hindrance to growth and investment, especially in more specialised areas of manufacturing and production.

There are some grim statistics to grasp that relate to education, Only two-thirds of 15–24 year olds in Africa have completed a primary education, which is roughly 20 per cent less than the world average, with less than one-in-five students continuing beyond primary school. These stats of course don't include the desire quotient of a hungry, determined young workforce. If the future is African manufacturing, then the first step is re-education, and creating the ground where workers can attain and create a massive shift out of the cycle of poverty and corruption and actually build an aspiration to build a middle class. This may sound Pollyannish to some, but in fact there are so many terrific stories that actually have what they call in America 'Rags to Riches.'

***

What are the pressing needs that most businesses large and small must confront? If I took a poll of every owner in medium and larger manufacturing and service businesses in Africa, 100 per cent of them will all respond, almost in unison, that the biggest and pressing need is for a trained, skilled and motivated workforce.

DOI: 10.4324/9781003453994-13

The question remains. If they get trained or upskilled, what are the options for young people to find skilled work?

In a highly mechanised business, such as furniture manufacturing and design, finding carpenters who can safely and expertly operate power tools is a big problem. Certainly, in the early stages of establishing the factory, I was unable to locate sufficiently qualified workers, which is a big headache for many companies like my own, we have resorted to importing skilled foreign workers.

This solution in the end is never ideal, because the added value diminishes as salaries, skills and steady employment leave the country and cause the costs of both goods and services to escalate.

I'm very adamant when I state that importing foreign skilled workers is not ideal nor is it sustainable and that the most positive and immediate action is that in Africa we must begin investing in intensive training of skills for these young people.

This chapter could be described as a call to action for investors, government policymakers and consumers that in Africa we are on the cusp of a gigantic manufacturing explosion.

However, we must learn from those who have already created a trained and skilled workforce, and then invest in their business ideas both large and small. Essentially, learn from those lessons and build upon them that make sense for Africa. I ask investors, where are those willing to bet on Africa as it is? And prevail?

★★★

'Big Ideas' in Africa often get marred by the myriad of problems it faces that are not front-page news. Many very good ideas get dropped or pushed back or shelved because the funding they require is just not there. There is also an overreliance on aid, particularity when it comes to health and education, and despite the millions of dollars, pounds and euros poured into African countries to support children and young adults, the actual verifiable results of educating and training the next generation is pretty abysmal.

This is not new nor is it provocative to reiterate what many economists like George Ayittey[1] have been writing about African functional illiteracy for many years, and his stinging words ring true. He quotes the Nigerian scholar Bayo Awokoya, writing in *African News Weekly* (26 August–1 September 1996, page 23):

> It is a sad commentary to call Nigerians 'the most unintelligent intellectuals on the face of the planet.' Although Nigerians are an academically brilliant group of people according to the US State

Department, applying 'book knowledge' to real-life issues and dilemmas has been a big problem for Africans and Nigerians in particular.

So then, if the top strata of African business and government elite society are basically functionally illiterate in terms of solving real-world problems, and they are actually running governments, education systems, schools, customs and tax collecting, power companies, where does the new working class who are looking to solve 'local problems and challenges find practical skills, like operating power tools, design techniques, upholstery finishing, packaging, all skills that manufacturers desperately need.

Yes, it is critical that Africans continue to train and invest in training doctors, lawyers, nurses, engineers, diplomats and the myriad of other professions to support the modernisation of Africa.

What I have noted, however, is that the stratum of educated elites receives the lion share of attention and support, and I'm not attempting to denigrate their success, but the voices of entrepreneurs are being mostly ignored. The irony is that almost every African manufacturer needs to have a skilled workforce, not only that creates good paying jobs for the vast underemployed, non-employed youth, but that creates all the massive socio-economic benefits of having a steady job. The first step out of poverty is often going back to school and getting upskilled.

As you can read in my opening of this chapter I've enumerated a lot of frustrations with the Nigerian education system and its failures. That is why in 2022, I along with my team at Majeurs, proposed prototyping and starting up a training academy. Below is our initial Curriculum Statement.

Majeurs Academy Guidelines and Curriculum Statement

Facts To Consider

Nigeria's Furniture Industry: The furniture industry in Nigeria is currently valued at 50 billion naira. This makes the furniture-making industry a very lucrative business opportunity and landscape. However, the potential in this industry remains largely untapped, viz: small-scale production, manual processes, the lack of machinery and technical know-how, poor finishing, the use of substandard materials, etc. Majeurs Holdings recognises this huge opportunity. After operating in the industry for over 13 years—serving different clients in Nigeria and the diaspora, it desires to train young people to be well-positioned for the abundant opportunities in the industry and to become successful in it. This is the rationale behind Majeurs Academy offering a training programme that solves all the challenges mentioned above. Our training programme and teaching methodology offer a huge opportunity to anyone who desires to tap into the full potential of the furniture-making industry. Being a part of the academy places you in a vantage position to learn, connect, and become a profitable furniture maker and business owner.

School Mission: The mission of Majeurs Academy is to compassionately educate and groom a new generation of furniture manufacturing leaders who demonstrate excellence in advancing professional, reliable and quality delivery. This mission is achieved through excellence in teaching, learning and assessment, strong partnership networks, and service to others.

School Vision: Our vision is to lead furniture manufacturing scholarships across Africa. Majeurs Academy will deliver significant economic benefits by creating jobs and skilling the local workforce. In addition, it will provide a hub that fosters creativity within the industry, create opportunities for innovation, and develop skills critical to the competitiveness and long-term future of the Furniture Manufacturing Industry.

School Values

Excellence

The focus on excellence is centred around students, faculty, and the community. Achievement of excellence requires the diligent and continual pursuit of professional knowledge and expertise and a faculty whose expertise complements the mission and vision.

Professionalism

We encompass values and behaviours foundational to furniture manufacturers and based on ethical principles and standards of practice. These values and behaviours are promoted through socialisation in the profession. For example, using evidence-based knowledge, skills and collaborative teamwork with other disciplines to ensure our students embrace accountability, dependability, responsibility, autonomy, and leadership qualities.

The words hold a lot of promise, but I also wanted to add the voices of the Facilitators who dealt with the first group on a daily basis, and of course speak about the practical and personal challenges they faced and how the solved the inevitable problems. I continue to be impressed by their energy, commitment to our cause and of course their willingness to teach beginners advanced carpentry and technical drawing skills. Our conversation was recorded, transcribed and edited for length.

Technical Drawing Facilitator, Lateef Balogun

Lateef Balogun is a graduate in mechanical engineering from University of Benin Edo State in Nigeria and also has a Master's degree from the University of Lagos, where he studied design and production engineering.

Lateef in fact is what I consider to be the next generation of leader in this industry and the boom in manufacturing. He had an industrial experience in engineering, before coming to the Majeurs Academy, he had seven years' experience in industrial design and engineering working with four different companies.

What makes Lateef such a critical hire for the academy? Number one is love for teaching, but also critical skill set. He likes to relate this story of how he was inspired, to study engineering—it is definitely worth repeating, because it gives a deeper insight to this kind of creative and inspirational faculty that I'm assembling at the academy.

> When I was a small boy, my dad was a Muslim. He was praying one night and…If you're quiet familiar with Muslims, you realize that they don't like being stopped when they are praying. My Dad was almost finishing his prayers, but on and on that night he suddenly stopped the

Figure 13.1 *Lateef Balogun working with academy students.* Image courtesy of Majeurs Holdings.

Figure 13.2 Lateef Balogun working with academy students, 2023.
Image courtesy of Majeurs Holdings.

prayer and called me to his side. He said, 'Look out there,' and pointed to the sky. There was an airplane flying overhead and blinking in the night sky This was very long time ago, and I was fascinated by that airplane and I asked myself, How could someone put something like that and something so big in the sky? That inspired me and I decided that I was gonna study engineering and learn how things are made and how people come up with structure. What is the design thinking behind a machine?

Lateef's passion, energy and skills are precisely what I'm looking for, his love of passing his knowledge to others.

Lateef and I also discussed all the problems we have in Africa in economic development, and training to fill the big gap of workers with skills.

As Lateef noted:

> We have raw materials and we have a lot of people in our population but there is a huge lack of skill and technical know-how so we needed someone in the furniture industry that is well experience[d] in industrial design in different material aspects. We need trained designers with technical skills, to be able to break down that knowledge for other people to assimilate and also to be able to replicate it. I really love that. I also have my industrial design company on the side. I love to teach the students so far, plus I'm still able to do my industrial design engineering work. That's how I got to know about Majeurs and that's how I was able to choose working.
>
> We have a huge body of very talented young workers. But either the school system something has failed on the way and they haven't that idea of having that sort of vocational skills. Those kind of things of that kind of training it…seems to be where your Academy it kind of fit filling in.

Lateef commented on his own schooling experience in Nigeria:

> It might interest you to know that while I was in school and during my first degree, I didn't learn digital skills in school. It was all theoretical and very few practical skills. During my internship I decided that I want to learn a practical skill. I want to learn AutoCAD. I was a 300 level when I heard about AutoCAD for the very first time.

I asked Lateef as a technical drawing facilitator, what he felt were the challenges to teach technical drawing which is by nature quite a complex subject.

Lateef was very honest:

> With my first rounds of students, okay, the first thing we did was that we have to structure the curriculum, in a way that it's easy for someone that had zero knowledge to pick up. someone that had a background in arts or in commercial or someone that dropped out of school, midway through the year, they were able to follow through because I had taught them the basics of technical background.

'And the biggest challenge?'

My main challenge was keeping their interest. Each student is quite different. Students had different reasons why they joined their Academy. They were more particular about their area of specialization rather than learning all the different aspects of the Furniture Design and making.

Okay, for those who are quite interested in carpentry they felt there was no need to learn technical drawing. So for them the class was a bit boring. But through our approach we started using technical board so that you understand, and how to draw a three-dimensional view isometric view and all that's before we migrate the data to AutoCAD. Fortunately, the Academy we have a partnership with Siemens Solid Edge. It's a 3D modeling software.

I feel that my challenge as a teacher was mediating between those that had low or zero technical background those people that already [were] grounded in technical drawing...because we were slow[ed] down a bit by those that had zero background and I had to take extra time to tutor them on the very basic things that I felt here should be easy for anyone to pick up.

I asked Lateef, 'What do you think makes someone good at technical drawing and who can actually make that leap and become a very skilled technique in technical drawing?'

It's actually...not being an expert in the use of tools. It's actually more or less asked to do with the curious mindset of the person and the meticulous ability to be put having attentiveness to details. You need to ask yourself: How does this thing comes together? Why is this made this way? How would I explain this to the person that is going to make it? Then ask what's the best materials that is suited for this region? What is the long life of this material?

You need to know the type of materials and understand what... all the components you are. If it is chair, how comfortable it is, what is the size, the color, the materials, and so on. Those are what is expected of normal for each furniture designer, but what makes a difference between them is the little details of accent yourself, you, have questions about who is going to use it, who is going to make it and also the products itself.

Then the last question to ask yourself, is what is our capacity as a company? What are our limitations? Because if we are trying to do something and aspects of that product is being outsourced to someone else that means [we] will be paying someone else for it and the influence of time and money.

I asked Lateef, what is his biggest success so far?

My biggest success. It's when my students were doing presentation[s] with the final projects. I was very impressed. I was very impressed and I was also excited. I realized that my greatest joy actually wasn't from teaching in the classroom…The joyful feeling was from having the satisfaction that I was able to replicate myself in someone else work.
　That's what a teacher is.

'Final thoughts, Lateef?'

At the Academy the skills we are teaching cover a lot of ground, that's very impressive because there's a lot of conceptual and then there's a lot of practical at the same time. So that's really interesting for them to build on.

Woodworking Facilitator, Damiola Ogunbiyi

I also asked our Woodworking Facilitator, Damiola Ogunbiyi, how he became interested in carpentry. His journey started with an early interest in learning carpentry skills, while self-learning by using the internet to train himself during secondary school because the facilities and instruction were not available to him.

He told me that by using his passion and zeal he was able to quickly find the skills online as well as he was hired by several different companies.

I started as an apprentice and moved up the ranks very quickly. In one place of employment after two months working there, my employer said, 'Wow, Damiola how did you learn this?' I told him by watching and learning. In two months I moved from apprentice to head of quality control. I also worked with a Turkish company and there I was taught…the ISO standards of quality and production control, which is very important. I also learned quite a bit about dealing [with] customer complaints and all aspects of furniture production. It was an long apprenticeship and working period of over eight years.

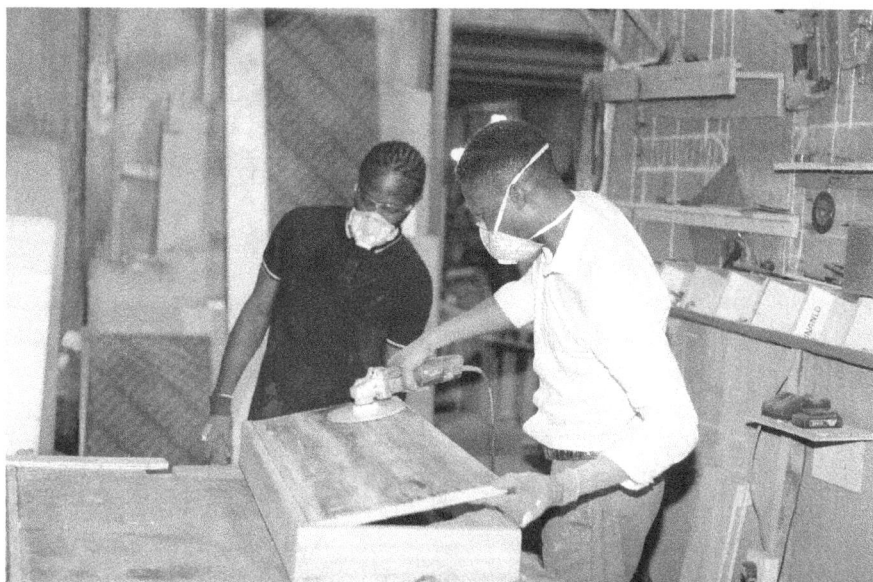

Figure 13.3 *Damiola Ogunbiyi in the workshop with students, 2023.*
Image courtesy of Majeurs Holdings.

Figure 13.4 *Damiola Ogunbiyi in the workshop with students, 2023.*
Image courtesy of Majeurs Holdings.

When I asked Dami to consider teaching at the academy, I'll admit he was slightly shocked when I asked him if he could teach carpentry skills to the highest standards but in a very short window. His easy-going style and demeanour seemed to be a perfect fit, and his story is not unusual for Lagos, with skilled workers in very demand and working a few side hustles.

> One of my facilitators in Builders Hub, who happens to be my friend called me over the phone and then asked me to come and replace him at Majeurs Academy. He was leaving Nigeria to run a programme for himself. While we were talking over the phone, I told him, I'm not ready to work for another organisation anymore because I am already working on building my own name and my own personal company. He pleaded with me to think about it and that he could not find any other qualified person to take on his role. He knew I'm very capable carpenter and could easily of take the position. I wondered why he has chosen me over others, and there is a reason why he wants me to come and replace him.
>
> I said to him, 'Okay, I'll give it a shot.' When I came to my interview at Majeurs Academy I was asked if I could teach carpentry skills over a short period of time. I asked myself, how is that possible? How is the student who have zero knowledge of carpentry skills, how would that be possible to, you know, acquire this knowledge within a short period of time? It took me eight years to master these skills and then build a career on. So I took that task upon myself. I started listening to this song by Sia, *Unstoppable, I'm Unstoppable*. This song inspired me to keep moving, to keep making my research, and then further help me to, uh, learn other ways of approaching the students to help them acquire the skill effectively.
>
> I sat down and did research online day and night to further help myself, and build better approach to help the students, so that they could acquire the carpentry skills effectively. I was also working with the Majeurs training manual that was given to me at the academy. So, with the best of my abilities combined with the willingness of the student as well, you know, trying to make sure that they also get the best out of the programme, in a very short period of time and that part of their time they're gonna working with me learning carpentry skills. All of these put together, we helped each other and we stood up to the storm of time. We completed all the class activities, and covered a lot of practical work in the shop. I'm proud to say that we got it all done in this very short time period.

'What were the major challenges for you and your students?'

We had a lot of challenges, you know, and at the beginning it...looks as if, though, they're not gonna get it right. I was able to encourage them as the facilitator, helping them realise that, because you fail the first time doesn't mean that you can't get it done. The times you fail mean that you have learned a better way to get things done right. It was not easy, all of this, you know, but with encouragement with my students, they quickly get themselves on the right track. We overcame a lot of personal and technical challenges, step by steps until we're get able to get to the final stage of the curriculum.

Sometimes the students find it difficult to meet up with class activities because of the financial constraint. At the time, there was a scarcity of cash in Nigeria. These financial challenges had to do with the government so it was difficult for everyone. The students were able to navigate their way through to the end. As for me, I was also happy that they found a way to also encourage themselves, to make sure that they acquired the skills, learn all the aspects of carpentry, and importantly learn how to handle basic hand tools and use them correctly and effectively. We also spent time learning about personal safety that is really important in working with carpentry skills. I can't afford my student getting injured while working at the academy workshop.

'What is your biggest success so far?'

That is a personal [one]—the success was teaching all this in a short time period, because I didn't think it was possible. I'm so happy that I'm able to prove to the academy and my students that my capacity, my competency, and my efficiency, and to take the students from zero knowledge of carpentry skill through the entire process of becoming a professional carpenter in the furniture industry by mastering the skill, the techniques of handling their tools, and creating self-awareness of safety in the workshop.

Now I believe that nothing is impossible if one can try, and no skill is difficult. If one can take time to learn it. As long as there is willingness, there is self-discipline and determination and focus to learn anything, anything is possible to achieve.

Dami's energy and commitment, skill and willingness to adapt to Majeurs make him and Lateef the ideal teachers/facilitators. They both embody the outstanding young creative and artisanal skills that are in fact make Majeurs and our academy an attractive option. I'll also state for the record that they are both totally unstoppable.

The Future of Our Academy

I truly believe that businesses and particularly the manufacturing sector will help save Africa from its current socioeconomic problems. There will need to be a lot of heavy lifting and committed 'teacher-preneurs'—like Lateef and Damilola—in order to do great business; we must equip our people with the knowledge, tools and skills necessary for future success and sustainability. I argue that Africa must industrialise to truly fulfil its potential. The plans we have developed are ambitious, but scale is essential in Africa, and big ideas don't need to crumble in the dustbin of history, nor should they be shot down by the elites, who may not see or care about the real-world advantages of having a trained and motivated workforce. I'll outline why we have started the furniture training academy in the hope that one day it will become part of a university that produces the future furniture manufacturers of tomorrow who will seize the opportunities that Africa has to offer with their creativity and foresight. We intend to train young Africans of ages 18–35 in the lessons that will allow the industry to grow and be a big player in the global economy. For the record, please read our mission statement. I should credit collaborators here for their invaluable support and commitment to get this plan up and running.

Note

1 George B.N. Ayittey. 1999. *Africa in Chaos*. St. Martin's Press (see Chapter 4: The Functionally Illiterate Elites).

What Are We Waiting For?

A Challenge for Challenging Times

> I feel sorry for the youthman today,
> The system is bad for the youthman today,
> Every day and every night they suffer
> The youthman want to sleep but no place
> The youthman want to eat but no food
> The youthman want good dress but no good dress
> The youthman want to buy but no money
> The youthman want to work
> If no work, how you expect him to eat.'
> —'Youthman' by Steady Bongo AKA Lanaga Sherriff

I'm concluding this book with a personal challenge to my readers. I'm issuing a challenge for business leaders, bankers, politicians, donors, competitors and tech specialists in Lagos, Nigeria and elsewhere in Africa to come to my factory and showroom and meet my team. (I'll agree that getting across Lagos in traffic will be a big enough challenge for some, but that is another story.) The challenge is that the invitee must sit in one of my leather sofas, much like Prince Charles did in my humble showroom in London many years ago, and we will talk about how we design and build the future for young Africans.

I'll sit with anyone who wants to brainstorm how we can find creative solutions to begin to build a pan-African job training and employment scheme that trains the youth for manufacturing jobs of the future. If an invitee can come up with a working plan, I along with my team, will create

DOI: 10.4324/9781003453994-14

a blueprint and then a prototype that can be replicated, taught and more importantly funded. I'll record our talk for my podcast called, *Start Up, Scale Up (SUSU)*, and it will be broadcast around the globe. The winners: young African men and women who are truly looking to find agency and employment. I'll post more on my website, www.DemiSamande.com.

Lessons and Learning

The truth is, as a businesswoman based in Nigeria, I have much to learn. Every day I wake up and worry that I am making yet another mistake, or making a wrong turn that will adversely affect my employees or to some damage to the business or the brand. I constantly worry that I am wasteful and not thinking big enough.

What has certainly helped me and inspired me to keep moving forward is connecting with other young entrepreneurs, who are based in West Africa and have already leapfrogged over the old stifling institutions that are inherently designed to sap their energy, by playing the old postcolonial mind games of being second class in everything that we make.

I'm not against helpful tax regulations or normal import or export duties, but new businesses need time to grow their wings and find consumers all over the globe.

Since relocating to Nigeria in 2017, the most visible and urgent need at this moment is to create viable, sustainable and satisfying employment for our youth. There is an urgent need for massive, smart and targeted capital to train workers and then build factories for a wide variety of products.

In our ever-connected world where every young person has a cell phone where they can see lifestyles of others in Europe, the UK, Asia, anywhere but Africa, they cannot see any future for themselves. In a book published in 2013 about African youth, *The Time of Youth*, the Mozambican academic Alcinda Honwana writes:

> The majority of African youths are today grappling with a lack of jobs and deficient education, After they leave school with few skills they are unable to obtain work and become independent—to build, buy, or rent a house for themselves, support their relatives, get married. Establish families and gain social recognition as adults. These attributes of adulthood are becoming increasingly unattainable for the majority of young people in Africa. They are forced to live in the liminal, neither-here-nor-there-state; they are no longer children who require care, yet they are not yet considered mature social adults, They lead a precarious existence; their efforts are centred on trying to survive each and every day.[1]

The generational shift is clear and these young people don't see any hope where they live, and feel they will never be able to build a future.

We need to begin to stanch the outflow of young African men and women who believe that their only chance of making it is to take the perilous journey to northern Africa and then pay exorbitant fees to illegal human traffickers. So many deaths of our young people in the Mediterranean Sea, innocent people seeking a better life.

They take illegal side-hustle jobs, such as smuggling cars and prostitution. These heartbreaking migration stories can be stopped, and I truly believe that the best, and least corrupt, path to providing employment is building a global hub for manufacturing in Africa.

The solutions are really at our fingertips. Without a doubt the creative class, and the Cheetah generation, are investing and reinvesting into their businesses, and supporting more and more employees. However, as I've argued earlier in my book, the capital to scale up is just not there.

In her book, Honwana[2] interviews a young Nigerian man, Akinde, who migrated to Lagos looking for work.

> I came to Lagos from a neighboring state as a teenager. I left secondary school midway…and proceeded to learn auto mechanics work…I began smuggling vehicles across the border myself. I feel smuggling is extremely more profitable…Nigeria is a country where everyone has to fend for himself, the government cares for no one, and those in power are only using their positions to enrich themselves. (Quoted in Oamnisakin and Ismail 2008, 17)

Sadly, there are many, many Akinde stories, of young men and women who are neither children nor adults who have to make very hard choices to survive.

★★★

As a young woman growing up in East London, I also witnessed plenty of 'disadvantaged youth'. I was different, perhaps privileged, because of my parents' insistence on education and entrepreneurship. I learned many valuable lessons about making a living while living at home, and they provided a stable, two-parent household and as role models taught me invaluable lessons about getting a university degree, and then employment.

I knew that I had to hustle, and this energy of not being content with the status quo, and always seeking a better way to support myself independently from my parents and learning that my unstoppable mojo, inner drive or whatever you want to call it, drove me to find side hustles like selling body shapers, and then working restoring and rebuilding leather sofas.

Considering all that I had in terms of family and community resources to build, it was a massively greater set of opportunities than the young people from my generation in Lagos and Nigeria have.

The larger question remains: if the Global North continues to ignore or underfunds manufacturing and new startups in Africa, what will be the consequences?

Certainly, a massive Mediterranean migration crises in Europe,[3] and all the social and politic ills that this human disaster has already caused. The UNHCR[4] numbers are grim and sadly growing monthly after a pause brought on by the pandemic. What is clear to so many African youths is that there not enough work, or places where they can see a future for their lives.

In Honwana's book, she details the very common struggles of Sami, a 27 year-old Tunisian man:

> Sami earned his degree at the university, and then went to Mahida, a town near the city of Sousse on the east coast to study information technology and management. Since finishing his bachelor's degree, Sami has been unable to secure full-time employment. While waiting to find a job, he earns some money as a day laborer in construction and agriculture…Sami confessed that he often becomes desperate about his situation, and he dreams of migrating to Europe, as some of his friends have done. But he said 'you need money to do that. You must pay the people, who take you across. It costs a lot of money, and for now I cannot afford it.'

If they make it to Europe, then the struggle continues for many of them to integrate into societies that are growing more and more hostile to migrants and more often than not, they are swept up by local authorities in Italy, Spain and Greece and many are now being sent back home.

★★★

The statistics of lost lives at sea are heartbreaking and staggering, but I believe that there is a better solution. It must be made in Africa, by Africans, for Africans, by drilling down past the statistics, and by scaling up, and by investing in sectors such as manufacturing and thereby creating massive work and education programmes with an emphasis on training for specific vocational skills, that are not available in traditional educational settings.

For the Samis, Akindes and millions of other talented, and motivated, African youths, there needs to be better alternatives than paying human smugglers exorbitant sums, as Honwana concludes:[5]

Hundreds and thousands of young men[…]risk everything in hope of finding work and prosperity in Europe. Their quest is not merely for survival but also for dignity, because *liggey* (work) makes one a respected person, capable of taking care of oneself as well as others. Young unemployed people in Senegal, Tunisia, Mozambique, and South Africa are fighting for subsistence and dignity by crossing borders with merchandise for sale, hawking goods in the streets, scavenging garbage dumps, and boarding crowded boats in dangerous journeys to Europe.

The socioeconomic tipping point is close at hand, as too many of our brightest and most talented youth are perishing at sea. That is why I am urging donors, funders, educators and colleagues through my podcasts and in my book to come together and invest and develop manufacturing hubs, training academies, such as we've done at Majeurs.

We have built and are testing the prototype in Lagos. We are purposefully ambitious—ready to expand our programmes anywhere in Africa.

I am honoured and eternally grateful that every day when my team shows up for work and puts all their creative efforts into creating gorgeous leather sofas, chairs, and the carpentry team turns out amazing wooden tables, that will be shipped and sold all over the globe. Beneath the busy hum of electric saws, screw guns and pneumatic staplers, is the quiet dignity that work and pride brings for a job well done.

I believe that each and every piece we build is infused with this pride and dignity, and if this spirit can be learned, and relearned and passed on to others, then many more manufacturers can succeed.

We must defeat the smugglers, and the false and criminal hopes that they represent, by building massive training and employment schemes in Africa. Then the desire that the foreign shores are more lucrative will quickly fade and they will stay within their home nations. Then Africa will in fact become the Next Factory for the World.

Aspiration and Creating High-quality Skills-based Education for Young Africans

My desire is not only to design and build furniture, but also create a scaled-up generation of savvy, educated African entrepreneurs who have access to capital to build on their dreams and then employ a new generation of talent. In effect it is a commercial solution to the actual on-the-ground realities for underemployed, unskilled youth.

Honwana succinctly writes:

> Young Africans' lives are amazingly varied, reflecting the cultural diversity and uneven economic development that characterises the continent. Their differing socioeconomic conditions and backgrounds affect their life chances and outlooks. On average today's youth are better educated than their parents. While many still fall far below global averages, some have qualifications that compare favorably with their counterparts in the global North. They are better connected with the rest of the world and gradually overcoming social and cultural factors that once limited their earlier generations of Africans, navigating the communications highway and gradually overcoming social and cultural factors that once limited their access to information and the world beyond their locality...*As a result, African youth are more determined to find ways to close the gap between the limited opportunities before them and what they perceive to be possible in the global arena. They seek to create better and more meaningful lives for themselves, not merely live out their days within the constraints of the situations they now inhabit.*[6]

This is precisely what I have seen on the ground in Lagos as a business-woman, and employer of 30 plus Nigerians in my factory and academy in Lagos. I see their determination to create meaningful lives that add value to their families, communities and of course to my manufacturing company. However, if some of these staff members branch out, and build small companies that feed into a larger supply chain, and they hire local skilled workers, then the impact will begin to take hold as more and more youth are attracted to make a better life for themselves, rather than look at the grim and precarious choice of migration.

In Lagos, a medium-sized company such as Majeurs that employs 30 personnel barely registers in such a huge sprawling city, which has close to 20 million inhabitants. However, if a hub of small, medium and large factories, that have the capital and constantly train their employees, so that upward mobility is a possibility, then Steady Bongo's 'Youthman' lyrics and music will be considered a relic.

Certainly, the conflicts and the possibilities for more youth-led riots, such as in Tunisia, Egypt and elsewhere in Africa has been created by both ignoring and then abandoning this generation to fend for themselves.

The African youth are being constantly linked to and reminded of the outside world on their smartphones, through the platforms of Instagram, X, Facebook and TikTok. They are not only knowledgeable about trends in music, fashion and design, they know how to recreate them and build communities and take opportunities that the platforms offer.

I have three general observations of social media and one is positive and the others more troubling. I am a big user of social media, podcasting and connecting my ideas to others.

Information Overload and Echo Chambers

While social media offers incredible opportunities for connectivity and idea sharing, it also presents challenges. One of the most concerning aspects is the overwhelming amount of information available. I often find myself scrolling after 20 minutes and begin to have a headache from the overload of content, how much can I consume before I am influenced to begin to think that the content is my viewpoint and I'm not simply being brainwashed? The constant influx of content, opinions and news can be mentally exhausting and lead to information overload. The old saying is still true, *you are what you consume*. A useful lesson is that I find that I must be intentional about curating my content in order to feel I'm feeding myself what I need to consume, as opposed to just grazing on what is placed in front of me.

The second and positive observation is that social media can educate and sometimes provide deeper a meaningful introduction into healthy lifestyles, and the bigger ideas that good paying jobs will allow you to purchase homes, purchase luxury goods and reinforce positives values such as building families and stronger communities.

The third observation, on the darker flipside, is the obvious pull that interconnectivity drives many to make bad choices, such as easier access to criminal activity, including theft, prostitution, smuggling, and many drop into the dangerous idea that it is better to migrate, which involves multiple and horrific layers of exploitation, physical danger and a high risk of mortality.

However, as businesspeople, and in the bigger picture for African nations, if we can tap into that youth and dynamic energy of their aspirations and a determination to be better educated, then over time, the idea of migration becomes a nonstarter, because the lure of steady employment in sectors such manufacturing, technology, will offer a much more sustainable idea of earning a paycheque with a good paying job, with benefits such as healthcare and a future.

Impossible, a pipe dream, for a continent that has a vast and mostly young population? Where do we start?

Skills-oriented Curricula

Honwana writes about the death of hands-on vocational training in African schools:

> Curricula do not focus on developing skills that meet current labor market demands. In a situation where educational prerequisites and skill requirements are rising sharply, many graduates are unprepared for the few available jobs. This issue has been the focus of contentious debates among educators, especially at the intermediate and higher levels, about 'ability-based curricula' and students' 'employability' as employers lack the 'transferable skills' required in the workplace.[7]

I could not agree more with her statement, and in fact, since the demand was so urgent for the long-term sustainability of my company and other manufacturing companies, we instituted a solely skills-based vocational-style academy. In fact, the undergirding motivation in curricula that we have developed and prototyped and put into action in less than 12 months addresses all of the structural weaknesses that the next generation are desperately seeking to overcome. Many are willing to pay for an additional skills upgrade, particularly if they understand that their employability grows tenfold.

Honwana does not pull her punches:

> Technical and vocational training in Africa suffers from a lack of resources and has been unable to provide young people with the skills that businesses demand. In addition, it became too expensive in the context of structural adjustment programs and public spending cuts. Only 2 to 6 percent of education budgets are devoted to this type of education. Skills-development strategies often fall outside donors' priorities. Inadequate investment in vocational education aggravates the mismatch between school curricula and job market needs. [8]

For entrepreneurs and business owners, who see that Africa is on the cusp of building a manufacturing hub, and the potential for very good profits, they will also need to see that partners in education and in particular vocational educational training is the answer for a sustainable future, but this topic is too rich and complex to contain within the pages of one book.

My overarching goal in writing this book was to hopefully inspire and create an entirely new class of African-based entrepreneurs who will have the opportunities to successfully develop and build new companies, particularly in the manufacturing sector, and who are willing to match or better my commitment to creating a new hub of production, manufacturing not only furniture but in a myriad of other sectors as well.

What Are We Waiting For?

Honwana concludes her book, stating:

> Young Africans in waithood cope with extremely precarious and taxing conditions in many ways. ...*Yet, the young people are not waiting passively for their lives to change, or expect others to solve their problems. They recognise that they have to fend for themselves in the best way they can, as the actions and words of young Africans I met so vividly show, they are using their agency by adapting practices and fashioning new types of livelihoods and relationships to mitigate their everyday problems.*

Her words are a powerful reminder that the next generation are not looking to their governments, nor to educational institutions, to give them the job skills to meet the demands of the global markets. Therefore, it falls on us—private businesses—to plug the massive training gap.

Dayo Olopade called it Kanju, operating just outside the legal rules, such as Nigeria's notorious 419 email and phone scamming organisations. I've called it the Industrial Revolution 4.0, where African youth seek out and build value-added lives by finding employment in manufacturing, technology and social political activism in an increasingly connected world. Whatever this generation seeks out, their futures will be entirely built outside the old school hegemonic power structures.

In the Preface of George Ayittey's powerful final book, *Africa Unchained*,[9] he sets up the argument for youth, and business, the Cheetah generation, to leapfrog over the old Hippo generation. He writes, 'The basic thrust of *Africa Unchained*: unleashing the entrepreneurial talents and energies of the real African people.'

In a recent NYT article in October 2023,[10] by Declan Walsh, he quotes Edward Paice, Director of the Africa Research Institute in London, and author of *Youth Quake: Why Africa Demographics Should Matter to The World*.[11] Paice states that Africa is entering a period of truly staggering change. He adds, 'The world is changing and we need to reimagine the world with Africa in it.'

I could not have said it better or more succinctly.

Will It Fly?

Will young Africans rise to this massive challenge? As a CEO of a new startup, I sincerely believe in investing in the youth of my community—it drives my organisation to be innovative, sustainable and responsible to the team of employees. I'll never waver from that. However, my larger goal is to fully engage the youth of Africa to build their own futures. It will take a structural, educational and yes, inspirational leap into the future. I am already working with partners in business, educational institutions and organisations that promote youth employment to launch and sustain our academy, and I believe it will help young Africans seize the opportunities and unleash their creativity by accepting the challenge.

As I draw the final curtain on this book, I want you, the reader, to carry with you the profound sense of hope and purpose that has been woven into its pages. If you have managed to read it to the very end, I want to first congratulate you for your hunger to do something truly amazing.

The journey we've embarked upon together within these chapters has been a testament to the boundless potential that resides within each of us.

While the path ahead may present its share of challenges, it is illuminated by the promise of a brighter future. It is a future where determination fuels our progress, where innovation guides our endeavours and where a steadfast commitment to nurturing the talents of our youth propels us forward.

This book has been a vessel, carrying within it the collective wisdom, experiences and dreams of so many of us. It has been a source of inspiration and a call to action, reminding us that we stand not at the sidelines of history but at its forefront.

As you venture forth, remember that you are not alone in this pursuit. We are part of a worthy movement, a collective force of change that seeks to reshape Africa's future for the better. Our journey continues, and it is filled with the promise of transformation, growth and the realisation of our shared dreams.

Thank you for being a part of this journey, for embracing the challenges and for believing in the potential of Africa and its youth. The future is bright, and together, we will write a story of progress, innovation and lasting impact. Together we will share the challenges and the burden to innovate the solutions that propel us all forward.

With hope in our hearts and determination in our souls, let us step boldly into the future and create a legacy that generations to come will celebrate and be proud to say that we indeed did the work that allowed them to charge even further forward.

Notes

1 Alcinda Manuel Honwana. 2013. *The Time of Youth: Work, Social Change, and Politics in Africa*. Boulder, Colorado: Kumarian Press Pub. Page 13.
2 Ibid. Page 13.
3 https://news.un.org/en/story/2022/06/1120132
4 https://data2.unhcr.org/en/situations/mediterranean
5 Alcinda Manuel Honwana. 2013. *The Time of Youth: Work, Social Change, and Politics in Africa*. Boulder, Colorado: Kumarian Press Pub. Pages 84–5.
6 Ibid. Page 13.
7 Ibid. Page 43.
8 Alcinda Manuel Honwana. 2013. *The Time of Youth: Work, Social Change, and Politics in Africa*. Boulder, Colorado: Kumarian Press Pub. Page 43.
9 George B.N. Ayittey. 2005. *Africa Unchained: The Blueprint for Africa's Future*. Palgrave. Page xxiv.
10 https://www.nytimes.com/interactive/2023/10/28/world/africa/africa-youth-population.html
11 Edward Piace. 2021. *Youth Quake: Why Africa Demographics Should Matter to The World*. Apollo.

For Product Safety Concerns and Information please contact our EU
representative GPSR@taylorandfrancis.com
Taylor & Francis Verlag GmbH, Kaufingerstraße 24, 80331 München, Germany